HUMAN HACKING

HUMAN HACKING

WIN FRIENDS, INFLUENCE PEOPLE, AND LEAVE THEM BETTER OFF FOR HAVING MET YOU

CHRISTOPHER HADNAGY

WITH SETH SCHULMAN

HARPER
BUSINESS

An Imprint of HarperCollins*Publishers*

The names and identifying details of some individuals discussed in this book have been changed to protect their privacy.

FIRST EDITION

Designed by Nancy Singer

Image Credits: Amaya Hadnagy and Christopher Hadnagy

Library of Congress Cataloging-in-Publication Data
Names: Hadnagy, Christopher, author. | Schulman, Seth, other.
Title: Human hacking : win friends, influence people, and leave them better off for having met you / Christopher Hadnagy; with Seth Schulman.
Identifiers: LCCN 2020028518 (print) | LCCN 2020028519 (ebook) | ISBN 9780063001787 (hardcover) | ISBN 9780063001794 (ebook)
Subjects: LCSH: Social engineering. | Hackers. | Interpersonal communication.
Classification: LCC HM668 .H3297 2021 (print) | LCC HM668 (ebook) | 302—dc23
LC record available at https://lccn.loc.gov/2020028518
LC ebook record available at https://lccn.loc.gov/2020028519

---

21 22 23 24 25   LSC   10 9 8 7 6 5 4 3 2 1

To Areesa, the love of my life. You are my best friend and one of the most beautiful humans I have ever met.

To Colin, watching you become the man you are has given me endless hope. I am so proud of you.

To Amaya, there are no words to describe the depth of my love for you. Your beauty and talent astound me.

CONTENTS

PLEASE READ AND SIGN
BEFORE CONTINUING

The tools contained in this book are uniquely powerful. Every year, criminals around the world use them to manipulate others to do their bidding, stealing trillions of dollars from businesses and individuals, wreaking havoc on the lives of millions, and altering the political destinies of entire nations. In sharing these techniques with you, I trust that you'll use them for the cause of good, not evil. You'll help others, not just yourself, and you'll refrain from behaving in ways that harm others. This is serious business—lives are at stake here! So, before proceeding, please read and sign the following pledge:

I, _____, solemnly swear _not_ to use these skills to manipulate people for selfish, one-sided gain. While I may use these skills to benefit myself, I will ensure that the others with whom I interact benefit as well, and that they don't compromise their own best interests by acceding to my wishes. Further, I promise to respect the privacy of others in using these skills, and I promise to use these skills to enhance my own self-awareness, so that I can become a better partner, family member, friend, colleague, and neighbor. Most of all, I promise to use these skills in ways that ultimately leave people feeling better for having met me. If I fail in this task, as I occasionally might, I promise to learn from the experience and do better next time.

Signed,

_____

(Sign and date here)

HUMAN HACKING

YOUR NEW SUPER POWER

It's one o'clock in the morning, and we're in a rented black Suburban, creeping along off-road through desert scrubland with our lights off. I squint in the moonlight, navigating around boulders, clumps of underbrush, and the occasional small tree. My buddy Ryan's knuckles are white as he grips the passenger seat. Every few minutes, he cranes his neck to make sure nobody is following us. I take deep breaths, trying to stay calm. Neither of us talks, save an occasional "crap" from one of us when we take a hard bounce or narrowly avert a boulder.

Going just a few miles per hour, we make our way toward a group of boxy, nondescript buildings illuminated by powerful floodlights and other scattered industrial lighting. More precisely, we head toward the ten-foot-high security fence topped with razor wire that stands between us and those buildings.

At one point, about five miles into it, I brake hard as a coyote darts in our path. We shouldn't be doing this, I tell myself.

About a quarter mile from the fence, I spot a large and deep gully cutting down into the earth off to my left. "How about there?" I ask.

"Fine," Ryan says.

I maneuver into the gully, trying not to scratch the car on the thick, dry brush that lines either side. I go as far down as I can before parking so that guards or workers walking around this dusty wasteland can't see the car. From here, we'll proceed on foot. "Any company?" I ask, shutting off the engine.

"Don't think so," Ryan says.

"Let's roll."

We get out and close the doors softly behind us. Rattlesnakes and scorpions abound in this habitat, so we tiptoe around, alert to the slightest movement. We open the back hatch and pull out an aluminum ladder and some lengths of rope. Aside from the ladder, we're traveling light—you never know if we'll have to make a run for it. "Okay," I say, pointing to a section of fence a bit to our left. "Over there, that dark area. Looks like a light is out. It's our best bet."

We walk, carrying the ladder between us. It's eerily quiet, save for a low hum coming from the buildings and the occasional, soft clanging of the ladder. We're fifty miles from the nearest town, unarmed and uninvited. If anything happens to us, nobody will know. And something might happen. I've been arrested and had guns put to my head. And those were easy jobs compared to this one.

I can't divulge what kind of facility this is, or where in the world it is located. What I can say is that beyond this barbed-wire fence a powerful organization is keeping watch over something immensely valuable. This "something" is so valuable, in fact, that the organization has spent tens of millions of dollars designing this facility and outfitting it to be, as we were told, "absolutely impenetrable," one of the most secure facilities on the planet. Besides the barbed wire, dozens of highly trained guards armed with automatic weapons patrol the grounds, making rounds throughout the night. Other guards stand watch inside high turret towers. Powerful spotlights illuminate the fence at regular intervals, with hundreds of cameras monitoring movements on the grounds and around the perimeter. An array of other costly and sophisticated equipment that I can't reveal is also in place, all with one objective: keep people like Ryan and me out.

We know about the security in such detail because we've spent weeks preparing for this mission. Working from a remote location, we gathered reams of detailed information via phishing and vishing (phishing phone calls) attacks. In the course of seemingly innocuous conversation, people working behind the razor wire and at other facilities maintained by this organization revealed operational plans, scheduling details, even the names of employees and managers who worked here—enough of them so that we could piece together large portions of the organization's management hierarchy.

In recent days, we continued to amass information while poking around the facilities in person. We had learned that the organization was building a new facility near this one, and that they were holding a groundbreaking ceremony this week. Although no information about the new facility's location was available online, that didn't stop us. Noticing that a local journalist had written articles about the construction, we hatched a plan to pose as this journalist and his colleague from the same news site. To learn the location, we had Debra, one of our female colleagues, call the facility's main office posing as an assistant to the journalist. "Hi," she said, in a cheerful tone. "This is Samantha over at WXTT [not the television station's real name]. I'm Pete Robichaud's secretary. He's coming out to cover the ribbon ceremony on Saturday at ten thirty. I just have a couple of follow-up questions."

"Hold on a sec," a man on the other end of the line said, probably checking that Pete (also not his real name) was on the guest list. "Go ahead."

"Okay, so first off, what kind of ID does he need to bring? He'll need a government ID with a photo, right?"

"Yep. Driver's license is fine, as is a passport."

"Great. So, next question, he's planning on bringing his own camera equipment. Is that okay? Anything he shouldn't bring?"

"That's fine," the man said. "We'll search him on the way in, though."

"Absolutely," our colleague said. "So, my last question is . . . I just want to verify. We seem to have lost his invitation, so I want to verify the facility's location and where he needs to go."

"No problem," the man said. He gave us exactly the information we needed.

It was a seemingly trivial conversation, lasting only thirty seconds. The man on the other end of the line probably didn't give it another thought. But there was more to the exchange than meets the eye. Debra only wanted to obtain one piece of information—the address— yet she posed two warm-up questions, eliciting basic information that we knew the man on the other end of the line would have no problem answering. This technique is what people in our line of work call "concession." The warm-up questions served to get the man comfortable *conceding to* the prospect of answering her questions. Once his brain had answered two of them, it would be better primed to answer the third, so long as that last question wasn't so outlandish as to arouse suspicion. Debra even threw out an answer to the first question for him, signaling that she knew what she was doing, had done it before, and everything was legit.

But Debra was deploying other techniques as well. When she posed the third question, she positioned it as simply "verifying" what she already knew. She was setting up the question by evoking its logic, making it seem a perfectly reasonable question to ask. And before that, when she asked if there was anything her boss shouldn't bring, she was playing dumb, implicitly asking the man on the other end to teach her. This massaged the man's ego, validating his authority and making him more comfortable and willing to talk—a task made easier by the gender difference between them.

Thanks to this conversation and others like it, we had been able to show up at the facility the day before and nearly gain access. Security personnel became suspicious and briefly detained us, but not before we'd learned numerous details about the security provisions, how the guards were trained, what weapons they carried, what kinds of threats they were alert to, what kinds of cameras the facility used, and so on.

Now Ryan and I are trying again to gain access, in a way that admittedly is far more dangerous. In the middle of the night, with two unidentified men dressed head to toe in black sneaking up to the fence, it would be easy for a nervous guard to shoot first and ask questions later. At six feet three, I'm hardly a small target. I try to push these thoughts aside as we make our way toward the fence, but it isn't easy. My mind keeps returning to the phone call I'd made earlier to my wife and kids, telling them that I love them. With every sound, my pulse races and I suck in my breath. We shouldn't be doing this, I tell myself again.

We reach the darkened section of fence and glance around—all clear. I rest the ladder against the chain link, and we use the rope to ease the razor wire down. With him video-recording on his phone, I climb up to breach the fence. I look around to see if we've been spotted, but fortunately, we haven't.

Over the next hour or so, Ryan and I explore the grounds, break into a couple of buildings and large machines, and take photographs and video-record what we see. Not once do the guards approach us. They apparently have no idea of our presence. Still, every second is pure temple-throbbing, adrenaline-coursing torment.

When we feel we have enough documentation, we head back to our truck and call it a night. Over the next few days, we'll use low-tech tools and psychological techniques to compromise this facility again from other entry points. We'll have guards shouting at us and putting guns to our heads, but only after we've spent hours again wandering around buildings and into the facility's most sensitive, highly guarded areas.

"Absolutely impenetrable"? I don't think so.

WHO WE ARE AND WHAT WE DO

You might think Ryan and I are government spies, high-end criminals, or fearless thrill seekers looking for another million YouTube followers. You'd be wrong. We're not any of those.

We're hackers.

Most people think of hackers as young techno-thugs who pound Mountain Dew and tap at their computers stealing data, crashing websites, or sending spam about Viagra. But there are good hackers, too, top-security professionals that governments and companies hire to *protect* them from the bad guys. And among these good hackers, there are a select few who don't specialize in the technical side of breaking into computers, but rather the messy, human side. This subspecies of hackers bypasses even the tightest security not by writing code to hack machines, but by hacking *humans*. They're con men, essentially, fast talkers who convince unsuspecting people to let them into machines and secured physical locations. The best of these hackers are so good that they not only get what they want, they make it so their targets *feel better for having met them.*

Ryan and I are hackers of humans. And don't worry, we're good guys. Thinking like the bad guys do, we apply advanced psychological principles and techniques to break into servers and physical sites. When we succeed, which is the vast majority of the time, we help our clients understand and fix their weaknesses, so that their customers and society at large are safer. That's what we were doing in the desert that evening—probing the security of this supposedly ultra-secure facility and identifying weaknesses, so that our clients could fix them before the bad guys broke in and wreaked havoc. We make our living getting perfect strangers to say or do pretty much whatever we want.

I've honed my techniques for more than a decade, using them to compromise the world's most secure facilities and computer networks, prompting one journalist covering the security industry to wonder aloud whether I'm "the most dangerous man in America."[1] That I'm not, but we do teach our methods to spies, military personnel, and security professionals around the world so that they can stay one step ahead of the truly dangerous bad guys. In this book, I'll reveal our secrets to you for use at home and at work. You'll learn how to read people effectively from their body language, how to get people instantly on your side by uttering exactly the right words, how to make requests in ways that dramatically increase your chances of a positive response, how to spot and thwart people who are trying to manipulate you, how to plot out an important conversation from beginning to end to increase your odds of success, and much more. Whether you seek to land a promotion, get people to give you free stuff, get people to tell you what they *really* think, or improve your relationships by learning to communicate better, our methods will be your new secret weapon. As you'll discover, hacking humans can help anyone win friends, influence people, and achieve their goals. It can help *you*.

A NEW KIND OF HACKING

The notion of hacking people instead of computers might sound strange. Who knew it was a "thing"? I didn't back in the day. In 1991, I got kicked out of college after only two months because of a little stunt I pulled. Actually, it wasn't so little—I messed around with the primitive modems we had on campus and wound up shutting down practically the entire phone system for Sarasota, Florida, for a full day.

Afterward, I drifted. I knew I had this strange knack for convincing people to give me stuff I shouldn't have, so I used it to land jobs that interested me. About a year after dropping out, I was working a job delivering papers when I walked into the office of a twenty-five-unit apartment complex and began chatting with the owner. I had never met this guy before, but in just a few minutes, I got him to tell me his deepest, darkest secrets. It turned out he had some personal issues he needed to resolve out of state. Two hours later, I had a well-paying job—with no relevant experience—as vice landlord renting out apartments and managing the complex. I was just seventeen years old.

I stayed for a while, leaving when I became bored. I got it into my head that it would be cool to be a chef, so I walked into a very fancy restaurant and, with zero kitchen experience, asked for a job. Two hours later, incredibly, I had one.

I got bored of that, too, so I talked my way into yet another job with no experience. Then another. And another. By the time I was in my late twenties, I was working as an international business negotiator for a company that, of all things, made stainless steel industrial products. I was traveling the world wheeling and dealing and making great money. But by that time, I had also talked this woman I loved into marrying me and having kids. Wishing to spend more time at home, I decided to leave and find something else to do.

It occurred to me, given my experience getting kicked out of college, that I might be good at hacking into computers. I went online and found a course offered by a security company on how to do it. I took the course and was the first person in the company's history to break into one of its most hardened servers. The owner offered me a job on the spot helping them to physically break into computer networks using technical methods.

There was one problem: despite having taken the course, I wasn't all that great at the technical methods. What I had going for me was my street smarts and skills as a fast talker. It turned out that this was all

I needed. For the next few years, I helped out the team in unexpected ways. My colleagues would be messing around with computer code, trying to find software or hardware vulnerabilities they could exploit to break into a system. They'd go at it for thirty hours, forty, fifty. Eventually, I'd pipe in: "How about I just call this guy and ask for his password?"

They'd shrug and say, "Well, you can try."

In ten minutes, we were in the system.

This scenario played out again and again. Sometimes I'd call people to extract information, other times I'd use phishing emails or just waltz into a facility with no fear and convince people to give me access to their servers. I wasn't using any preexisting methods, just my intuitive people skills and street smarts. But it worked, so much so that I suggested to my boss that we create a course on these methods. To my surprise, he told me to go ahead and make one up. "No way," I said. "I have no clue how to write a course. I never even finished college."

"It's easy," he said. "Just find every book you can that might have relevant psychological theory or research and think about what you're doing every day on the job. Write all of this down and organize it into a simple framework that you can teach to people."

His advice made sense, so I accepted the challenge. In 2009, after almost a year of studying and thinking, I had my framework written. I posted it online, and then largely forgot about it. A few months later, a publishing house cold-called me and said they'd seen my framework. They wondered if I would like to write a technical book for people in the security business. I turned them down at first, telling them I was just a greasy little hacker, and nobody was going to read anything I wrote. I told my boss about the offer, thinking he'd find it as funny as I did. He almost jumped out of his seat. "Are you crazy? Call them back and write the book!"

Again, I took his advice, and *Social Engineering: The Art of Human Hacking* came out in 2010. It was the first "how-to" book on hacking humans and has sold more than 100,000 copies, which is crazy for a nerdy technical book. In framing what I did as "social engineering," I appropriated a term first coined in the late nineteenth century and popularized during the 1990s and 2000s by the prominent hacker Kevin Mitnick. As I explained to readers, social engineering was "the act of manipulating a person to take an action that *may or may not* be in the 'target's' best interest."[2] I have since altered his definition, distinguishing between influencing people to behave or think as you wish and manipulation, which is the darker art of forcing or coercing them to do so. Given the ethical constraints in which good hackers operate (discussed in a moment), the vast majority of what social engineers like me do is influencing people. We sneakily get them to divulge sensitive information, and we refrain in almost all situations from coercing them.

Cross paths with us, either in person, on the phone, or online, and you'll think you had a delightful if perhaps trivial encounter with another human being. In some small way, you'll feel better off for having met us. But because we framed the conversation in exactly the right way, using specific words and paying close attention to your reactions, you'll almost certainly have also given us a password, a Social Security number, or some other piece of information we needed. The truth is, a well-trained social engineer doesn't need to use manipulation. Influence techniques are powerful enough.

You know that nice old lady who called you yesterday soliciting a charitable donation, and who chatted you up for a few minutes? Or that friendly UPS guy who in the course of asking for directions remarked on your company hat, cracked a joke, and queried you quite innocently about your work? I don't mean to scare you, but she might not have been nice, and he might not have been innocent. These strangers might have been malicious hackers, trying to squeeze you for information. They almost certainly weren't—let's not get carried away—but they could have been. Millions of people get hacked by criminals using influence techniques masquerading as an innocent conversation. The victims don't know they've been had until one day they discover that someone has taken out a small business loan in their name or locked down their computer and demanded a ransom.

Social Engineering laid out the basic principles and techniques for hacking humans, so that security professionals could use them to thwart attacks and keep us safe. In retrospect, I'm not proud of this book—it's pretty weak. But it did help put social engineering on the map. And for me personally, *Social Engineering* was a turning point. Excited about the reception it received in the security world, I started a company that evaluates companies for weaknesses by performing "penetration tests" such as the one depicted earlier, and that trains security professionals in how to hack humans effectively.

In the ten years that we've been in business, my firm has used the principles of social engineering to send 14 million phishing emails and more than 45,000 voice-phishing phone calls. We've broken into hundreds of servers, and physically compromised dozens of the world's most tightly guarded corporate and government facilities, including banks, corporate headquarters, manufacturing facilities, warehouses, and defense installations. If we'd been real thieves, we'd have obtained highly sensitive state secrets, stolen untold billions, and wreaked havoc on millions of lives by stealing people's identities and leaking their most sensitive information. We've been so successful that the FBI has recently invited me to train new agents in their Behavioral Analysis Unit. I've also partnered with law enforcement and used human hacking techniques to catch pedophiles online through a nonprofit I created, the Innocent Lives Foundation.

My team and I think of hacking humans as a super power, a psychological martial art, that we can use to get people we meet to do almost anything we want, and feel better about themselves—and us—in the process. In some ways we're tricking people, but more fundamentally we're wielding finely honed empathy and social savvy to our advantage. Applying insights from psychology, we cue in closely to how people are thinking and feeling, and use that information to nudge them so that they *want* to comply with our requests. Used correctly, social engineering enables others to feel happier, calmer, stronger, and just *better* about themselves by helping us out. They get this small, emotional "gift" from us, and they naturally return the favor, giving us what we want. All in the course of a few minutes of pleasant conversation.

HACKING HUMANS IN EVERYDAY LIFE

Imagine that you could harness these skills in your personal and professional life. You can. Not long ago, my wife, daughter, and I were in London's Heathrow Airport waiting for our plane. I was dragging around a cart piled high with our luggage, and as I approached the check-in counter, the cart hit a bump and some of the luggage fell off. Mindful that a major highway in London was named the M5, I made a joke: "Oh, a big American accident on the M5." The lady behind the counter laughed, so I said to myself, "Okay, great. At least she's in a good mood."

My wife chatted with this woman for a few minutes. "Before we check in," my wife said, "can I just tell you, your makeup is so immaculate, it matches your scarf beautifully. I'd love to buy one of those scarves. Is there any way I can do that?"

The woman was delighted at the compliment, not least because she'd probably been spending much of her shift until now taking requests from stressed and disgruntled passengers. She and my wife chatted for a few minutes more about scarves and makeup, and the gate attendant become visibly more relaxed—a smile on her face, the lines in her forehead easing, her shoulders relaxing. My wife wasn't trying to butter this woman up, nor was she piling it on. She genuinely liked the woman's makeup, and was happy to tell her so. The woman could sense her authenticity.

As for me, I sensed an opportunity. Leaning over, I put my arm around my wife and smiled, while tilting my head slightly. "Hey, you know," I said, "while you're checking us in, I'm wondering . . . I know we probably can't afford it, but is there any way you can just tell us how much it would cost to upgrade from economy? You know, maybe just to premium economy or something?"

She looked at my wife, not at me, and whispered, "Don't tell anyone." She typed furiously on her keyboard. "I'm putting all three of you in first class."

"What??? Thank you," we said. "That's amazing."

Let's break down what happened here. Whenever we meet someone for the first time, four baseline questions pop into our minds:

1. Who is this person?
2. What does this person want?
3. How long is this encounter going to take?
4. Is this person a threat?

If you think back to your most recent experience meeting someone, surely these questions were salient for you, even if only in the background of your awareness. To get a person you're meeting for the first time to do something for you, you have to quickly and deftly answer these four questions for them so that they can relax and feel comfortable. Otherwise, you're screwed. You can say whatever you want, and they'll be wary of you and unenthusiastic about complying.

When I arrived at the baggage counter, three out of these four questions were immediately answered for the attendant, simply from the social context and the way I looked. With my cart full of bags,

I was almost certainly a passenger, and I almost certainly wanted to check in. Our encounter would most likely only take a few minutes, as these encounters usually do. The only question that was not answered was the fourth one—was I a threat? Likely, I wasn't, but the attendant couldn't be absolutely sure. Maybe I was drunk and would become loud and violent when told I couldn't get an aisle seat. Maybe I was not drunk, but still a belligerent jerk who hated the airline and was looking for trouble. Maybe I was sick with COVID-19 and was about to cough all over her and expose her to the illness.

When I told that little joke, I settled question #4 for her in my favor. I was in effect throwing up what we call a "verbal softball." I just launched that joke with the attendant and other passengers within earshot, not knowing who would respond and "catch" the softball. Whoever did would become my "target," or as I also call it in this book, my "person of interest." That the attendant responded was a positive development, since she had something I wanted. My joke allowed me to build just a tiny bit of initial rapport with her. She laughed at the joke, and we made eye contact. To her, I was no longer a potentially threatening stranger, but rather a fun, self-deprecating American. We were off to a good start.

Then my wife, bless her heart, spontaneously did something amazing. She felt moved to compliment the woman, in a way that was not calculated or off-putting, setting in motion what we call "the liking principle." When it comes to influence, we tend to like people who like us. So, in addition to seeing me and by implication my family as nonthreatening, the gate attendant now liked us, or at least my wife. My wife also built a sense of common understanding with this woman— they were able to connect over makeup and scarves. Meanwhile, the compliment gave the attendant a chemical boost, causing her brain to release oxytocin and dopamine, molecules that create trust and produce the feeling of pleasure, respectively.

Amid this chemical soup, this mini-storm of connectedness, happiness, and pleasure, I knew that any request I made that was not outlandish would be more likely to elicit a positive response than it would otherwise. In that context, it would be easier for that attendant to honor my request, which she did. And then she took it a big step further by not charging us. We'd given her a "gift," and she'd given us one in return.

My students and I have used these and similar techniques to get seat upgrades, rental car upgrades, sought-after reservations to restaurants, and many other goodies. We've also used them to fix family relationships, get a big promotion at work, deal with difficult colleagues, make new friends, feel more comfortable at cocktail parties and in other social situations, and much more. Of course, we've also used it to protect ourselves against others who might like to manipulate us to take action that isn't in our best interests. Social engineering is a generally applicable approach that, when mastered, will allow you to win friends, influence people, and achieve most goals you might have—all by being kinder, more empathetic, and more giving.

Empathy in particular is foundational to human hacking. Popular culture often portrays empathy as inherently good, a view supported by psychologists such as Simon Baron-Cohen, who has theorized that cruelty is made possible in part by a relative lack of empathy.[3] But other scholars have linked the presence of empathy to a range of negative phenomena, including cruelty and tribalism.[4] I tend to regard empathy as a value-neutral concept, defined as the act of imaginatively inhabiting someone else's emotional experience. Criminal hackers and con men are amazing at the perspective-taking that is at the core of empathy—they just deploy it maliciously to benefit themselves. They are keenly sensitive to what others are thinking, and they deploy that sensitivity to say or do exactly the right thing to manipulate others.

We can use the same empathetic mindset, but channel it more

positively, influencing others to decide to help us rather than forcing them to do so through manipulation. As I know you'll find, taking the empathetic leap makes it far easier to achieve whatever goals we might be pursuing. By displaying empathy, we can simultaneously address others' needs, too, leaving them better off for having met us.

The Foundational Principle of Hacking Humans

To influence others to obtain what you want, cultivate an empathetic mindset. You must make a habit of getting outside of your own head, imagining what the other person is thinking and engaging with them in ways that respect and address their needs, beliefs, and emotions.

If you take anything away from this book, make it the cultivation of an empathetic mindset. All of us can empathize with others to a greater or lesser extent, and all of us can cultivate that ability by working on it. In fact, the tools we'll explore in the following chapters all amount to different ways of practicing, channeling, and expressing empathy. By mastering these tools, you can become so awesome at empathy that it becomes a way of being, something you instantly and unconsciously apply as you move through the world. You'll be amazed at how much easier it is to achieve your goals, and how much better it feels.

It might surprise you to hear that something as benevolent as empathy (coupled, as I'm suggesting, with a serious dose of kindness, respect, and generosity) underlies something as seemingly malevolent as hacking, but it's true. Understand people better, communicate with them better, treat them better, and you'll get more of what *you* want, too. Think of social engineering as the art of asking nicely, of behaving diplomatically, of reading others and respecting their needs, of practicing the social niceties, all rolled up into one powerful approach that you can mobilize at will to whatever end you choose.

ABOUT THIS BOOK

I first knew I needed to write *Human Hacking* a few years ago when I noticed that laypeople were spending thousands of dollars to take my social engineering course, even though it was marketed explicitly to security professionals. A salesman was taking it to learn to sell more effectively. A Zumba instructor was taking it to improve personal relationships. A high school teacher was taking it to learn how to engage more fruitfully with her students. A mom was taking it to come out of her shell more and engage more effectively with her kids. These people had all heard about the course from friends and made the connection with their own lives.

Curious, I followed up with these people after the course was over, and found that they were achieving epic, even life-changing results by hacking humans. They were getting ahead in their careers, solidifying their romantic relationships, parenting their kids better—you name it. Many of these students were introverts who were painfully shy when they first came to my class. A week later, I had them running around the city asking bold questions of complete strangers. Over the following weeks and months, they were making new friends, networking with colleagues, and engaging with the world in other ways that they never would have imagined.

These are difficult times in which to live as a human being. Technology has rendered us more isolated from one another and more socially awkward than ever before (and pandemics like COVID-19 don't help, either). We live in our little social bubbles, reluctant to connect with people in our immediate vicinity. Tribalism compounds the problem: entire categories of people seem so different from us that communication seems impossible. Meanwhile, as long-standing rules for social conduct are demolished before our eyes, it's no longer clear how we should communicate with our work colleagues, people we meet at social events, members of the opposite sex, or even our kids.

All of these developments may leave us feeling powerless, insecure, and anxious when communicating with others. But if we learn how to hack humans, we can regain some of this power. We can learn how to read people and their emotions better than before, and thus become wiser when dealing with them. We can handle conflict with others more adroitly, and even better, prevent it from arising in the first place. We can ask for what we want and need in ways that seem natural and reasonable instead of off-putting. We can spot opportunities when they arise, getting more of what we want (as I did at Heathrow Airport). We can learn to protect ourselves against malicious hackers and scam artists, allowing ourselves to feel calmer and more confident in any situation. Critically, we can learn to become far more self-aware about how we're communicating. When we do commit social miscues—and as we'll see, even the most masterful hackers do—we can learn from them and get better going forward.

The chapters in this book take you through the topics that every expert hacker of humans knows and masters. We start with a powerful tool you can use to help you understand communications patterns better—your own, and others'. After all, if you understand what a person in your life is likely to respond to, you can tailor your communications accordingly to be far more effective. Subsequent chapters teach you how to:

+ establish rapport with people;
+ develop effective pretexts for conversations;

+ influence people to do your bidding;
+ get people to divulge information they might not otherwise feel comfortable sharing;
+ protect yourself against would-be manipulators;
+ frame conversations so that you are more likely to succeed;
+ use body language to your advantage; and
+ plan out important interactions in advance, integrating the many tools covered in this book.

Work through these chapters individually, taking time to practice the skills using the "missions" or exercises I provide. With diligence on your part, you should see improvement in your abilities as a communicator and influencer within just a few weeks. Hopefully, you'll continue practicing and improving much as you would with a martial art or a musical instrument, recognizing that as good as you might get, you're never "done."

You can also use this book to prepare for specific, "big" conversations in your life, like a job interview, a negotiation, or a difficult conversation with a colleague or loved one. Instead of going into such conversations cold, you'll have a whole set of tools to fall back on, as well as a plan and the confidence that comes with knowledge and mastery. Read each chapter with your upcoming interaction in mind, thinking how you might apply the skills in question to this particular "hacking humans" challenge. Then use the book's final chapter to map out a detailed plan for how you'll handle it. If you've ever tried to prepare for a big conversation before, I think you'll find that this book will help you take your readiness—and your confidence—to a whole new level.

I just have one request of you: *Don't Be Evil*. Can you manage that? As you read this book and begin practicing its techniques, you will quickly understand the potential of this new super power you are cultivating. Like any super power, hacking humans can be used for good and for evil. And when it's used for evil, the effects both on individuals and society can be devastating. Mindful of these effects, my team and I adhere strictly to a formal code of ethics. There are a number of parts to it, but in essence, we won't break the law in order to hack into a server or secure location.* We won't tell the world about the vulnerabilities we uncover. We won't threaten people or use other manipulative tactics that cause them to suffer. We *will*, in every inter-action we have, leave others better for having met us.

In my courses, I have students agree to this code of ethics before I teach them the material in this book. In sharing it with you, I ask that you read the code of ethics at the beginning of this book and agree to abide by it. None of us are perfect, but I believe that the vast majority of readers will hack humans in ways that do leave others better off for having met us. A few readers might put my techniques to immoral or criminal ends, but on balance, spreading our hacking techniques will make the world kinder, more considerate, more empathetic, and more welcoming. For every person with ill intent, a thousand will use this book to become more successful and happier while also treating others in ways that they like, too.

Be one of that thousand. If you've been struggling to get ahead in any area of your life, or if you simply want to build on your existing success, this is the book you've been waiting for. Learn the skills, prac-tice them, and master them. Do yourself and the rest of us a favor. Get off your butt, stop slacking, and start hacking. Humans, that is.

---

* Technically, we do violate the law by breaking into buildings, sending phishing emails, and so on. However, clients contractually allow us to take these actions, specifying, for instance, that we have their permission to break into their buildings. What we *won't* do is take any illegal action that our contracts don't permit.

CHAPTER 1

KNOW YOURSELF, SO YOU CAN KNOW OTHERS

Become more aware of how you and
"persons of interest" in your life tick.

Before you can master the art and science of hacking other humans, you must first hack yourself. That is, you have to understand your own communications patterns, so that you can adjust for tendencies that might not be working to your advantage. As you become more self-aware, you can take your communications to the next level by considering others' personalities and the communications styles they favor. Tailoring what you say to each particular "person of interest" in your life—your boss, your spouse, your kids, strangers you happen to meet, anybody at all—maximizes your chances of success, no matter what your objective might be.

In 2018, a scammer convinced Marian Simulik, the treasurer of the city of Ottawa, Canada, to wire almost $100,000 to a phony vendor. The scammer deployed a phishing attack, sending an email that

purported to be from Steve Kanellakos, the city manager and Simulik's boss, asking her to wire the money. Actually, this was a particular
kind of phishing attack, one that individually targets an important
person inside of an organization—what we call a "whaling" attack (get
it? Whaling?). Here's what the email said:

> Okay, I want you to take care of this for me personally, I have
> just been informed that we have had an offer accepted by a
> new international vendor, to complete an acquisition that i have
> been negotiating privately for some time now, in line with the
> terms agreed, we will need to make a down payment of 30%
> of their total, Which will be $97,797.20. An announcement is
> currently being drafted and will be announced next week, once
> the deal has been executed, for now I don't want to go into any
> more details. Until we are in a position to formally announce
> the acquisition, I do not want you discussing it with anybody
> in the office, any question please email me. Can you confirm if
> international wire transfer can go out this morning?[1]

Would you have fallen for this scam? The email was well conceived, deploying a number of powerful techniques we'll discuss later
in this book. Before we get to those, let's consider how adroitly this
message was framed with Simulik in mind. If you had to guess, you'd
probably assume that a city treasurer responsible for handling millions of dollars in taxpayer money would be a diligent, conscientious
person—very private, disciplined, systematic. It's a stereotype, but
most stereotypes contain at least a kernel of truth. If you're a scammer,
a kernel is all you need.

In this case, the scammer wrote this message to appeal to a diligent, conscientious person. The language is precise, conveying relevant
and believable facts about the apparent deal. The tone is serious and

businesslike—no chatting about the kids or LOLs here. The scam's pretext—that Kanellakos has been "privately" negotiating a sensitive deal—is something a precise, restrained, private person would readily "get." The first line asks Simulik to "take care of [the wiring] for me personally," suggesting that the matter at hand is extremely sensitive and requires discretion and judgment. That Kanellakos is making this request at all suggests that he trusts the treasurer and her judgment over that of other team members. Later in the message, the scammer asks Simulik to show discretion and not discuss this very sensitive matter "with anybody in the office." He *knows* she's conscientious and appreciates that about her. Although the scammer (impersonating Kanellakos) says that Simulik can feel free to email him, he indicates that he doesn't "want to go into any more details"—precisely because he, too, is precise, professional, and conscientious.

The scammer probably didn't *know* that the treasurer was a particularly conscientious person. Chances are, he had never met her or otherwise interacted with her. The FBI actually caught this scammer, who turned out to be some guy living in Florida, thousands of miles away.[2] This scammer probably had met treasurer types before and taken an educated guess about *this* city treasurer. If he had been wrong, and this treasurer had not been especially conscientious, private, or diligent, the email likely would have rung false, and she would have spotted it as a fraud. As it turned out, the scammer was right, and she fell for it.

Think about the power of this kind of attack. Simulik wasn't a newbie on the job. She was a twenty-eight-year veteran and a "highly respected senior manager," as a newspaper account reported. Also, not long before receiving this email, Simulik had received another email asking for money that appeared to be from the head of the city library, and that they recognized was fraudulent. And yet this time Simulik had still fallen for it. The scam was only discovered promptly because the scammer got greedy. Days after Simulik had wired the money, she received another email asking for even more money. That subsequent email prompted her to chat with the city manager and learn that she'd been scammed.

There are important lessons here for us all. First, and most obviously, *don't automatically send a wire transfer when requested by email. Always follow up personally.* And second, when making a request of someone, *always consider their communications style and preferences and tailor what you say accordingly.*

KNOW THYSELF

Actually, if you think about what was likely going through the scammer's mind, there's a third piece of wisdom here for us: *Know your own personality and be sure not to let it impede your communications goals.*

My company was launching a new conference for people in the security industry—a big deal for us. We had months to prepare, but I needed my people all in, especially Shayna, my assistant. My natural inclination when interacting with others is to be really blunt with them and order them around, drill sergeant–style. I tend to just blurt out thoughts, not considering how others around me might feel. People have called me forceful, confident, blunt—and they were being charitable. I've heard words like "jerk" leveled at me, too. In this instance, I might have gone up to her desk and said, "Hey. We need this conference to succeed, so like everyone else, you're going to have to work your butt off. That means staying late when we need it and working weekends. Do it, okay? Don't disappoint me!"

For most employees, a request proffered in this way wouldn't be terribly motivating. On the contrary, it would be off-putting. Fortunately, I didn't ask Shayna in this way. About a decade ago, I became more aware of my own personality and communications style, the good, the bad, and the ugly. I was giving my first-ever week-long training on social engineering, and true to form, was leading the class like a drill sergeant—shouting at people, ordering them around, projecting authority. It was exhausting for me, and probably annoying for my students.

My friend Robin Dreeke, bestselling author and former FBI behavioral expert, was co-teaching this class with me, and afterward he pulled me aside and said, "Dude, you've got to change your training style. You're just barking orders out left and right." I disagreed with him at first, but because I respected him, I took his advice and stopped barking out orders. What a difference that made. Students actually smiled as they sat in class. They participated more. They seemed more eager to absorb the material. Wow, I thought, this is powerful.

Over time, I adjusted my communications style, ditching the drill sergeant persona and becoming much more outgoing, jovial, and lighthearted. I also became much more aware minute to minute of what I was saying, how I was saying it, and how it was coming across. I started to focus more intently on understanding other people's personalities and crafting my communications accordingly. Did I become far more effective as a hacker of humans? Heck, yeah!

Instead of ordering Shayna to put in her best effort, I thought about her personality and the communications style that would likely appeal to her, just like the Ottawa scammer had done for his target. I had an advantage in that I knew Shayna quite well—I wasn't taking much of a guess. I knew she was conscientious, very organized, and private, like the scammer assumed his target was. She liked boundaries and preferred to stay out of the limelight. So, a very private, personal gesture on my part would likely prove most effective—certainly more so than my lavishing public praise on her, say, and then asking her to please put in her best effort.

I bought Shayna a gift card for a store I knew she liked, attaching a personal note thanking her for all the professionalism she has brought to our company, and telling her what a difference it has made. I mentioned that our conference was coming up, and that I really needed her to continue doing the great job she had been doing.

Shayna *loved* it. The gesture touched her and inspired her to keep working hard. By all appearances, I could have handed her a million-dollar check and she wouldn't have been as motivated. All because I had been aware of my own worst impulses, had resolved to bypass them, had taken into account the personality of my "subject," and had shaped my communications accordingly.

You can't become an effective hacker of humans unless you've developed at least some awareness of your own communications tendencies— your strengths and weaknesses—and have developed the habit of uncovering relevant personality traits of those you need to influence. If I were trying to break into the headquarters of a big company, and I deployed my blunt, drill sergeant style (for instance, pretending that I was a senior executive from another office, and ordering the guards to let me in even though I didn't have a badge), that might resonate with some security personnel who react well to that style. But it would almost certainly backfire with many others who don't. So I would instantly be limiting my chances of success to just 50 percent (or less). In addition, by jumping in and communicating in my own style, I'm not giving any thought to crafting the interaction to my benefit, using the tools I'll share later in this book. I'm increasing my chances of making a dumb mistake.

In our daily lives, our obliviousness to how we naturally like to communicate leads to untold problems. A former employee at my company—I'll call her Camilla—and I worked together closely for years. For much of that time, we struggled to get along with one another, and I wasn't sure why. It turned out that our communications styles were completely different. Because I was so direct with people, Camilla often saw me as a complete jerk. Meanwhile, she preferred to communicate more deliberately, thinking her ideas through first before speaking. Because she didn't react quickly and decisively to what I was saying, I often viewed her as being completely apathetic about her work and our business.

Day after day, we talked at cross purposes with one another. On one occasion, when we had to choose a health care plan for our company, I did some research and was pretty sure about which plan I wanted us to go with. I sent her a short email outlining my logic and asking her what she thought. A few minutes later, I called her up and asked if she got the email. "Yep," she said, "I'm reading it now."

"So what do you think"

Pause.

"Okay," I said. "I'm going to go this route, okay?"

"I guess you can . . . [pause] . . . if you want to be a jerk about it."

"Great, thanks, that's all I need."

Click.

Later that day, I learned that she was upset at me. I couldn't understand why—I had asked her opinion, and she had said yes. When I asked her, she explained that I hadn't given her any time to read the email and make a thoughtful decision. "I said you could, if you wanted to be a jerk."

"I didn't hear the 'if you wanted to be a jerk part,'" I said.

"You never hear that part."

She was right, I didn't. And I also didn't get that she really did care about our company and making the right decision—she just needed more time to think before speaking up.

You might have the best of intentions when you have an encounter with a spouse, colleague, friend, or someone else in your life. You might be trying hard to communicate well and have an awesome conversation. And yet, you might find that you're failing to connect, that the other person isn't quite getting what you said, or that they're becoming upset. Perhaps this other person is in a bad mood, and it's coloring what they hear. Perhaps you lack some context about them or their experiences, and you inadvertently offend them. But perhaps the *way* you are communicating with them doesn't conform well with how they're inclined to communicate. In so many cases, such mismatches make our relationships more difficult and cause us untold angst and pain.

Failing to understand our own communications tendencies also leaves us vulnerable to being influenced by others in unfortunate ways. When I was fifteen, my family moved from upstate New York to Pennsylvania and then down to Florida. I was pale as a lightbulb but, like many teenage boys, eager to impress the ladies. Picture me and a bunch of girls lying on the sand one cold January day by a fire. All of the guys are out surfing in the water. "Ahhh," I think to myself, "this is paradise. I've got all these babes to myself." Then one of the guys comes in and says to me, "Hey, Chris, you gonna sit there like a wimp, or are you gonna paddle out like the rest of us?"

Now, the water on this day isn't just frigid, but rough—six- to eight-foot seas. I haven't surfed before, not even a little bit. If I say yes, I'll open myself up to likely humiliation. "Some other time," I say. "I don't have a bathing suit."

"You have underwear on?" the kid says.

"Well, yeah."

"Go in that."

Turning away from the girls, I strip down to my underwear and make for the water. I grab a board, strap on its leash to my ankle, and hit the water. In addition to being freezing cold, it's rough as heck—the waves slam into me, knocking me around. I can barely make it out thirty feet, and I even feel like I might drown in the shallow water. I know that in my awkwardness I'm humiliating myself in front of these girls. Finally, one of the guys swims over and tows me out, causing me even more embarrassment.

Farther out, the waves are coming in bigger than a house. There is no way I should be out there. But, egged on by the other guys, I paddle for a wave. I manage to stand up, but just for a second, before losing my balance. The churning water pummels me and smashes me down hard on a sandbar. When I manage to surface, I'm gasping and can't find my underwear—the combination of wave and sandbar has ripped it off me. I look around for my board and find it smashed to pieces. So, picture me now having to make the walk of shame, buck naked, freezing cold, pasty white, past all of those girls I've been trying to impress.

It was an epic fail—not only was I humiliated, but I wound up catching pneumonia from the cold water. I allowed this unpleasant situation to unfold for two reasons. First, I was a testosterone-laden teenager who didn't have any friends and was eager to make them. But second, and just as bad, I lacked any sense at all of my own communications proclivities. As someone who favors a dominant, aggressive style of communicating, I tend to respond well to challenges. If someone dares me to do something, I'm going to take the bait and accept the challenge. The guy who convinced me to jump into the water dared me—was I "tough enough," he implied, or was I a wimp? If he had asked me in a quieter way, I probably wouldn't have gone in. If he had levied the challenge, and if I understood myself well enough to know that I was susceptible to that kind of appeal, I also probably wouldn't have gone in—I would have made a smarter decision and found a way to decline the invitation. Since I utterly lacked self-awareness, this other guy was able to trigger a favorable response in me. I paid the price.

FOUR TYPES OF COMMUNICATORS

When I train people to become security experts, I introduce them to a classic psychological profiling tool called DISC, which they can use to analyze their own communications behavior, and which they can deploy before and during conversations to quickly size up how others prefer to communicate as well. Although DISC has both fans and critics, many companies use it when hiring employees and assembling teams, and experts in professional fields like dentistry have advocated for its use as well.[3] There's a good reason: research suggests that DISC is both reliable and helpful, increasing people's performance and making workplace interactions easier.[4] My students and I agree. When it comes to the hacking of humans, both professionally and in everyday life, DISC is invaluable and even transformative, regardless of whatever imperfections or limitations it might have.

DISC is based on the pioneering work of the psychologist William Moulton Marston, who, during the 1920s, came up with the idea that we can separate people into four distinct "types" based on how they tend to express their emotions.[5] Generations of psychologists have since developed and commercialized tests based on Marston's model that people can take to determine which type best describes them. My team buys one such test and incorporates it into the social engineering courses we teach, allowing our students to obtain a scientifically valid assessment of how they communicate. As I tell my students, DISC isn't a personality test like the better-known Myers-Briggs assessment. Rather, it helps us understand our communications tendencies, which might reflect elements of our personalities. (Our personalities, after all, are defined by way more than our self-expression. They encompass other kinds of behavior on our part, as well as how we make sense of the world.)

I can't reproduce the specific test we use in this book (our provider would sue me!), but I can draw on my general knowledge to give you the gist of DISC. That should be enough to help you understand better how you communicate and how you might better interact with others. In particular, let's take a closer look at those four types, so that you can begin to see how you and others around you might map onto them. I'll emphasize right up front that the DISC model is value neutral. No one type among the four is better or worse than any other. You're not smarter or more skilled or possessed of a certain set of values just because your communications fall into a given pattern. You just communicate in a specific way that has advantages and drawbacks, depending on the social context and the people with whom you're interacting.

Some people are Dominant (D) types—they're confident and focused on bottom-line results. Others are oriented around Influencing others (I)—they're enthusiastic, optimistic collaborators. A third group of people are known for their Steadiness (S)—they're sincere, calm, and supportive of others. Finally, you have your Conscientious types (C), people like my assistant Shayna who are known for being organized and very factual. "D"s and "I"s tend to favor more direct communications styles, while "C" and "S" types favor indirect styles. Individuals who are "I" or "S" tend to focus on connecting with people more, while "D" and "C" types are more focused on getting things done in their communications.

To help people understand these four types, I find that it helps to connect them with celebrities. Foodies out there will be familiar with celebrity chef and television personality Gordon Ramsay. Now, that dude is *definitely* a "D" kind of person: he's direct, sharp, forceful, task focused—and that's putting it mildly. (Oh, how I love that guy!) At times, "D" people seem to not care about others and their feelings. That's not necessarily true—they might care very much, but they focus so much on results that other considerations fade into the background as they interact with others. They come across as overly harsh, severe, abrupt, pushy, or domineering, especially in stressful situations. Other celebrities who exhibit strong "D" tendencies are Simon Cowell from the TV show *American Idol*, CNBC personality Jim Cramer, and former GE CEO Jack Welch. In the workplace, Dominant types tend to gravitate toward leadership and managerial roles—careers in which they can be in charge of others.

The prototypical Influencer type might be someone like former president Bill Clinton. He is a natural with people—expressive, exuberant—as Influencers tend to be. They love to be the center of attention. If you're not laughing at their stories and enjoying yourself, there's something wrong. Influencers also like to talk about themselves, and they tend to do it in ways that get them noticed (by speaking loudly or in an animated fashion, for instance). Other well-known people whom I'd classify as Influencers include Jimmy Fallon (and a good number of other television hosts), Tina Fey (and many other comedians), and quite a number of salespeople I've met during my time. Many motivational speakers, teachers, and courtroom attorneys are also natural "I" types. And yet, "I"s can sometimes struggle to connect with certain types of people. Sometimes Influencers are so enthusiastic and outgoing that they seem fake, superficial, or manipulative, not to mention egotistical. To other non "I"s, they might come across as impulsive or excessive, speaking too spontaneously and throwing too much information or emotion at you too quickly. And because they're so cheery, "I"s can often seem overly optimistic.

Actors like Tom Hanks or Hugh Jackman are steady "S" types. Like Influencers, they're people-oriented, but they tend to exude a quieter presence, standing out of the limelight and serving instead as supporters or wing people. They're happy for others to shine, and they tend to talk about others in their lives. Many people in helping roles—nurses, therapists, teachers, counselors—tend to be "S" types. They come across as agreeable, reliable, and accommodating—the person on your team who would fall on their sword for you. Their goal is for *everyone* to succeed, and they take pleasure in having the team get credit and feel good about what they've done, not just them. But because they stand back so much, "S"s also can come across as apathetic and slow. They don't like to rock the boat, so at times they can seem stubborn and unwilling to change. They can also appear overly passive-aggressive. You know they're feeling something, but they just aren't coming out and *saying* it.

The final DISC type, Conscientious, or "C," tends to be more reserved, but also more detail oriented. An actress like Meg Ryan, who is very private and has professed to hate the spotlight, might be a "C," and famous recluses like the authors J. D. Salinger or Harper Lee might have been, too. Conscientious types are discreet, and they also tend to be orderly and methodical in how they communicate. "C" types might naturally gravitate toward careers as accountants, researchers, doctors, or pilots, since these roles reward people who attend to the details and remain oriented to completing the task at hand. The challenge: "C" types can come across as nerdy, aloof, awkward, distant, or hard to know. If you ask them a question and don't happen to like detail, they might bore you with a long-winded answer, giving you way more information than you feel you need, because they revel in the details. They might struggle in fast-moving situations that require spontaneous disclosure of information, or situations when openness and spontaneity with others is a plus.

In describing these types, I'm broadly generalizing about people and how they interact with others. In truth, all of us express all four of these communication behaviors to varying degrees. When I say I'm a "D," what I mean is Dominance traits tend to come out most strongly in me. I also have some "I" and "C" traits, but they're not as pronounced, and I'm really weak on the "S" trait, but it's still there. Also, we tend to bring out more or less of these traits depending on the situations we're in. Someone who comes across most strongly as an extroverted "I" type might express those traits in a public setting like a cocktail party. Get them with their family, and other behavior might emerge, even if their communications overall still remain pretty strongly in "I" territory.

GET YOUR DISC ON

When I teach DISC, students often rush to apply it to others around them—their spouses, bosses, and so on. "Whoa, calm down," I tell them. "Let's first use this to figure out *YOU*, because that's going to let *you* become much more powerful in the social situations you encounter each day."

I invite you now to perform the following exercise:

Take a moment to think about your own communications tendencies, using the DISC cheat sheets located in the Appendix at the back of the book. Do you tend to be more people oriented, or do you focus on the task and obtaining specific results? Do you tend to adopt a more direct communications style, or indirect? Asking these two questions can help you locate where on the grid you roughly are. Once you've identified your dominant type, think about its strengths and weaknesses. How does your behavior serve you well—or not so well—in specific situations and with specific people (at home with your family, at work with your colleagues, during the weekend with your friends)?

As you understand the strengths and weaknesses of your primary communications style, pay special attention to the weaknesses. When might your style risk alienating others that you might otherwise wish to attract or feel close to? Here's another exercise to try:

Over the next few days, notice times when you accomplish something in collaboration with others, and times when you come into conflict with others. In the moment (that is, right after the experience), think about how your communications tendencies just contributed to the win or the disagreement. If you're like my students, you'll find yourself coming up with small epiphanies, saying to yourself, "Oh, that's why that conversation ended in an argument," or "That's why that email didn't get the reaction I'd hoped."

As you become attuned to how you operate socially, the next step is to exert more control over your behavior. Understanding tendencies of yours that rub others wrong, you can work on softening those "rough edges." As a "D" I know I'm often overly direct and abrupt with people. In the past, when I received an email that upset me, I tended to fire back and tell the sender what I *really* thought. That behavior ticked people off, which meant that they were less inclined to go along with my requests and felt more distanced from me emotionally. I challenged myself to take a breather every time I received a challenging email. "Chris," I told myself, "get up and walk away." That technique didn't work for me—I wound up stewing about the email. So I tried something else: when I received that challenging email, I let myself write the email response I wanted to write in my moment of anger, but then I told myself to walk away before clicking send. That worked: I got my emotions off my chest, but I didn't respond in a stereotypically "D" kind of way. After my break, when I reread the email I was going to send, I usually found myself editing 90 percent of it.

My advice for people with other communications profiles would be similar: find a way to get outside any emotional response that is triggered in you, and to avoid the baseline communications behavior to which you'll automatically revert. If you're an Influencer type, you might wind up alienating others by talking too much about yourself in the course of a conversation—how you feel, what you think, how you reacted. To smooth out this "rough edge," take a step back, and then challenge yourself to let others talk more and to practice active listening. Resist the urge to think about what you'll say next, and refocus yourself (repeatedly, if necessary) on what others are saying. If you're speaking in person or on the phone with another person instead of via text or email, you might have to do more than simply walk away. Explain to the other person that you need a few moments to calm down or take a break, and that you'll then be happy to continue the conversation.

If you tend to behave along the lines of a Steady type, passive-aggressive responses might pose a problem. The next time conflict arises with someone in your life, step back and practice active listening just as an "I" type of person might but focus on understanding the other person's viewpoint rather than winning the argument. "S" types are extremely people oriented, so they tend to find it disturbing when someone raises an issue with them. It's hard for them not to react defensively, and as a result they often can't process another person's perspective. Focus on stepping past your emotional response, putting yourself in the other person's position, and really "getting" what they're saying.

If you're a Conscientious type and you're in a confrontation with someone else, you're going to feel tempted to blast the other person with a million and one reasons why what they did sucked. If you lay it all out there, you presume, you'll win the argument by sheer force of logic. If you're in a real-time conversation either in person or on the phone, challenge yourself to take a break for a few minutes to get outside of the emotion. Upon returning to the conversation, focus on actively listening rather than talking. If you find yourself resorting to a litany of facts, stop, take a breath, and focus on listening once again. Ditto if you find yourself spewing a litany of facts into an email or text.

Think about three specific and recurring social situations (conversations you have, situations in which you receive certain kinds of email or text messages, and so on) in which your dominant behavior type causes you to behave in ways that others don't like. For each one, think of a more specific strategy for how you might compensate for the unhelpful parts of your communications profile. Over the next several days, deploy your strategies and see what happens.

The point here is to make a habit of thinking about the weaknesses of your dominant communications style, so that you can correct for them consistently and in the moment. You want to behave more *mindfully* in social situations, and you want to get to the point where you're doing it automatically. That takes time and practice. It's like learning a foreign language: you must focus on it daily for weeks on end, maybe longer. But becoming a master hacker of humans requires nothing less.

TAKING DISC TO THE NEXT LEVEL

Once you've got a better handle on your own communications tendencies, you can enhance your behavior further by applying DISC to other people and adjusting your own communications to better match their needs. When you're about to have a significant conversation, or if you need to write someone an important email or letter, prepare in advance by creating a DISC profile of that person. I have every member of my company take a formal DISC assessment when they come on board, and I make these available for everyone to see. Before a big conversation with an employee, I'll look up their profile and on that basis generate a strategy for the conversation. You can do something similar for key people in your life. Based on the description of DISC provided above and the DISC worksheet provided at the end of this book, sit down before your big conversation and think about how the person—whether it's your spouse, your teenager, someone on your team, your landlord—tends to communicate. Run through the four types—can you more or less identify one of them as that person's dominant type?

Once you do, use the DISC Cheat Sheet to think more closely about the other person and his or her inclinations and needs. You don't want to speak to a "D," say, in the same way as you would an "S." A "D" wants you to speak directly to them and to focus on results, while an "S" wants you to try to get along with them and validate them in a more relaxed, easygoing way. Since you're preparing in advance, you can craft what you'll say with this difference in mind. If you're planning a conversation with an "S," make sure you mention some reasons (truthful, of course) why you think they're important. Take your time with the conversation—don't rush to get straight to the point. Don't get too excited or impassioned in making your argument. Listen carefully to what they say and validate it. The DISC Cheat Sheet provides advice about what people falling into each type want out of social interactions, how they tend to communicate, how you can best communicate with them, and how you can help them communicate better with you.

You don't have to wait for a big conversation before performing a DISC analysis. When my student Brannon took my course in 2013, he had never heard of DISC. He found himself getting goose bumps as he read through his own profile, and was, as he remembers, "shocked because there were things in there that I wasn't prepared to admit to myself." Looking around the room, he saw "person after person, row after row, having the exact same reaction to their test results. It was really astounding, an almost surreal experience." Learning that he rated strongly for the "D" and "I" types, he realized that he had been "a bull in a china shop" for his entire life.

At the time, Brannon was having trouble with his marriage—he and his wife were constantly arguing and angry at one another. Learning about DISC, he realized that his wife had a different profile than he did—she was a very strong "S" type. Talking about it together, they realized that their differing communications styles accounted for a good part of their conflict. As an "S," his wife tended to shrink away from direct confrontation, while Brannon favored it. When issues arose, she just wanted peace, while he wanted to talk the issue to death until they reached some sort of resolution. Understanding her communications style allowed Brannon to spot occasions when it was better to let his wife cut a conversation short instead of pushing through until it was "over" in his mind. Brannon and his wife eventually split up, but understanding one another's profiles has allowed them to get along better as they co-parent their kids. "Now we can talk more objectively about the things I'm doing to tick her off," Brannon says, "and the things she's doing to tick me off. It makes life easier."

Applying DISC can also help you when you're dealing with people you don't know all that well, or whom you're encountering for the first time. As you work with DISC, you might find yourself spotting behavior that "seems like something a 'C' would do" or that is "very 'I'-like." No, you're not performing a scientific analysis. Yes, you're coming to a superficial conclusion. But superficial conclusions, while they can often prove wrong, are sometimes correct. When you're dealing with people you don't know well, a superficial conclusion is better than having *no* insight into those individuals. At least you have something to go on, even if you wind up having to adjust your behavior midstream as you discover more about them and the kinds of communications behavior they prefer. See the DISC Cheat Sheet for some quick pointers on how to spot people matching the four types "in the wild."

With practice, you can become adept at quickly classifying people you meet and adapting your speech and action accordingly. To make it second nature, start by jotting down notes immediately after conversations. Given what the other person said or did, how might you best classify them? Did they use a lot of detail? Were they direct? Did they talk about themselves a lot? Did they direct attention toward others, to the exclusion of themselves? And so on. Again—I can't emphasize it enough—active listening is *so* important. When you first start dabbling with DISC, don't think about classifying someone during a conversation. Listen as intently as possible, soaking everything up, really engaging with what you hear. Once the conversation is over, take a few moments to recall what you heard and analyze it while it is still fresh. Over time, you'll find that you don't need this extra few minutes of deliberation—you'll naturally perform the analysis in your mind at the conclusion of the conversation. And with even more practice, you'll find yourself instantly and unconsciously doing it during the conversation, even as you actively listen.

Imagine being able to approach someone and know immediately what is more likely to resonate with them, and what isn't. Your quick analysis might be off, but even if you assess correctly 20 or 30 percent of the time, that makes a big difference. I've gotten to the point where I can determine a person's communications profile with at least some degree of accuracy within seconds of meeting them. When I'm approaching the reception desk of a corporate headquarters and trying to break in, I concoct a running theory of the receptionist's type based on how they greet me, what kinds of pictures are on their desk, their body language, and so on, and I frame what I do and say accordingly. It's quite amazing—and I'm even more accurate if I have gone online in advance and reviewed the receptionist's social media postings. Which brings me to our next exercise.

Look up the Twitter accounts of three of your favorite celebrities. Closely review their postings. What can you discern about their communications style? For example, Bill Clinton's postings are those of the classic Influencer. He talks about himself a lot, speaking in the first person and highlighting people whom he likes. In general, his postings are quite energetic, exuberant, and "loud." Bonus points: for each of the four DISC types, see if you can come up with five celebrities other than the ones mentioned in this chapter who evoke that type.

And here's another exercise you might try:

To practice quick DISC analyses, go to a crowded public place and people-watch for an hour. Watch groups of people, and see if you can figure out which individuals fit under each category.

SUMMARY

Lao Tzu, the Chinese philosopher and founder of Taoism, once said, "He who knows others is wise; he who knows himself is enlightened."[6] This chapter has been about being both enlightened and wise: knowing yourself better, and also your people of interest. As I think you'll find, communications profiling is amazingly powerful when it's fully developed, underpinning anything else you do to hack humans.

Although most bad guys probably don't use DISC, they do use their own versions of quick-and-dirty profiling to choose their victims and make their approach. Terrorist networks are known to scrape social media platforms like Twitter or Facebook, searching for people who are expressing hostility toward Western governments. In particular, they're looking for individuals who feel a certain type of disillusionment and frustration, and who likely harbor a specific set of emotional tendencies. The extremists tailor what they say and how they say it to lure these people in. Young people become vulnerable, as they have no idea of the sophistication of the seemingly sympathetic people they're encountering.

You can use profiling for good, deploying it to improve the quality of your relationships and interactions. In essence, profiling works because whether we're classifying ourselves or others, we're directing attention away from where it usually is during social encounters—on ourselves, our needs, our desires—and onto where it should be: onto other people. We're trying hard—maybe for the first time in our lives—to think deeply about others and how they're approaching and experiencing a conversation. We're developing empathy for other people, so that we can begin to connect with them on *their* terms, not just ours.

Empathy truly is fundamental to human hacking, but as we'll see, it goes far beyond profiling. Con men, security experts, and other professional hackers of humans draw on empathy to frame conversations from the very outset so that their victims are more likely to do what they want. If you're sitting at your desk working, and a stranger calls you up and says, "You don't know me, but I want you to wire five hundred dollars to the following account number," you're not going to do it. But if a caller identifies himself as a representative of your energy company, says that your bill is past due and that your service will be cut off if you don't pay five hundred dollars within an hour, you just might (and even more so if you looked at your caller ID and the call seemed to be coming from your energy company's number). This scam is extremely common,[7] and it works because many people feel anxious at the thought of losing their power. The scammers know this—they've made that empathetic leap—and have developed that insight into a compelling "pretext" for holding a conversation with you. Conversely, it's very difficult to win friends, influence people, and get what you want if you haven't mastered what we might call "the art of the start." Let's explore how to initiate conversations more deliberately, so that you're evoking positive emotional responses in people that will make them *want* to engage further with you.

CHAPTER 2

BECOME THE PERSON YOU NEED TO BE

Create a context or "pretext" for a social encounter that will set you up for success.

"Honesty," the comedian Richard Jeni observed, "is the key to a relationship. If you can fake that, you're in."[1] If that guy wasn't a social engineer, he should have been. To exert influence and get what you want, it helps immeasurably to devise a plausible and compelling pretext for having a conversation and making a request, and to play your prescribed "role" within that pretext flawlessly. In other words, you have to frame the meaning of the social encounter for your target at the outset in such a way that you appear unthreatening and even likable.

There's a big retail brand—I can't say which—that's much more secure today because of a visit they received from a certain, very helpful Waste Management sales representative. Yes, I have one of those outfits, too. My challenge in this assignment was to see if I could get inside an incredibly secure warehouse, where I would take videos and pictures of unsecured entrances. Then, on a separate occasion, I was supposed to see if I could enter through an unsecured entrance and steal the valuable merchandise stored there.

When I say these warehouses were incredibly secure, I mean that entering them was like getting into a maximum-security prison. You approached glass doors made of tinted, bulletproof glass, pressed a buzzer, and someone watching you on a video screen asked for identification. Once you got through that barrier, you went to a second security barrier, a ceiling-to-floor metal mantrap, like the kind they sometimes have to let people into and out of subways. While you were inside the mantrap, a security guard had to use a badge to unlock it and spin you out the other side. After that came a metal detector, and then another security counter where you presented government-issued ID and they issued you a visitor's badge.

How the heck was I going to get through all of that security? Garbage, that's how. Using images on Google Maps street view, we spotted a giant Waste Management trash compactor in the back of the warehouse. Comparing the image of the compactor to one on Waste Management's website, we identified the exact model of compactor the warehouse had installed. I downloaded all of the schematics and made myself an expert on these compactors. Then I donned a Waste Management uniform, complete with logo, hat, badge, and giant clipboard.

Showing up at the warehouse's outer door, I announced myself as someone from Waste Management who had come to speak with the warehouse manager about the trash compactor. The security agent buzzed me in. When I reached the mantrap, the guard there asked me what exactly I had come to discuss. I told him that a select number of our trash compactors contained motors that were subject to a recall. I needed to check the serial number on the motor to tell them if we needed to recall theirs. When the agent expressed doubt about letting me in, I told him that he could go back and check the serial number himself—that would be just fine. He replied that he didn't know where the motor was located on the unit, so I told him that I could either describe it to him or I could just go back to check myself—it would take me five minutes. He swiped me through the mantrap.

I proceeded through the metal detector and up to the security counter. I had known that I would need a government-issued ID but did not want to use mine, since it displayed my real name and address. When they asked me for it, I flashed a look of extreme disappointment and told them that I'd left my wallet in the car. "It's this big, George Costanza thing," I said. "It wrecks my back it's so thick."

That got a chuckle, but the security agent was unmoved. "I can't let you in without a government ID."

I pretended to be flustered, telling them that I couldn't go through all that security again just to do a five-minute trash compactor check. Then I pretended to have a bright idea. "Oh, you know what," I said. "I've got this Waste Management corporate badge right here. It has my picture on it, my date of birth, all of my information on it. Can I just use this?"

He nodded and said, "Yeah, okay, this looks the same as a license, we can just use this." For the next ten minutes, I roamed around the warehouse, taking the video and pictures of unsecured entrances, noting where I would be able to break in and steal merchandise. When I was done, I walked back through the security checkpoints. "You're all set," I said, smiling. "Your serial number isn't on my list, so you're great, you don't need a recall." In this way, I left them feeling great for having met me. In their minds, they had served their organization well, helping to avoid a potential problem. "Thanks for coming out," they said. "We appreciate it!"

I used this method with seven warehouses for this retailer. I got in all seven times. And the reason I got in was that I nailed the pretext for requesting entrance into the facility. I had an impeccably logical reason for venturing into the warehouse: I was a Waste Management guy, with a pressing task to accomplish, one that benefited *them*. Everything I wore, had on my person, or said screamed Waste Management. Why *wouldn't* they let me in?

PRETEXTING AND THE CRIMINAL MIND

Pretexting is the art of creating a *context or occasion* for a conversation so that you're more likely to achieve your goals. When you create a pretext, you're presenting a rational justification, explanation, or "excuse" for pursuing a social encounter of some kind. You're also assigning yourself a role to play during the encounter. Pretexts work by triggering emotions, positive or negative, in the people with whom you're dealing. In his book *Talking to Strangers*, Malcolm Gladwell popularizes the "Truth-Default Theory," the idea that "our operating assumption is that the people we are dealing with are honest."[2] A good pretext keeps this assumption intact, easing anxieties or concerns your person of interest might have, and even arousing positive emotions, such as love, happiness, or a sense of well-being. With a baseline sense of trust, your person of interest becomes much more willing—even happy—to comply with your requests. Conversely, a bad pretext arouses negative emotions such as fear or anger and activates your person of interest's critical thinking capacity. Instead of "going with the flow" of their positive feelings and complying, they become suspicious, thinking of reasons they shouldn't comply, and placing the burden on you to prove their suspicions unfounded. As Gladwell notes, "We *stop* believing only when our doubts and misgivings rise to the point where we can no longer explain them away."[3] A bad pretext "triggers" our unwillingness to trust in others.

Scammers, con men, and hackers everywhere know all about how pretexting works on people—it's their stock in trade. A man in the Texas community of West University allegedly rang people's doorbells, purporting to work for the municipality's water authority. While he was engaging a homeowner in conversation and building rapport (a topic considered in the next chapter), another crook allegedly broke in and stole whatever he or she could grab.[4] That's pretexting in action. The role of the "helpful water authority person" was the rationale the crook needed to get homeowners to do what he wanted: open up the door and engage in a few minutes of seemingly innocent conversation.

Pretexting occurs in electronic form as well, and in fact figures prominently in our current epidemic of online fraud. In Hong Kong, hackers took over the WhatsApp account of a man's sister, using it to impersonate her and convince him to buy "points" for virtual games, so that he could resell them at a higher price and make some easy money. The only ones to score a bonanza here were the hackers, who netted $55,000 in a matter of hours.[5] Likewise, crooks emailed parents of a student at St. Lawrence College, purporting to be from the college and asking them to make an early tuition payment in order to receive a discount. Some parents fell for it—and lost their money. In the first case, criminals adopted the pretext of the helpful or loving sibling who cared about the victim's financial well-being. In the second case, the pretext was that of the helpful college administrative representative emailing with a potentially attractive offer.[6] Both pretexts established the rationale crooks needed to get unsuspecting victims to take the desired action, which entailed parting with their money.

Perhaps the greatest criminal pretexter of all time was Victor Lustig, known variously as "America's greatest con man" and "the man who sold the Eiffel Tower. Twice." At least we think his name was Victor Lustig. Nobody really knows—the guy had no fewer than forty-seven identities. During the mid-1920s, Lustig impersonated a French government official, telling prominent members of the French scrap metal industry that the government was planning on demolishing the Eiffel Tower, and soliciting bids for it. The pretext of a government official offering an insider deal on valuable scrap metal seemed both perfectly reasonable and alluring to this audience. The metal guys fell for it, submitting bids, with one of them eventually forking over $70,000 for the tower. When the scam was discovered, the victim by one account "was too embarrassed to go to the police." Buoyed by this success, Lustig apparently tried the scam again without getting caught.[7]

A closer look at this scam reveals an important truth about pretexting: it isn't just about what you say, but also what you do. Pretexting can include how you behave—whether you appear calm, nervous, happy, sad. It can include the location you choose for a conversation, as well as objects or "props" that bring to life the role you're playing or identity you're assuming. In his Eiffel Tower scam, Lustig didn't just call up his victims and spin a tall tale about who he was and what he wanted. He had stationery created that had his name on it, and that also bore "the official French government seal." He summoned the scrap metal bosses to a meeting at a fancy French hotel—something that a connected government official might have done. He was also alleged to have presented his pretext using language that betrayed a bureaucrat's familiarity with his subject matter: "Because of engineering faults, costly repairs, and political problems I cannot discuss, the tearing down of the Eiffel Tower had become mandatory."[8] Note especially the phrase "I cannot discuss," an expression of apparent discretion that was exactly what a scrupulous official privy to sensitive discussions might say. Lustig's pretext included all of these elements, just as mine in the story above included my uniform and my company ID, as well as the seemingly informed explanation I gave to the warehouse guards.

Pretexts can consist entirely of actions and props, with no verbal explanation offered. In 1935, the secret service arrested Lustig, locking him away in Manhattan's federal detention center, a facility reputed at the time to be "inescapable." It was inescapable—for other prisoners. Tying bedsheets together to create a long rope, he hoisted himself out the window of his prison cell and lowered himself down the building. People on the ground gawked at him, so he passed himself off as a window cleaner, making use of a rag he had carried with him. The rag, his position on the building: these contributed to a pretext in the minds of the onlookers (not for a conversation, but for his own presence there on the side of the building). When Lustig reached the ground, he took a bow and scampered off, and it took a month for the law to catch up with him again. Afterward, he would relocate to a prison that really was built to house criminals like him: Alcatraz.

THE EVERYDAY ART OF PRETEXTING

Given Lustig's colorful exploits, it might not seem that pretexting holds much relevance for normal, law-abiding citizens. Surely you're not going to adopt a whole new, fake identity like I did just to convince a family member, colleague, or neighbor to do something you want. And you're not (I hope) going to invent some false rationale and role in order to steal unscrupulously from people in your orbit. Legal scholars have cast a suspicious eye on the practice of pretexting among attorneys and police to obtain information, regarding it as deceptive and unethical. In an article entitled "Pretexting: A Necessary Means to a Necessary End?," one scholar came out strongly against pretexting, arguing, "The legal system and the profession can ill afford the use of any dishonest or deceptive means to gather information."[9] The

Federal Trade Commission has likewise defined pretexting as an inherently dishonest, criminal act: "Pretexting is the practice of getting your personal information under false pretenses. Pretexters sell your information to people who may use it to get credit in your name, steal your assets or to investigate or sue you. Pretexting is against the law."[10]

Rather than justifying pretexting on the grounds that "the ends justify the means," as some in the legal profession do, I would contend that pretexting in everyday situations isn't fundamentally about lying, dissimulating, and playacting. When I dressed up as a Waste Management guy, I was telling a bald-faced lie, but I was taking part in a specific assignment in which my client and I predetermined (as we always do) that certain forms of lying were fair game. I would never deceive others like this while pretexting in everyday life—and I wouldn't need to. Pretexting in everyday life entails *selectively presenting parts of the truth* in order to create an advantageous context for a conversation, so that you can quickly build rapport. Pretexting can be as simple as posing as an interested customer if you happen to own an ice cream shop and want to check out a popular new competitor that has opened up in your neighborhood. Or if you're thinking of moving to a new town but want to know what people *really* think about the schools, it can be calling up a broker and saying, "Hey, we're moving to the area, we have a couple of questions."

The ice cream store owner might not be primarily interested in buying a cone when she goes into that new neighborhood store—she wants to learn about her competitor. But, since she's paying for a cone, she also is a customer. You might not be looking to close on a property next week, but the initial, "what if?" phase of looking is still part of the process of buying a house. So, pretexting isn't an outright lie, but rather a representation of reality rooted in the truth. If you have any doubts about how far to go when setting up a pretext, remember this: you need to leave people better off for having met you. If your pretext is so distant from the truth that for whatever reason you won't be able to leave people better off, then don't use it.

We create pretexts all the time, almost always without realizing it, by taking on "roles" for ourselves to fit particular situations. A long-standing debate in psychology concerns whether personality or specific social contexts determine our behavior. Both seem to matter: our stable personalities shine through in our behavior, but we project certain parts of them most fully in the right settings, and we might even look to insert ourselves into situations in which we can bring out certain parts of ourselves—our gregariousness, say, or our propensity to seek out novelty.[11] As Christopher Soto of Colby College has written, "On any one occasion, a person's behavior is influenced by both their personality and the situation, as well as other factors such as their current thoughts, feelings and goals."[12]

When devising pretexts for our conversations, we emphasize particular dimensions of our personalities to fit the needs of the moment. If my daughter has done something wrong, I might sit her down and have a stern discussion with her, adopting the pretext of the "tough, disciplinarian dad." If I have a problem with one of my adult employees, or if I'm trying to resolve an issue with my wife or my best friend, I can't play that fatherly role—the people with whom I'm interacting would find it insulting and demeaning. So I might play the role of the empathetic boss. Or the frustrated but compassionate spouse. Or the concerned best friend. In all of these situations, I'm the same person, but I'm allowing different sides of me to come out in hopes of achieving my goals.

We instinctively embrace these different roles because we sense that the specific pretexts we choose can help determine whether we get what we want out of our social interactions. Let's say your elderly mother is in declining health, and you must have a difficult conversation with your sister, with whom you are not particularly close, about generating funds to move her into a nursing home. If you framed the occasion for the conversation as "I want to talk to you because I need you to give me ten thousand dollars by the end of the month," and if you held the conversation in a crowded, noisy bar right after a long day of work, when your sister was stressed and tired, the conversation might not go so well. When your sister hears the words "I need you to give me ten thousand dollars by the end of the month," she might experience any number of negative emotions, including fear ("How will I possibly come up with that kind of money, and so quickly?"), resentment ("Who are *you* to ask me for that kind of money?"), fatigue ("Yet another thing I need to deal with? I'm stressed out already!"), or frustration ("Why are people always asking me for money?"). Your sister's critical faculties will fire up as she thinks about all the reasons she can't, shouldn't, mustn't come up with the money. But if you call your sister and say, "I know we haven't spoken recently, but I'm really worried about Mom. We need to figure out together what the best option for her care is," and if you suggest meeting for lunch over the weekend at a quiet place you know your sister likes, you won't trigger these emotions, and her critical faculties won't immediately engage. You'll stand a better chance at eventually getting what you want: a $10,000 contribution from your sister.

Pretexts elicit emotions by implicitly answering (or failing to answer) the four key questions that, as we saw in the introduction, everyone asks when beginning an interaction with another person: Who is this person? What do they want? How long will the interaction take? Is this person a threat? Depending on the situation, some of these questions will of course already be answered: Your sister in the above scenario obviously knows who you are and should know you aren't a threat. But she might not know the answers to the other questions. If your pretext fails to answer them, the resulting uncertainty could elicit fear or doubt in her. Disturbing answers suggested by your pretext will trigger these emotions as well. By asking your sister straightaway for the $10,000, you might be identifying yourself as someone who poses a threat to her lifestyle—you're demanding her money. If you've had long, torturous conversations in the past about money with your sister, the open request for money might leave her anxious that a long and painful conversation will ensue. By approaching the situation as a concerned family member who just wants to find the best care option for your mother, you probably won't come across as a threat. Instead of fear, your sister might experience love, gratitude, or a sense of validation.

Most of us don't give much thought to pretexting. Although we might project different sides of ourselves in different contexts, we don't do so strategically to match our needs. As a result, we might find ourselves falling back habitually on certain pretexts, even when it doesn't help us. We get used to playing the disciplinarian mom or dad at home, and then replicate that at work or with our friends. We play the fun friend at school, forgetting to shut that off when we're talking to a boss or other authority figure. When our habitual pretext and the associated role or identity don't work for us, we often blame our failure on the other person. In the above scenario, we might come away without the ten grand we wanted and gripe that our sister was "being unreasonable," or that she "didn't get it," or that "she's a total jerk." Maybe our sister really is an awful person. But maybe *we* didn't do such a great job of framing a helpful or appropriate pretext. When we retain the same pretext even in inappropriate situations, we also tend to throw up our hands in the face of failure and say, "I'm sorry, that's just who I am, that's my personality." Uh, no, it's not who you are—it's just a part of your personality. If you try, you can cultivate other parts of your personality in specific situations, crafting your pretexts strategically to influence others and get the results you want. Hackers do it for evil purposes all the time. Why can't you do it in a more positive, benevolent way?

Tonight, before you go to sleep, think back on the many social interactions you had during the past day or so. How many different roles did you play? Were you the concerned parent, the fun friend, the stern, unforgiving boss? Were you the concerned neighbor, the happy, loving spouse, the curious student? Make a mental list of these roles, and think about how effective each of them was for you. Were you unconsciously projecting a role appropriate in one situation into other situations where they proved less helpful?

Think of a recent situation in which someone asked you for something, and you agreed. Think of another in which you refused a request. What pretext did the person in each situation use? Why was it effective—or not?

You might object that crafting pretexts strategically, while not outright lying, is still bad, as it involves calculating and plotting in your interactions with others. But I'm not asking you to be fake with your family and friends. Being more deliberate about what you say isn't being fake. You're still allowing "you" to come out, just taking a bit more care in determining which part of yourself to express. And if you're an ethical person, you're not manipulating another person, which I define as tricking or forcing them to comply with your desires to their own detriment (see chapter 6). Rather, you're making it more attractive for them to comply by giving them something *they* want, too. So many conversations unfold thoughtlessly, leaving everyone frustrated and worse off. Isn't it better and wiser to deploy just a bit of strategy to make our interactions more pleasant and productive?

Let's say your supervisor approaches you in the hallway and says sternly, "I need to meet with you tomorrow at three." When you ask what's up, she refuses to tell you what the meeting is about and why it's so urgent. Unless your boss's goal is to manipulate you by eliciting fear, she's just deployed a horrible pretext. The invitation will likely seem ominous to you, and you'll spend the next twenty-four hours fretting that you've done something wrong and are about to be fired. It would have been so much easier—and kinder—if your boss had said, "Hey, last week at our client meeting, there were just a couple of small issues, nothing serious, but I'd like to talk to you about them tomorrow at three." With that framing, you'd be less anxious and better prepared to handle the actual substance of the conversation. You'd also be more likely to react positively to whatever your boss says, giving her what she wants.

Pretexting is a more compassionate and productive way of entering a conversation because it entails doing something incredible, almost radical: *taking a moment to think about the other person's emotional needs.* As mentioned in the last chapter, most people jump into conversations thinking about what *they* want out of it. To frame a strong pretext, you must make that empathetic leap, putting yourself imaginatively into the other person's mindset, and adjusting your pretext accordingly. As a boss, you'll avoid leaving a cryptic "meet me at three tomorrow" message because you understand the power differential between you and your employees, and you anticipate the fear that a cryptic message would generate in your subordinates. As someone seeking their sister's help in caring for their aging mother, you'll ask in the kindest, least threatening, most respectful way because you're anticipating that your sister might find it hard to fork over ten grand. I wish more people thought about the feelings, needs, and desires of others before they opened their mouths. The world would be a gentler place. And all of us would get much more of what we want.

TO PRETEXT LIKE A PRO, YOU HAVE TO PREPARE

Now that you're familiar with pretexting and why it works, let's talk about how to do it. Throughout my life, I've performed pretexting naturally (and I'm guessing that almost all successful hackers, con men, and hustlers have similar experiences). Even as a kid, I tended to plan out instinctively how I'd want conversations to unfold, taking into account the person I was dealing with and what their needs, desires, and mindset might be. This approach became so ingrained that I'd do it spontaneously and almost instantly when encountering people minute-to-minute. It looked and felt a lot like "winging" these interactions, but in my mind I was setting them up and framing them. Only recently, as I've tried to teach others how to pretext, have I taken a more analytical tack. Reverse-engineering my mental process, I've developed the following seven-step formula for successful pretexting when instigating a conversation with someone else:

PREPARE
1. Problem: Identify the issue you're trying to solve.
2. Result: Specify your desired outcome.
3. Emotional State: Identify the emotions you want to see in your subject.
4. Provocation: Anticipate the emotions you need to project or display in order to generate the desired emotions in your subject.
5. Activation: Define your pretext, which should be very clear now.
6. Rendering: Determine the specifics of where, when, and how best to deliver or render the pretext.
7. Evaluation: Mentally evaluate your pretext to make sure it's strongly rooted in truth and allows you to leave people better off for having met you.

In sparking a conversation, you first need to clarify in your own mind what issue you need to solve, and the outcome you seek (steps #1 and 2). You might hear that your teenage daughter Natalie has been secretly texting with a college guy named David, despite your express instructions that she avoid all contact with him. That seems like a pretty clear problem, but you can be more specific: in texting with David, who incidentally has recently been arrested on drug charges, Natalie not only deliberately broke a house rule, but also lied to your face about it (you'd asked her whether she'd been in touch with David, and she'd denied having any contact with him).

Clarifying these nuances of the problem gives you a better sense of what's at stake in the conversation. Many parents in a situation like this might jump straight to meting out a punishment, failing to understand the root causes of a behavior problem. In confronting Natalie about her texting, you might decide that you're especially bothered by the lying and the possibility that Natalie's friend David is linked to drugs. Your goal for a problem of this magnitude thus might not be just to get her to take responsibility for her actions, but rather to get her to speak openly and honestly with you about what she did and why. You need to understand what is going on with her, whether she is using drugs, and why she felt like she could sneakily break your house rules. If you can get to the root of the problem and work together to resolve it, you might lay the foundation for a more trusting relationship, which in turn would yield more honesty and better behavior on her part going forward.

Clarifying your goal will in turn allow you to address step #3. Causing Natalie to feel emotions like anger, fear, or shame will probably not make her want to confide in you around this topic. If you could induce a mild sadness in her as well as some compassion for your worries and fears, that might work. Given that you're aiming for low-level sadness, you should consider what emotion you need to convey during the conversation to evoke sadness in her (step #4). In many situations, you can elicit emotions in others by expressing those same emotions yourself. If Natalie sees that you're empathetic and a bit sad, she'll probably feel that way, too. This insight in turn sheds light on your pretext (step #5). You can't initiate a conversation by saying that she's screwed up bad and you need to talk about it. That will only elicit fear. Rather, you'll want to play the role of the "kind and considerate parent," framing the conversation in a quieter, more empathetic way. You might tell her, for instance, that you'd like to talk to her because you want to get her feedback on an important issue that's come up around the house. Your delivery of this pretext (step #6) will likewise feel calm, quiet, and empathetic to match the pretext. You might go over to your daughter, tap her on the shoulder, and say something like, "Hey, sweetie, can we talk for a second? I know it's getting late and you're probably tired—you've been doing homework all night. But there's something that's really bothering me that I'd like to discuss."

Now that you've framed your pretext and planned its execution, you must ask yourself: Is it ethical? The answer, hopefully, is a clear yes. The "kind and considerate parent" might be a significant part of who you are, so you're not lying. The pretext and its execution will leave Natalie better off for having met you. If it engenders trust in her, helping her to open up with you, you'll both enjoy a better relationship over the long term. In the short term, she'll feel as if she is loved, respected, and cared for by her parent. Other ways of executing this pretext probably wouldn't have passed the ethical test. Imagine if you had never tried drugs as a kid, and in the guise of being the kind and considerate parent you chose to tell her this elaborate, painful, and false story of how you had been a heavy cocaine user, saw people overdose in front of you, had gotten arrested, and learned firsthand how bad drugs are. In the short term, the story might have its desired effect, convincing her to stay away from drugs and her friend David, but if she ever discovered that the story was false, she would feel hurt and betrayed. The conversation would leave her feeling a lot worse for having met you, perhaps permanently damaging your relationship.

Note that you might find it necessary to adopt a new pretext midstream, depending on how our conversation unfolds. If you learn in the course of talking with Natalie that she's been texting David because the two of them are planning to run off together, you might want to ditch the "kind and considerate parent" pretext and adopt the role of the stern, "disciplinarian parent." If you learn that she hasn't been texting with budding drug czar David, but rather with another boy named "David" from her social studies class who is her age and a good kid, then you might apologize for being suspicious, congratulate her on her honesty, and tell her how proud you are of her, adopting the pretext of being the "strongly supportive parent." The complex interactions we have with others in our daily lives often do (or should) lead us to adopt multiple pretexts as a conversation takes unexpected twists and turns. Still, the most important pretext we adopt is the initial one, as that will determine whether a conversation can even begin to unfold productively. If your daughter felt anger or fear at the outset, she probably wouldn't have been able to respond logically to what you were saying, or to feel empathy with your position. Your conversation would have gone nowhere.

I've developed a parenting example here, but you can use the PREPARE framework in any setting to get conversations off to a productive start. At a big industry conference where my company was holding an event, members of our team were racing around doing a million things to make sure that our event was a rousing success. One of our team members, a bright twentysomething man named Vince,[13] was missing in action, and nobody knew where he was. I called him, texted him—nothing. I was ticked. Where *was* this guy when we needed him?

A half hour later, Vince surprised everyone by emerging from under a table. For the past ninety minutes he'd been lying down there, taking a nap. My first inclination was to fire him on the spot. But I calmed myself down, ran through the seven steps of the PREPARE model in my mind, and had a very different kind of conversation. Approaching him, I adopted the pretext of the "empathetic boss." My goal was to learn what had been going on with him to produce this behavior, so that I could determine if there was anything I could do to fix it.

"Hey," I said, "we were really stressed out looking for you. We'd all planned out what we'd be doing to prepare for the event, and how important every person's role was. When you weren't here, we were worried. We didn't know if you were dead or alive. Can you please explain why you disappeared for an hour and a half?" Vince reddened and said he was embarrassed and didn't want to talk about it. "I'm sorry it's embarrassing," I said, "but I just need to understand that you're okay." Vince told me that he'd strained his back and was in great pain, so he took some medicine he'd been prescribed, sat down on the floor, and wound up crawling under the table and falling asleep. He had been in so much pain, he said, that he just couldn't move.

If Vince had answered differently, telling me that he'd fallen asleep because he was an alcoholic and had gotten tanked the night before, I might have abandoned the "empathetic boss" pretext and become the "stern boss," telling him that he had to pull himself together because his behavior was impeding his performance and affecting our team's ability to deliver. But now that I'd heard his explanation and found it reasonable, I could stick with "empathetic boss." "Look," I said, "I get that this is embarrassing. I've had injuries like this before. The next time it happens, just tell me about it. I'll probably tell you to take an hour if you need it, or even to go home if you're in too much pain to work." Vince thanked me, and went on to do his job well for the rest of the conference. Since then, he's informed me when his back pain has flared up, and we've made accommodations. Hearing about my gentle and reasonable reaction, other team members have come to me to talk about physical problems they're having that might be impeding their performance. I've averted any number of misunderstandings with my employees and built up much more trust—all thanks to the magic of pretexting. If I'd just ripped into Vince out of anger and fired him, I wouldn't have learned about what had really happened. He'd be out of a job, and I'd be stuck trying to find his replacement. Both of us would have lost.

WORKING WITH PREPARE

Try using PREPARE to, yes, prepare for important conversations in your daily life. The first few times, write out the steps on a piece of paper, just to make sure you get them. Doing so might take you five to ten minutes, but don't worry. After a few days or weeks, you'll find that pretexting has become second nature, and that you'll be able to develop a pretext in a matter of a few seconds on the fly, without writing anything down. More broadly, you'll get in the habit of thinking about conversations before beginning them, including what you want out of them, what the other person's mindset is, and how best to frame a conversation to have the desired emotional impact. You'll also develop the critically important habit of breaking away from your emotions during interactions, regaining your composure, and engaging with others more calmly. All of this will leave you far more confident in your social interactions, and more conscious of the pretexts that others are using with you.

As you consider the emotions you seek to evoke in others and those you wish to display yourself (steps #3 and 4), check that those emotions aren't negative. Again, your ultimate goal here is to get what you want while leaving the other party better off. It's unlikely that the other party will feel better off if you're evoking a negative emotion in them, like fear or anger. Every step in the PREPARE framework has to either leave people better off or align with that aim. Otherwise, you're likely veering into the darker realm of manipulation, where you win and the other party loses as a result of your interaction. Don't go there.

Check as well that the pretext you're choosing really is consistent with you and your personality. No matter how hard I might try, I will never pass myself off as a twenty-five-year-old college girl when breaking into a building—it just won't happen. Even if that would be the ideal pretext for a given situation, I'll need to come up with something else. In my personal life, I'll never be able to pull off the "wild and crazy bachelor friend"—it's just not who I am, and none of my buddies would buy it.

Some ways of delivering an otherwise suitable pretext will also blow up in our faces because they, too, seem at odds with the people others take us to be. If you're asking your sister to help out with your aging mother's care, and instead of inviting her to dinner at one of her favorite restaurants, you take her away for a spa weekend, even though you've never done anything close to that before, your sister will probably feel manipulated once you pose the question to her. The conversation will appear calculated and inauthentic, since you've done something that's perceptibly out of character for you. On the other hand, if you've often gone away for spa weekends before together, this might be exactly the way you'd want to execute the pretext.

You might suppose that you should stretch a little when creating a pretext so as to accommodate the other party. I hate golf, but if I'm trying to make a potential business partner feel comfortable so that I can have an easier time negotiating a deal, and if I know that this person loves golf, shouldn't I just suck it up and arrange a game for us? Not at all. Since I hate golf and am terrible at it, I'll spend the entire outing frustrated and stressed, which will prevent me from expressing the emotions required to evoke the desired emotions in my potential partner. If it became obvious that I really disliked golf, my potential partner would start to feel as if I had been inauthentic in setting up a game. Just because you're focusing on the other person and their emotions doesn't mean you should neglect your own. Arrange an outing that conforms reasonably well with both of your personalities and tastes, so that you can both relax and enjoy yourselves.

One caveat: Let's say your sister loves golf, and you hate it. If you have to arrange a conversation to ask her for help with your ailing mother, you might still suggest a golf game if you set it up as follows: "Look, next year it looks like I'm going to have to go out golfing because of some client meetings I have. Could we go out on the course next week and play three or four holes so that you could show me how to play? I know you really love it, and I don't want to embarrass myself with my clients." Assuming that you really would have to golf with clients next year and were worried about embarrassing yourself, this would be a great pretext for a conversation with your sister. She'll be in an environment she loves, and you'll get some golf instruction, which you really need. Meanwhile, you're putting your sister in a position of authority, leaving her feeling empowered, validated, and important— all positive emotions that might make her more receptive to your request about your mother.

As you consider how to execute your pretexts, remember: everything you do or say has to align with them, or your pretext will seem flimsy. If you're attending a school meeting for your kid and your pretext is "the responsible parent," don't reek of pot and wear a T-shirt with a decal of marijuana leaves on it. If you're claiming to be the "patient and attentive friend," don't check your iPhone every three seconds. And if you're trying to be the "empathetic dad," don't blow your top and say things like, "What the hell is wrong with you?"

Be sure as well not to let an initial failure prompt you to abandon your pretext too quickly. Imagine how inauthentic you would appear to your sister if, when asking for help caring for your aging mother, you hear a no from her and then angrily blurt out: "I knew you were going to be a selfish pig! How typical!" You're far better off staying in pretext and responding with something like, "I know, this is a huge ask and a ton of money. That is what I am struggling with, too. What do you think we can do if we both can't afford it?" Such a response keeps the conversation going, allowing you to continue to validate your sister and request her help. You might not obtain everything you want, but you could still get something. Maybe your sister will reply, "Look, right now I just had a massive car repair, and I don't want to re-mortgage the house. I can afford to contribute two or three thousand dollars now, and I'll give more as I can over the next eight to nine months. Is that okay?" She might never have put forward this offer if you had broken your pretext and yelled.

Parents will find this dynamic familiar. You're sitting there on the couch, and your precious, beautiful, little five-year-old daughter comes crawling up on you. She gently hugs you and kisses your cheek and says, "Daddy, I love you." As your heart swells with love and happiness, she says, "Can I get this new toy I want online? Pleeeeeaassseeee, Daddy?" You look at her and say, "Sorry, honey, not right now." Her face reddens, and she says, "WHY ARE YOU SO MEAN??" She just broke with her pretext.

Conversely, my own daughter Amaya and I were once in a meeting, and I told her three or four times to stop running around and making so much noise. "If you do this again," I said, "we'll go in the back for a spanking." Guess what? She did it.

I stood up and told her to come with me, saying the normal, ominous dad thing: "You know what has to happen now." When we got to the back room, I said, "Amaya, I told you five times not to make noise, and you know the consequences, so now there has to be some discipline."

She looked up at me, grabbed my hands, and said, "Daddy, I'm sorry. I know you warned me and now it's time for my spanking, but before you do, can we just sit here for a minute so I can give you a hug to tell you how sorry I am?"

"Do you think this is going to get you out of discipline?" I asked.

"No, Daddy," she said. "I know you have to do this—you warned me. But I am really sorry." And with that she threw her arms around me and hugged me really tight. She kissed me on the cheek and then said, "Okay, I'm ready."

Not only did she not get a spanking that day, but she never received one again in her life from me. Sticking with pretext is *so* important.

It's also vital to keep your pretexts and their execution simple. You don't need to think through every last detail. Consider the example of my employee Vince who was MIA because of his back pain. If I'm trying to initiate a conversation by the "compassionate boss," I don't need to tell Vince in excruciating detail about every last time I experienced a terrible injury that affected my on-the-job performance, in the guise of conveying my empathy. A couple of well-chosen details will do. If I say too much, I might frustrate Vince by boring him to tears. Even worse, I might come across as "trying too hard" to forge a connection with him. He'll suspect that I've scripted this conversation with my own ulterior motives in mind. He'll see me as fake and be less inclined to confide in me.

When executing pretexts, up your game by mobilizing the DISC analysis we discussed in the last chapter. Let's say you're a boss, and you need to alert your underperforming employee to what they're doing wrong and motivate them to put out more effort and do better. If your employee is an "I" type who is very outgoing, effuse, and emotional in their expression, you might wish to deliver your pretext in writing while also offering a follow-up conversation in person or over the phone. If you present the feedback initially in conversational form, they'll likely become defensive, arguing with you point for point. You'll wind up having a debate rather than a productive conversation. Delivering your feedback in writing will allow them time to get past their emotions and process what you're saying.

If your employee is a "C" type, by contrast, a phone call or in-person meeting might be preferable. Your "C"-type employee will want to understand your feedback in detail, and a conversation will allow you to explain yourself fully and handle your employee's clarifying questions. A phone call or in-person meeting might also be indicated if your employee is a "D" type. "D"s don't need a ton of detail—they want you to be direct with them and get quickly to the point. Send a D a lengthy email, and they're more inclined to become frustrated with your feedback, regardless of its substance and veracity.

A more general point here is to do your homework. Gather information about your person of interest beforehand, as I did with the warehouse I was seeking to compromise. The more you know, the more clarity you will have about which pretexts will or will not work. It might sound creepy, but when I'm gearing up for a difficult conversation with someone, I'll check their recent social media postings, searching for clues about developments in their life that might relate to the problem we need to resolve. Sometimes, such clues help me define my goals for the conversation more clearly or frame a pretext that is more likely to seem relevant or interesting to them. Information I uncover also prevents me from saying or doing something that is almost guaranteed to turn them off. As an extreme example, if I learn via social media that a friend whom I plan to approach for a favor has lost a beloved pet, I obviously wouldn't initiate the conversation by asking how his dog is. Instead, I might offer my condolences.

As important as preparation is, you don't want to take it to excess. If your story is too perfect, or again, if you include too much extraneous detail, you set off alarm bells in your person of interest's mind. Aim for a balance between spontaneity and preparation, as that will give the conversation a ring of authenticity. As I tell my students, you can actually practice being spontaneous, as contradictory as that might sound. Challenge yourself to visit a public place and hold unscripted conversations with complete strangers with the aim of eliciting from them a single, simple piece of information, like their full name or date of birth. Don't map out your pretext—just approach people and start conversations. Try different opening lines and see what happens. Sometimes you'll succeed, other times you'll fail. As you hold a number of these conversations, you'll find yourself improvising new opening lines or making small, impromptu tweaks to your previous lines and to your delivery. You'll walk away with a better sense of how to engage with strangers, and you'll feel much more comfortable doing so spontaneously.

THE POWER OF A GOOD BEGINNING

As we've seen in this chapter, pretexting is the art of setting up conversations so that other people will agree to continue them, in situations when they might otherwise slam the door unceremoniously in your face—indeed, when reason or conventional wisdom almost dictates that they should. If you deliver an amazing pretext, eliciting the right emotions in others and short-circuiting their critical thinking processes, you can keep that little door of theirs cracked open for the time being, because you're making them *want* to give you a chance. Even the seemingly impossible can remain in reach.

I mentioned in the introduction that I once managed to convince the owner of a fancy restaurant to hire me, even though I had zero experience. My ability to deliver a compelling pretext on the spot was critical. I was bored in my new career, and eager to try something new. Spotting a road sign that said, "chef wanted," I asked to speak to the head chef. Instinctively adopting "the uber-confident-but-not-cocky job applicant" as my pretext, I shook his hand and said, "Hi, I'm Chris. I'm your new chef." I wanted him to feel confident in me, trusting that I could do the job. To elicit that emotion, I decided that I would display confidence myself, tempering it with a sense of lightheartedness and fun.

"Okay," he said. "Where's your résumé? What credentials do you have?"

"I don't have any credentials," I replied. "I don't need them. You should taste what I can cook. My meal will be my résumé."

"Fine," he said, gesturing behind him toward the industrial refrigerator and the stovetop. "Cook me something."

I went to the refrigerator, took out some meat, vegetables, coconut milk, and spices, and made him some Thai food (thanks to my wife, who is of Thai descent, I had learned to make some pretty great curry dishes). Watching me cook, he said, "This is the most unorthodox job interview I've ever done."

I nodded. "Yeah, we can go through this whole process of multiple interviews, where I sit and talk on and on, but in the end, you're not going to hire me until I cook you something. So let's just cut to the chase."

When the food was ready, I placed some into a dish and handed it to him. He studied the presentation, sniffed the dish, and took a taste. His eyes lit up. "You're hired."

Of course, now that I was hired, I had to deliver—not easy given my lack of experience, but I made it happen. My new boss asked me to cook him some other recipes that we could perhaps put on the menu. Since I didn't have any, I went home and spent days researching and practicing a couple of recipes. Over the next few months, I finagled it so that he and others in the kitchen taught me basic cooking skills as we did our daily work, without ever doubting my competence. For instance, I didn't even know how to julienne vegetables. When my new boss asked me to do it, I said, "You know, everyone juliennes differently. Why don't you show me your perfect method so that I can copy you?" He did, and I did. Thanks to my willingness to learn on the job, and my ability to shift and dodge around tricky situations, I quickly became a valued employee. I stayed on the job for two years, only leaving because I got bored and wanted to try something else.

Pretexting got me in the door, enabling me to talk my way into a senior-level position with zero experience. But it was only a beginning. Something similar holds true in any conversation you might have. Once the door is open, you have to know how to follow up, or you won't get anywhere. Hackers build on their effective pretexts by creating a very special space of common ground between themselves and their "targets." They do this in a matter of seconds and almost automatically, before their target has even realized it. If this common ground is established, they're well on the way to achieving their goals, whatever those happen to be. If it's not, they haven't got much of a prayer (unless they're willing to depart from ethics and start manipulating people, which I'm not). Professionals call this act of creating common ground building rapport, and as I think you'll find, it's relevant to virtually any social encounter you might have, from meeting strangers at a cocktail party, to reconnecting with an old friend, to telling your spouse what's *really* bothering you. Let's take a look at rapport, and how to become better at building it than you ever imagined.

CHAPTER 3

NAIL THE APPROACH

*Build instant rapport with almost anyone so
they'll be more likely to agree to your request.*

Now that you've established the context for a social encounter, it's time to initiate that interaction to your best
advantage. I'll introduce a process you can apply at cocktail parties, professional conferences, stores, and anywhere else to convince people instantly that you are a
safe, trustworthy member of their tribe. Imagine being
able to walk up to friends, acquaintances, and even perfect strangers, saying just the right thing so that they like
you and feel more inclined to help you.

I'm not a smoker. I hate the smell of cigarette smoke. But I do know
one thing: smokers tend to bond with one another over their habit, especially with all the public censure that surrounds smoking these days.
Not long ago, this bit of common knowledge helped me break into the
central administrative headquarters of a major health care provider.

My client had challenged me to access the executive floor and
find sensitive material lying around the office. While researching the

company, we had learned that a construction project in the area had triggered an invasion of tiny spiders in surrounding buildings. I dressed up as a pest control guy, complete with a real spray canister, walked up to a public entrance, and mobilized many of the tricks I'll show you in this book to bypass security and enter the building. None of it worked. "Look," security personnel explained, "your name isn't on my list, so you can't get in." I tried again at a second entrance and got shut down again. It was a total bomb.

Although I felt a little dejected, I was happy to see that my client had stopped me so quickly. But I had to come up with a plan to try again, as that is what they had hired me to do. I exited the building and meandered around the side, unsure how to proceed. Spotting five or six employees sitting near a side entrance and smoking, I got an idea. Carrying my pest control gear, I approached them and said, "Hey, mind if I stand here and breathe in the fresh air?" That got a chuckle out of them as well as an inquisitive look or two. "Yeah, man," I said, "I just quit for, like, the tenth time."

"I know what you mean, brother," one of the employees said to me. "I've tried to quit fifteen times myself."

"I'm not even trying to quit," another said. "I've quit quitting!"

A third employee held out a pack of cigarettes. "Want one?"

I waved him off. "No, I'm really trying to quit this time, but maybe if I just stand here the smell will kill my urge."

"Sure," they said, "no problem, you can stand with us."

And like that, within no more than sixty seconds, I became a member of their in-group. I hung out with them for the next five or six minutes. When their smoking break ended, they strolled together back to the entrance, with me in tow. When we reached the side door, which was only accessible to employees with a badge, they opened it and walked into the building, allowing me to enter without giving it a thought. Bingo—I was in. Just a few minutes later, I was up on the executive floor, rifling through all kinds of sensitive documents.

In this instance, I improvised a believable pretext for myself, that of the veteran smoker struggling to quit, but this move only enabled me to begin a conversation. To achieve my goal, I had to pursue the conversation in a way that continued to answer the four baseline questions people instantly and unconsciously pose when they first meet a stranger (Who is this person? What does this person want? How long will this encounter take? Is this person a threat?). I did that by building quick rapport with these unsuspecting smokers. With just a bit of carefully crafted banter, I could affirm to these strangers that I didn't pose a threat but was rather a perfectly innocuous and friendly member of their tribe. We were just one big, happy family of smokers. When the time came to return to work, they thought nothing of letting me into the building. In their eyes, I was one of them.

OF SKATER DUDES AND OXYTOCIN

Building rapport might not seem especially complicated at first glance. It's not complicated at second glance, either. We might live in a world of smartphones and skyscrapers, but our brains are wired as they were when we subsisted in tribal groups roaming woodlands and foraging for food. We feel more inclined to help others with whom we maintain some kind of communal attachment, whether our bond is based on a shared social class, profession, ethnicity, belief, life stage, affinity, or experience.[1] If you want someone you've just met to comply with your wishes, you stand a far better chance of succeeding by first establishing common ground, making them feel like they're interacting with a fellow group member.

In my classes, I introduce the concept of rapport by asking would-be human hackers to remember what lunchtime was like at their high school cafeterias. If your high school was anything like mine, you and your fellow students sat with your respective tribes—the jocks, nerds, punks, skaters. Everybody knew where they belonged, openly identifying with a tribe through insider language, demeanor, and dress (fact: I was part of the skater tribe, which meant I wore baggy pants and a chain wallet). Such identification served to establish at least some kind of initial rapport between students who might not have otherwise known one another very well. If the new kid at school who happened to dress like a skater sauntered up to the nerd table and posed an innocent question about, say, the upcoming school dance, the four baseline questions would have posed a hurdle, because the nerds didn't know the skater. These nerds would have wondered: Why *are* you here? What *do* you want? How much of my valuable time *will* you take up? *Are* you a threat? But if the skater approached the skater's table and, affecting boredom and nonchalance, asked the same question, most or all of those questions would have been answered in the skaters' minds, because they would have accepted the new kid as a member of the tribe based on visual appearance alone.

As researchers now know, these annoying high school social dynamics are rooted in human biology. Rapport building helps trigger the release of a powerful hormone called oxytocin. In a series of studies, researchers linked the presence of oxytocin in the brain to experiences of trust and acts of generosity. As they also found, arousing feelings of empathy in people prompted their oxytocin levels to rise, which in turn led to generous behavior. In one study, researchers elevated oxytocin levels by exposing people to a video that portrayed a child desperately ill with cancer. Those higher levels of oxytocin in turn "predicted larger donations to the charity that produced the video." Oxytocin has also been linked to other "positive social behaviors," like making eye contact or recognizing other people's emotions.[2]

When we build rapport, whether it's in high school cafeterias or in our homes or workplaces, the sense of connectedness we establish produces a tiny hit of oxytocin in others, leading them to feel trust, connection, and generosity toward us. It's a powerful dynamic and one that shrewd operators deploy to induce potentially reluctant targets to do their bidding. Shady salespeople don't just approach you at the car dealership and ask you flat out to buy a car that's overpriced and well beyond what they know you can afford. No, they chitchat with you, get to know you, offer you coffee, rejoice in the fact that you both attended the same high school or love the same football team. Seasoned politicians don't just come out and ask for your vote. They flash their million-dollar smiles, shake your hand, hold your baby, or make a comment that suggests their familiarity with your local culture—all attempts to make you feel like you're a fellow tribesperson, if not a close, personal friend. And of course, successful scammers rely heavily on rapport to get unsuspecting victims to willingly hand over their money, information, or other valuables.

In one common scam, crooks pretending to be from companies like Microsoft or Apple call people up, claiming they want to help them resolve a computer software problem. If the victim provides certain information or clicks on a seemingly innocuous link, they inadvertently provide the scammer access to personal information like bank accounts, passwords, and the like; the scammer might even hijack the computer and demand a ransom.[3] To build rapport, scammers will seem friendly and polite, engaging victims in light conversation. In the United States, they'll usually come across, via their accents and tones of voice, as being females from India. Since people in general tend to regard women as nonthreatening, and Americans tend to associate Indians with customer support roles, victims think nothing of doing as these scammers ask. They assume that the stranger on the other end of the line shares their basic sense of decency and have no reason to think otherwise. Having deftly established this common ground, the scammers have the oxytocin flowing in their victims' brains. Rapport equals oxytocin equals trust equals a first-class ticket into a victim's bank account.

Expert hackers of humans need only a few seconds of well-tailored interaction to build rapport. That's because we humans aren't merely tribal. We also tend to make snap decisions about people we encounter based on stereotypes. And we make these judgments by assessing a few key factors that are primarily nonverbal, such as dress, hairstyle, skin color, and so on. To build rapport, you must quickly size people up, arrive at a clear but superficial understanding of who they are and what tribe they might belong to, and find a way to connect personally. You're not establishing a deep or enduring friendship, just enough of a bond so that people don't raise their psychic force fields and begin questioning your motivations.

As with pretexting, you can use body language as well as words to establish common ground. Bestselling author and former FBI behavioral expert Joe Navarro told me of a memorable occasion in which he had to take over the handling of an informant (or in FBI lingo, a "human asset") from another agent. It was a delicate business: informants risk their lives to cooperate with the FBI and provide evidence against criminals. They depend on the trusting relationship they have with their handlers. Disrupt that relationship, and the informant might disappear or stop cooperating, fearing for their safety. Joe had to establish a strong working relationship with the informant, somehow retaining and even building on the trust that the previous agent had established.

The challenge was especially great given that the informant—I'll call him Boris—was a Russian-speaking man in his eighties, and his previous handler at the FBI was an experienced agent in his mid- to late fifties. Joe, meanwhile, was all of twenty-five years old, a recent recruit to the bureau. How would he possibly establish common ground with a man from a different cultural and linguistic background who could have been his grandfather? "I had a plan for building rapport," Joe said, recalling their initial meeting, "but when I walked into the room to meet him for the first time, everything changed." Sizing Boris up, Joe realized that the standard approach that an agent in this situation might take—projecting his professional authority, speaking very formally to Boris and assuring him that he would remain safe—wouldn't work. "This guy was obviously an accomplished individual," Joe said. "He had lived through the Soviet occupation [of his country]. He knew how to read me—what was pro forma and what was from the heart. And he knew that as a twenty-five-year-old, I barely knew my job. So, as they say, don't deceive a deceiver—and in this instance, I wasn't about to do that."

Joe perceived that Boris had an old-world mentality; respect and deference shown to one's elders mattered. Instead of projecting his authority as an agent, he bowed his head slightly while first shaking Boris's hand, avoided eye contact, and sat down at an angle to him—all of which suggested deference on his part rather than an attempt to assert dominance or control. When Boris requested tea, Joe did the same, even though he preferred coffee. Instead of refraining from divulging personal information during their conversation, as an agent would normally do, Joe spoke openly about his family's painful history—how his relatives had barely escaped Fidel Castro's Cuba, and how his father had been arrested and tortured. "I could see his facial muscles begin to relax, and it was then that I came over to the couch and sat with him," Joe said. In just a minute or two of conversation, he had established rapport. "I humbled myself before him and then just proceeded to let him know that in my eyes he was venerated." It was the beginning of a successful, three-year relationship between the two men.

BUILD RAPPORT WITHOUT SACRIFICING YOUR SOUL

Reading a story like this or learning about my own experience making friends with smokers, you might find yourself harboring some of the same concerns about rapport building that people sometimes have about pretexting. Wasn't Joe being "fake" by approaching his encounter with Boris so strategically? He wouldn't normally show such extreme deference to informants. He also asked for tea even though he preferred coffee. As for me, I perpetrated an outright lie in passing myself off as a smoker pretending to quit. In both of these instances, it seems that the builder of rapport was deploying guile and deception—not something most of us would want to do in the course of our everyday dealings.

I'm not advocating that you lie to build common ground—I was only doing so in the context of a professional engagement that permitted this kind of subterfuge. In everyday life, anything you say or do in the course of building rapport should be at least rooted in truth, and it should leave people better off for having met you. A scammer who is making small talk with you while pretending to be a customer service representative is breaching an ethical line (not to mention a legal one), as is the unscrupulous car salesman who can't stand football but who pretends to love your favorite team to make the sale. In both cases, lies are told and the person building rapport isn't leaving their target better off for having met them. This is exactly the kind of conduct that good, law-abiding people like you and me must avoid.

By contrast, Joe Navarro might not have ordinarily shown such deference to an informant, but he did show deference to elders in other areas of his life, so doing so was not inherently at odds with his authentic self. Even if he preferred coffee over tea, he didn't absolutely detest tea. Partaking of it was a small gesture of kindness on his part, an offering made with the simple intention of helping Boris feel venerated. Joe might have ventured a bit out of his comfort zone, but not too much. And his actions left Boris better off while also inclining him to comply with Joe's wishes. With that hit of oxytocin coursing through his brain, Boris felt happier and more connected than before their interaction. The two of them were now both in a position to possibly deepen their level of rapport over time.

Like pretexting, rapport building involves the application of a certain amount of strategizing or posturing. But here again, that strategy is: a) unavoidable and b) a good thing. Most of us naturally try to build relationships with others in the course of our daily lives, whether it's engaging in a bit of friendly banter with our next-door neighbors, schmoozing with our business colleagues before the start of a meeting, or smiling and asking a grocery clerk how they're doing as they weigh our deli meat. By mastering the skill of rapport building, we're just doing this work of connecting emotionally with others more deliberately and often. While we might have a selfish purpose in mind, we're still making life just a little bit better for those we encounter, both strangers and people we already know.

So often, we go about our day distanced from others and oblivious to their needs. We bury our noses in our phones and forget to interact as we step into an elevator. Sealed away in our comfortable media bubbles, we find social, cultural, and political differences so daunting we don't even try to negotiate them. By becoming skilled at rapport building, however, we can train ourselves to think about others and reach habitually across the chasm to make or deepen a connection. We can make a habit of building common ground rather than ignoring or trying to persuade others who don't espouse our beliefs. Our violently polarized society needs *more* rapport building, not less. As we'll invariably find, just a little bit of social nicety goes a long way when it comes to getting people to comply with our wishes.

It might not always seem clear how far to go when trying to ingratiate yourself with someone. When I'm hacking professionally, targets sometimes ask me in the course of my rapport building to agree with opinions I find abhorrent or to behave in ways that violate my religious beliefs. It's an occupational hazard of being a security professional. Although it would certainly help me to swallow hard and behave as my target expects, I will always decline and try to find another way to establish common ground. Once when posing as an employee of a particular company, I had to approach a group of employees at that company to try to obtain information from them. Before engaging them in conversation, I heard them complaining about "Kathy," a female boss at the company, calling her a "stupid bitch" and much worse. When I introduced myself, they not only continued to denigrate this boss but invited me to join them in thrashing women in positions of power. "Thank God Kathy isn't your boss," they said. "She's such a [fill in with the swear word of your choice]."

I might have easily and instantly joined their tribe of angry men by agreeing with them and hating on female bosses I've had in the past, but I couldn't allow myself to do that. Our code of ethics and my own personal beliefs prevent me from making "offensive comments (verbal, written, or otherwise) related to gender, sexual orientation, race, religion, or disability."[4] Having encountered similar situations in the past, I also knew I could continue to build rapport with them without compromising myself. And that's what I did. "Oh, yeah," I said, "I had a boss like that. This guy I worked for at my last job, he was terrible. That's why I started to work here." Rather than find a common ground rooted in misogyny, I found one rooted in a frustration with bad bosses irrespective of their gender.

Think of a situation in which you might find yourself in a quan-
dary when trying to build rapport. Maybe you're in a locker
room trying to connect with a bunch of guys without engaging in sexist locker room banter. Or maybe you're at a gathering with your family, most of whom think differently about
politics, or religion, or any other topic, than you do and are
quite vocal about it. How might you engage creatively to build
rapport?

It's often hard in social situations to defy others' expectations,
especially if you're engaging with a group of people. We tend to
fear we'll be excluded from the tribe if we don't "go along," and so
we find ourselves sacrificing our beliefs to conform. With practice,
however, you can train yourself to step back from your fears in the
moment, so that you can quickly look for and find an alternate way
of building common ground. You can also pre-plan for difficult social situations that might arise, thinking through how you'll handle
them.

On one occasion, I was breaking into a building (at a client's request) and encountered employees in the lobby heatedly debating
whether to allow teachers in schools to arm themselves. I was trying
to build rapport and become a member of their tribe, but I realized
I was in a no-win situation. It wasn't that I had strong beliefs about
gun control—I can identify with people on both sides of this issue.
Rather, I sensed that anything I might have said for or against gun
control would have risked alienating half of the group. At one point,
someone turned to me and asked point-blank (no pun intended) what
I thought. I paused for a few seconds to think. Finally, I said, "You

know what I think? I think dead children in schools are the worst thing that can happen in this country. And having to send your kids to school worried about them dying is a horrible, horrible place to be." The whole group went silent. Although they were bitterly opposed on this issue, there was indeed a common ground to be found—and I had found it.

Chances are you have a relative, neighbor, or business colleague who subscribes to some belief you find abhorrent or who you feel shares little in common with you. Rather than avoiding these people, you can learn to extend a hand, without sacrificing your core values. Since you already know these people, you can use rapport-building skills to increase the (relatively low) level of rapport that already exists, whether or not you have a specific request with which you'd like them to comply. If you're shy or fearful in social situations, you can become far more confident and outgoing, again regardless of whether you have an agenda of your own. Why wait for someone to bring you out of your shell? Learn how to bring them out of theirs. The more you develop a discipline around rapport building, the more you realize that the seemingly impossible distances that keep us from others are in fact usually bridgeable. Furthermore, you realize that it's not necessarily these other people who are preventing us from making or deepening a connection—it's us.

Think of someone in your life with whom you have a difficult relationship. Perhaps you're estranged, or perhaps you're in contact but some long-standing grievance is weighing down your relationship. Think of three ways you might establish common ground during your next interaction, while still remaining true to your beliefs and values.

ENGAGE YOUR WAY TO RAPPORT—
AND USE THE "EIGHT"

Here's a challenge for you. Go into a Starbucks and speak to a stranger sitting at a table or standing in line. Don't look for someone your age or who seems to share your race or socioeconomic background. Pick someone at random and try to become a member of their tribe. Can't think of anything? Do what I do and fall back on your smartphone. Let's say you have an Android phone. Walk up to someone with an iPhone and say, "Hey, I'm thinking of switching from Android to iPhone. What do you think of your phone?" In my experience, iPhone users will blab your ears off telling you why their phone is a million times better than an Android. As you ask them why and show interest in what they're saying, you validate them as a person, if only in a small way. You've established common ground. No, you're not both iPhone users, but you're both in the tribe of people interested in talking about why iPhones are so great.

Confronted with a challenge like this, students of mine often ask for some easy rules or guidelines for developing rapport in social situations, whether spontaneously or in pre-planned encounters. They want me to tell them something like: "When you're trying to talk to a member of the opposite sex, do these five things," or "To connect with a millennial, say this." Sorry, there are no rules I know of that apply broadly. Each situation is different, and you have to think on the spot, devising your own strategy for building rapport. That might seem daunting, but it really isn't. The thought process I follow boils down to six simple steps, what I call ENGAGE:

ENGAGE

1. Establish your person of interest: Identify the person with whom you'd like to build rapport (if you're planning

for a conversation in advance and have already developed a pretext, then you've already completed this step).

2. Note: In a second or two, create a quick and dirty profile of the person, noting their apparent tastes, socioeconomic background, likely beliefs, ethnicity, gender, and so on (if you already know the person well, quickly call to mind that person's profile).

3. Generate: Based on your profile, generate a few possible pathways you might use to create common ground.

4. Arrive at a decision: Choose a pathway to try, realizing that if this one doesn't work, you can switch gears and adopt a second one.

5. Give it a try: Execute your selected pathway.

6. Evaluate: As you execute, pay attention to how your person of interest is reacting. If your approach clearly isn't working, switch quickly to an alternate pathway.

ENGAGE might sound like a lot to remember, especially since you need to run through these steps in a matter of seconds during an unplanned encounter. To help you master ENGAGE, go to the resources section at www.HumanHackingBook.com and download a small, wallet-sized card printed with the six steps; you can carry it with you and consult it just before entering social situations. After you practice rapport building four or five times, these steps will begin to feel second nature. Think of the ENGAGE framework as mental training wheels that readily fall off as you practice rapport building. But you do need to practice—starting now.

Of all the steps in ENGAGE, beginners struggle most with the fifth, "Give it a try." As you frame your next interaction, borrow some wisdom from bestselling author and former FBI behavioral expert Robin Dreeke. Here are *eight killer techniques for rapport building* to bear in mind when seeking common ground with others in everyday situations:

Technique #1: Establish artificial time constraints

You know from reading this book that time matters in social situations—it's one of the four items that automatically arise when someone first approaches us. If we sense we won't be able to help someone in the limited time available to us, we're more inclined to refuse the request. Many social encounters have natural time constraints. If you start a conversation with someone in line at Starbucks, they'll feel pretty sure that the interaction will only last until one of you has paid and has gotten your coffee. That expectation might make a stranger more willing to spend a minute or so talking with you.

In situations where time constraints aren't natural or obvious, you can facilitate your efforts to build rapport by subtly inventing artificial ones. You might say something like: "Hey, can I bother you for two minutes? I'm new to the area, and I just want to find a good diner to eat at." Make the time constraint realistic—if you ask for two minutes, be prepared to spend only two minutes, knowing that you'll extend the conversation if you sense that your person of interest wishes. Don't just ask if someone has "a second," because that isn't realistic—the second has already passed. You can also implicitly calm a person of interest by making a statement like "I'm just heading out but . . ." or "I was about to meet someone but I'm wondering . . . ," since both of those imply a conversation of short duration.

Technique #2: Adjust how quickly you speak

When I visited my sister in Tennessee, we went to a barbecue restaurant for dinner. The waiter came over and asked if we were ready to order. "I'll take an iced tea," I said, "and the ribs, and a side of corn bread."

"Whoa, whoa," the waiter said, "slow down, city boy."

I placed my order again, speaking more slowly. I will admit, I was somewhat miffed, perceiving that the waiter was disrespecting me and trying to put himself in a position of dominance. As I thought about it, I realized I had ignored an important fact about communications. We all talk at different speeds depending on our personality, age, regional dialect, and larger social context.[5] Americans residing in the Deep South speak slower than some of their northern counterparts.[6] There's nothing good or bad about that—it's just reality.

When trying to build rapport, it helps to think about the person you're interacting with and tailor your speech at least somewhat to them. You don't want to overcompensate the way people sometimes do when speaking with a child or someone from another country. That will only insult or confuse them. Try to be considerate of the other person's needs as you speak, with an eye toward making them more comfortable. And if you're one of those verbose New Yorkers who look down on people who speak more slowly, or one of those slow-talking southerners who like to take their time, you're in luck: as linguistic specialists have observed, people who speak more rapidly tend to be more authoritative and persuasive, while slow talkers often strike us as friendlier or more approachable.[7]

Technique #3: Request sympathy or assistance

Humans are altruistic creatures—we naturally want to help others in need. In fact, one of a social engineer's most powerful phrases is a simple "Can you help me?" That said, we must take care not to ask for too much lest our person of interest find the request—and our very presence—threatening. As a general rule, tailor any request for help to the level of preexisting rapport. If you're interacting with a stranger, make your request for help simple and light. When I show up at a building seeking to hack into the server room, I can't just say to the receptionist, "Hey, would you mind showing me into the server room?" I need to start small—I'm just trying to get the initial gatekeeper to let me pass so that I can go on to the next gatekeeper. I'll ask a simple, innocuous question: "Hey, I've forgotten my badge, can I just use this ID?" or even, "Hey, I'm here to see so-and-so, but I don't know who her assistant is. Can you help me?" Maybe the receptionist will simply identify the person's assistant and leave it at that, or maybe he or she will tell me the assistant's floor and let me through so I can chat with the assistant in person.

Take care not to make these requests in a flirtatious or sexually suggestive way. Students of mine who happen to be physically attractive will try to do that, and as I explain, flirting usually won't make the other person feel better off for having met you. Once they realize you aren't really interested in them in that way but are trying to achieve some objective, they'll feel used or tricked. As most of us know, that isn't so fun.

Technique #4: Suspend your ego

Broadly speaking, Western societies are much more individualistic than their more collectivist-minded Eastern counterparts.[8] Such cultural tendencies carry over into professional contexts in which Westerners find it difficult to suspend their own egos and prioritize others. Associating humility with weakness and confidence or competence with strength, they feel like they have to know everything and project authority and control. That's precisely the wrong approach when it comes to hacking humans. Think of someone in your life who is good at suspending their ego, to the point where they come across as genuinely humble. When you're with this person, how do they make you feel? Chances are words like "affirmed" or "validated" pop to mind.

Humble people have the ability to make us feel great about ourselves. When you're trying to get someone to comply with your wishes, that's strength, not weakness.

To build rapport, suspend your need to be "right" or in charge. Don't try to change people's minds. Let them see the world as they want or need to without feeling threatened. You'll have a much easier time reaching common ground, because you aren't implicitly separating yourself from others by placing yourself above them. When Ronald Reagan was president, people criticized him for being too old for his office. He could have been offended, reacting defensively by attacking his attackers. Instead, he chose to suspend his ego and joke about his age. While debating another candidate for president, for instance, he began his opening comments with the famous line: "I will not make age an issue of this campaign. I am not going to exploit, for political purposes, my opponent's youth and inexperience."[9] A quip like that got everyone laughing, including his opponent, instantly building rapport. Some observers even believe Reagan essentially won the 1984 election with that answer. If you can avoid getting into a subconscious "battle of egos" with your target, you implicitly put him or her at ease.

It's not always easy saying things like "I don't know" or "I'm sorry," nor is it easy to take words like "I" or "me" out of the equation. If you spent years earning a medical degree, it may seem strange not to introduce yourself as "Doctor." It might seem difficult to refrain from offering an opinion and instead solicit opinions and feedback from others. But the more you can behave in these ways, the easier it will be for you to connect with others.

Technique #5: Validate the person of interest

Suspending your own ego is a good first step toward helping others feel good about themselves and thus more inclined to help us, but you can build on that by actively listening to others, affirming their ideas and opinions, and offering compliments. Of course, you'll always want to behave in ways appropriate to the existing level of rapport. Guys make mistakes all the time here, trying to establish rapport with women by complimenting their physical appearance. It comes off sounding condescending or creepy, because the guys in this situation haven't built up enough of a friendship. Be kind, but try as well to put yourself in the position of your person of interest. What might *they* like to hear? And what might *they* find awkward or offensive coming from someone they don't know very well?

Technique #6: Connect with the quid pro quo

As a professional hacker of humans, I might seek to get someone to divulge sensitive information. Instead of bluntly asking for that information, I often volunteer some innocuous information of my own. Let's say I'm coming up to a receptionist's desk and want her to tell me where the server room is located. If I notice a photograph of her family on the beach during their vacation, I might invite her to converse with me by saying something like: "Hey, I'm about to take my two sons on their first beach trip. I don't know anything about beaches. This one looks great!" Later on, when I ask her in passing about the server room, she'll feel more comfortable divulging it because I've already told her something personal about myself. In addition, I'm implicitly asking her for advice about beaches, which validates her and puts her in a position of authority. I've given her something, and she can now give me something. Quid pro quo, baby.

Technique #7: Give to get

Shrewd hackers of humans take quid pro quo to the next level by seeking opportunities to bestow gifts on others. The idea is called "reciprocal altruism": many animal species, like human beings, feel inclined to do something nice for others who behave kindly toward them. Even rats do this.[10] Sometimes the gift you give can be a physical good, but just as often a nonmaterial gift of kindness or consideration will work.[11] The key is to make sure the gift has some value to the other person, whether or not you happen to find it valuable.

On one occasion, Robin Dreeke and I were renting a car to go to a training. The model we'd rented was ridiculously small—I couldn't even fit my legs into it. We headed toward the counter seeking an upgrade. Upon arriving, we noticed many customers were having problems with their cars. Some were even screaming at the middle-aged, female customer service representative, who remained calm but seemed frazzled.

We stood in line, and when our turn came up, Robin did something absolutely genius. Instead of just asking the customer service rep for an upgrade, he said, "Ma'am, it looks like you're having a really bad day. Why don't we just stand here for a minute? You can take a quick break."

Just like that, the muscles in the woman's face relaxed. "Really?" she asked, glancing over at her supervisor. "You would do that?"

"Sure," Robin said. "Everyone's been screaming at you." He pointed at her water bottle, which was standing behind her on a table. "Why don't you just go over and take a drink, and we can pretend we're talking."

It was as if we'd given her the greatest gift on planet earth. Boom—instant rapport. A few moments later, when she had collected herself, she asked us what we needed. We mentioned we wanted to buy an upgrade, and not only did she find a really nice luxury car for us on short notice, she gave it to us for free—without us even requesting it. We had given her a gift that was immensely valuable to her in the moment. Afterward, it felt far more natural for her to do something special for us.

Technique #8: Manage our own expectations

There's an awful term in the social engineering world, the "kill shot." You've been working hard to get "in" with someone, making a connection, building rapport, inching closer to your ultimate goal: obtaining a piece of information, say, or having the person buzz you into a secure facility. The "kill shot" is that final action or speech that prompts your target to give you what you truly want. You've gone in for "the kill" and nailed it.

"Kill shot" sounds so heartless. I like to think of myself as a nice, caring guy, not a hired assassin. Besides, such an approach is totally counterproductive. Second-rate hackers of humans obsess about their end goal when building rapport. They're constantly looking for the "kill shot." As a result, they tend to rush, overly eager to get what they want and leave. They make mistakes, say the wrong thing, and wind up alienating their "targets." These hackers would be better off managing their own expectations, forgetting about their end goal, and instead crafting an interaction that promises to leave the other person better for having met them.

Listen carefully to what others say. Seek common ground. Enjoy the interaction. Make it real. You'll wind up behaving more thoughtfully and compassionately toward others and building rapport more quickly and effectively. That in turn will increase the odds you'll achieve your ultimate goal. It can be hard to dispense with the "kill shot" mentality. If an interaction is going well, you're feeling great, too. Oxytocin is coursing through your brain, and that might lead you to jump too far ahead in the conversation. In managing expectations, you also have to manage your own emotions. Remind yourself to breathe. Don't rush. Make the experience of others your top priority. You won't go wrong.

Pick one of the eight rapport-building techniques and practice it with a complete stranger. When you feel you've mastered it, go on to another, and another. When you've mastered many or all of these, practice combinations of these techniques at the same time.

A NOTE ON PROPS

I love disguises and costumes. They're a professional social engineer's best friend. When interacting with others in everyday life, you obviously won't be pretending to be someone you're not in the course of presenting a pretext and building rapport. Nevertheless, certain kinds of physical props can help, not least because they shape how you think about yourself. Dress and appearance are particularly important. In one classic study, researchers asked students to take a test while wearing a white coat they found hanging in the testing room. Researchers told one group of students that the coat was a painter's coat and another group that it was a professor's lab coat. Students who believed they were wearing a professor's lab coat performed better on the test. Those who believed they were wearing a painter's coat worked through the test more quickly and scored lower. As researchers found, students who felt they were wearing a painter's coat lowered their own expectations for themselves. You know that old adage that you should "dress for the job you want, not the job you have"? There's some truth in that![12]

When I was trying to land a job as a chef at a fancy restaurant with no experience, my clothing choices figured prominently in my pretexting and rapport-building efforts. I didn't go in there wearing ripped jeans and a T-shirt, nor was I wearing a three-piece suit. I wore a button-down shirt and dress pants—formal enough, but not overly so. The outfit left me feeling confident enough, and it helped me during rapport building because it didn't distract or arouse suspicion in my would-be boss. Running my own company, I've sat on the other side of the table and encountered a number of job applicants who didn't dress appropriately. They couldn't build rapport with me, because all I was thinking during our interaction was, "This person has no clue how to dress."

It might sound obvious, but I'll say it anyway since many people mess this up: think carefully about all aspects of your appearance. If you're paying a sales call to someone, you probably won't want to go in there with uncombed hair, excessive piercings, or food in your teeth. If you're wealthy and trying to connect with someone who isn't, maybe you shouldn't wear all of your expensive diamonds or your $3,000 Louis Vuitton handbag. If you're on a first date with someone, check whether you're wearing too much cologne or perfume. In many situations when you're trying to have a serious conversation with someone, avoid pesky distractions like your smartphone. In any situation, think about the other person and how you might use physical props to make them as comfortable as possible, so that you can leave them better off for having met you.

HOW TO HACK A HACKER

We can boil down the concept of rapport building to two words: *be friendly*. But don't let the simplicity of that imperative fool you. There's sophisticated science behind rapport, and some serious artfulness is required to master it. If you do master it, you'll discover that the simplest things in life are sometimes the most powerful. Joe Navarro told me how he once used the principles of rapport building described here to convince a teenage boy on an Indian reservation to confess to a crime he had committed. The teenager had hit another person with his car, perhaps while driving under the influence. But he wouldn't talk to any of Joe's colleagues, despite repeated attempts on their part to engage him. Sensing that the teenager was overwhelmed, Joe took him for a little walk, away from the scene of the accident.

Joe took a deep, cleansing breath, and then another, and then another. Seeing him do this, the teenager took breaths of his own. And like that, in a matter of seconds, Joe had established rapport, creating a tribe of two stressed-out human beings trying to relax. "I really screwed up," the boy said, without Joe even asking him to tell him anything. From there, the boy went on to reveal everything that had happened.

Rapport building is so powerful that even highly trained hackers aren't impervious to it. At our big conference every year, my company hosts a blowout formal party with a very exclusive guest list, just our clients and a few close friends. Our fellow hackers know about the party, and every year some of them try to sneak in, just to say they did. Not long ago, a guy approached me at the conference and said, "Chris, we've never met, but I'm a big fan of your books and your podcast. Here, I have a gift for you, just to thank you for everything you do for our community." He handed me a bottle of Glenfarclas 25, my favorite scotch.

I was blown away. Inspecting the bottle, I said, "How did you know this was my favorite?"

"Well, I heard you mention it on your podcast." He told me which episode, and he was right—I had mentioned it.

I thanked him for the gift and then felt the impulse to do something nice for him. "Hey," I said, handing him a special wristband, "we're having a private party tonight, why don't you come? You can use this to get in."

"Wow, man," he said, "this is so cool. Hey, I have some friends with me. Can I bring them?"

"Of course," I exclaimed, happy to repay the gift. "How many do you need?"

"Five."

Five extra invitations was a pretty big ask for someone who wasn't a client or close friend, but this individual had just given me a gift that meant something to me, so it felt hard to say no. Without thinking much about it, I handed him five more wristbands. He thanked me profusely and went on his way. That night, he and his five friends partied it up on our dime. They had quite the story to tell their colleagues back at the office.

This guy was good. He hadn't manipulated me into doing his bidding—not at all. He'd built rapport by accomplishing several tasks in just a few seconds. He'd affirmed that he and I were in the same tribe of security professionals. He'd validated me while implicitly suspending his own ego. And he'd bestowed a thoughtful gift that meant something to me. The oxytocin was surging through my brain like the mighty Mississippi, creating a situation in which I *wanted* to comply with his wishes. When I did so, he went on his way, leaving me better off for having met him.

This guy had hacked a seasoned hacker. All by mastering the art of friendliness. Practice rapport building diligently, and you might hack someone like me, too. Even if you don't, you'll get more of what you want and leave others in your life a whole lot happier. In a small but important way, you'll have done something to build community and heal our fractured world.

CHAPTER 4

MAKE THEM WANT TO HELP YOU

Get what you want by subtly nudging
people to agree with you and to act.

"If you would persuade," Benjamin Franklin said, "you must appeal to interest rather than intellect."[1] Influence is the process of making it easy for someone to behave or think in desirable ways. Master the seven principles in this chapter and you'll soon find yourself winning arguments, making new friends, and convincing others to comply with your wishes.

I was standing in the parking lot of a corporate headquarters. My goal: get inside and access the executive offices. As I approached the front entrance, a guy in a shiny new BMW Z3 sports car zipped past me and into an executive parking spot. He was talking into his Bluetooth headset, and from the frown on his face and his flailing arms, it appeared that he was having a spat with someone and was quite upset. "Hmm," I thought, "I've got to walk slowly past this car to try to hear what he's saying." I knew I couldn't walk too slowly—that would seem creepy. But I was carrying some papers (part of my pretext) and pretended to read them so that I could quite reasonably shuffle slowly past. As I passed the car, I couldn't make out what he was saying, except for one thing: "I really don't want to do this today. It's going to hurt a lot of people." What was happening? Was he going to fire someone? Would there be layoffs? Would he announce some other bad news?

I continued walking to the front door, went inside, and approached the receptionist's desk. The monitor before her was tilted at an angle so that I could just barely make out what she was gazing at. And guess what? She was playing a video game. For an instant, I ceased being a hacker of humans, and just behaved like an ordinary, concerned person. If that angry, agitated executive walked in and caught her playing a video game, who knew what would happen. So, I said to her, "Hey, before I tell you why I'm here, I just want you to know: I think I saw your boss outside in the parking lot, and he's in a really bad mood. If he sees that on the screen, he's going to freak."

She shut down her game, turned politely to me, and said, "How can I help you?" Just then, the angry executive walked in. He passed by the desk in a huff and said, "Beth, in my office."

She got up to go, and as she was turning around, she mouthed "thank you!" to me. At that point, my "hacking humans" hat popped back on my head—I knew this would end well.

I sat down to wait for her to come back. Six or seven minutes later, she reappeared, a bit flustered, and said, "Oh, I'm so sorry. I can't believe you waited."

"Oh, no," I said, "I figured you'd be able to help me. So, I just thought I'd wait."

"Where were we?" she asked, sitting down.

"Oh," I said, "you were about to buzz me in because I'm late for my meeting in HR."

She shot me a look—no, it was a slow, full-on stare—that said, *I know that isn't true.*

I glanced down at my watch and sighed. "Yeah, I'm really late." "Yeah, you're right," she said. She hit her buzzer and let me in.

As a result of this one little encounter, my colleagues and I were able to hack this entire company. We gained access to *everything*—all of their data and documents.

The approach I used here wasn't rapport building—I didn't have time for that, nor was I able to convey a clearly defined pretext. I jumped straight to another set of tools that professional hackers of humans also keep in their toolboxes: principles of influence. Pretexting and rapport building can suffice to induce others to behave as we'd like, but more often they function as a prelude to deliberate efforts to influence. If you're trying to get your siblings to contribute money to pay for your aging mother's care, or your employees to put out extra effort so your team can succeed with a big project, you'll communicate your request in specific and strategic ways once you've already initiated a conversation so your siblings or employees will be more likely to say yes. Professional hackers don't leave these efforts to chance or "gut feel." They deploy proven techniques rooted in the science of human psychology, techniques so powerful they almost seem like mind control. In fact, hackers can often dispense with pretexting and rapport if they need to and just use influence to get what they want, as I did here.

The specific technique I used with this assistant is called reciprocation. It's similar to the "give to get" rapport-building technique described in the last chapter, with an important difference. "Give to get" is generic: you don't know much about the other person so you give them something small that everyone likes in hopes they'll do something good for you as well. Your goal is simply to get them to like you so that at some future moment you can *then* nudge them in a specific direction. With reciprocation, that moment of influence has arrived, and your altruism is now keenly targeted to elicit a specific act of goodwill that seems both commensurate and natural to the other person.

You know something about your person of interest and what they regard as valuable. You intentionally prepare the way for your imminent request by giving them this valuable gift so that they'll feel indebted enough to say yes to you.

In this particular hack, I had a goal in mind: I wanted the receptionist to let me into the building. Guessing that the executive I'd seen in the parking lot was her boss, I gave her something I knew she'd find valuable: a chance to avoid a potentially nasty encounter. Although it might seem hard to believe, I gave that gift selflessly, without my end goal in mind. I was just acting on impulse to help her. But it instantly dawned on me that I had stumbled upon the perfect gift to give her so that my impending request would seem both commensurate and natural for her to fulfill. I could now ask for what I wanted and receive a favorable response. I had unwittingly triggered the reciprocation dynamic.

You, too, can use reciprocation and other principles of influence to win people over and prompt them to act on your behalf. You're probably using some of these principles in your daily life right now without realizing it. Imagine what would happen if you honed these skills and deployed them deliberately. Imagine, too, how great it would be to recognize when others are trying to influence you—you could break free of their spell and make informed decisions that are in your own best interest.

SEVEN PRINCIPLES THAT WILL CHANGE YOUR LIFE

With one exception, the principles of influence I use and teach aren't original to me but rather come from Robert Cialdini's classic book, *Influence: The Psychology of Persuasion*.[2] Before encountering this book, I had intuitively practiced these principles, but had been only dimly aware of what I was doing. Cialdini crystallized these principles for me and introduced me to the underlying science, and for that I feel greatly in his debt. To become a master hacker of humans, read Cialdini as well as the other authors listed at the end of this book. In the meantime, begin building your skills and seeing results by integrating the following seven key influence principles into your daily interactions.

Principle #1: Reciprocation

Rounding out what I've said on this, let me emphasize the importance of breaking out of your own bubble and paying close attention to your person of interest. The Golden Rule presented in the Bible has us treat others as we would want to be treated. In applying reciprocation, you'll want to practice what businessman and author Dave Kerpen calls the "Platinum Rule": treating others in line with *their* wishes.[3] Since you're trying to arouse feelings of indebtedness in others, what matters is their subjective frame, not yours. Think of a gift they would find sufficiently valuable to inspire their gratitude or feelings of obligation to you.

Remember, gifts you bestow don't have to be expensive or fancy. Sometimes handcrafted objects or thoughtful gestures are the most valuable to people. And both gifts and requests can be quite subtle. Posing a question, for instance, creates an "obligation" to answer. Divulging a piece of information might create a sense of obligation to return the favor. Laughing at someone's joke might create an obligation for them to laugh at your joke. And holding the door open for someone might leave them feeling obliged to do something equally chivalrous for you.

In the above example, the "gift" I gave the receptionist turned out to be perfect for *her*, to an extent I couldn't have imagined. A few weeks after the incident, when I debriefed her and others in the organization about our break-in, I asked her why she let me in. "Because," she said, "I got yelled at three times already for playing computer games at the front desk because it's such a boring job. You saved me from getting yelled at again, and I was especially grateful because my boss was in a bad mood. When I came back and you said I was already in the process of letting you in, I knew that wasn't true, but you had just saved me from being humiliated. And I thought, 'Well, this nice guy can't be a bad person.' So, I decided to let you in." I had lucked into a gift that cost me little (just a few minutes of my time) but was so valuable in her mind that she breached important security protocol. Even though she knew something wasn't quite right it felt natural for her to agree, and she might have even felt obliged on some level to do so.

If you plan to make a request of someone, think in advance about that person's needs or desires and any gifts that might arouse feelings of indebtedness or obligation commensurate with your request. If you aren't sure what your person of interest values, observe them carefully, listening for "pain points" they might express—problems that you might help address with a modest outlay of time, effort, or money. Don't make your gifts larger than the level of rapport that exists, as that will backfire. Reciprocation is potentially an open-ended process in the context of everyday relationships. Gifts you give might allow you to extract positive responses to your requests, paving the way for you to give other, more valuable gifts and make bigger requests going forward. In effect, the act of mutual gift giving allows you to build progressively greater levels of rapport. You've left other people better off for having met you and thus created a positive impression in their minds. Since people like you more, you can increase the value of what you bestow and request.

If my neighbors watch over our house when we're on vacation and I reciprocate by doing the same for them, we've created a certain level of goodwill and trust between us, making it possible for either of us to do the other an even bigger favor—say, spending several hours to help the other figure out why their Internet isn't working—and ask a similar favor in return. As time passes and our relationship develops, we might find ourselves taking in valuable packages for one another or eventually watching one another's pets for the weekend. If either of us had asked the other to care for our dog Ralphie when we'd first met, it would have come across as strange and excessive. We'd have engendered distrust, rendering future cooperation less likely. But the same is true if one of us had bestowed a huge gift in anticipation of making a request. The other party might have found it strange and suspected that it came with some pretty big strings attached.

Any of the influence principles discussed here can create positive feelings in others' minds, raising baseline levels of rapport and enabling even greater influence. Rapport and influence are thus mutually reinforcing. The more rapport you build, the more influence you can potentially wield, and vice versa.

Principle #2: Concession

Years ago, after my family adopted our dog Logan from the Humane Society, we received a call soliciting a donation. "How is Logan," the woman on the phone asked. "Is he still healthy?" When I responded that he was and thanked her for checking in, she informed me that they were raising money for their annual charity drive to benefit animals under their care. "Most of your neighbors have been donating two hundred dollars today."

"Wow," I said, "two hundred is a lot of money."

"Yeah, you're right," the woman said. "I know times are hard right now so maybe a donation of fifty dollars would help. Could you manage that?"

"I don't know, maybe I could do forty. Would that be okay?"

"Perfect," she said. "Would you like to donate that now by credit card or by check?"

If the woman had called and not set that initial amount of $200, I probably wouldn't have donated $40. I would have reasoned that I was already doing my part by taking care of a dog. Or maybe I would have given a token amount, like $10. By starting at a high number and then conceding to something smaller, she made me feel like I was "getting something" from her and doing the deal on my terms. I felt more comfortable conceding to her and contributing the $40.

As the near ubiquity of the Golden Rule suggests, we humans like the idea of treating others as we've been treated (whether we actually do it all the time is another question).[4] This idea goes well beyond the reciprocal gift-giving described above. If someone concedes something to us, we'll be more likely to concede something to them. Further, as research in social psychology has also demonstrated, we are more likely to agree to requests if we've first agreed to a smaller, but related request—what is known as the "foot-in-the-door" technique.[5] A potentially useful pathway to compliance is thus to first use concession to get your person of interest to agree to a relatively small request and then progressively increase the scope of your requests as you build mutual trust and rapport. Now that I'd agreed to donate $40 to the Humane Society, I was more likely to comply with a follow-up request for a $60 or $75 donation, had that been their ultimate goal.

Another trick is to concede something that seems valuable to your person of interest, but that isn't valuable to you. The Humane Society might have decided that their target donation was $25 per person. Starting at $200 and conceding $160 of that was an effective approach. Before you deploy this technique, make a list of possible concessions you might make and compare them with the concessions you're seeking to ensure the balance is in your favor.

If you're not using concession in your parenting, you're missing out. When my son Colin was eight, he went through a phase of asserting his independence by refusing to eat breakfast. He just wouldn't do it, no matter how much I begged, cajoled, or threatened. He even began waking up later and getting ready for school just before the bus arrived so that he didn't have time to eat breakfast. One morning, I had an idea. I woke him and said, "Hey, you have a choice this morning. Do you want eggs, cereal, or oatmeal?"

He thought about it for a moment and said, "I'll take oatmeal." And like that, I'd won. I'd appeared to concede something by re-linquishing control and offering him a choice, thereby giving him a chance to express his independence. In return, he conceded some-thing to me: he would eat oatmeal for breakfast. All I really cared about was that he ate something—it didn't matter what it was. I'd done to him what the Humane Society had done to me. I'd given him a choice knowing that whatever he chose, I'd win. In both cases, the person deploying concession got their person of interest to willingly agree to what they wanted, leaving them better off.

Technique #3: Scarcity

According to social psychologist Timothy C. Brock, commodity the-ory holds that "any commodity will be valued to the extent that it is unavailable."[6] In other words, scarce goods are valuable goods. Hackers of humans mobilize this simple principle, designed to explain the psy-chology underlying consumer behavior, to move targets to a desired outcome. You can, too. Are you trying to sell a product? Announce that it will be around for a limited time only. Want to get someone to confide in you? Tell them you don't feel comfortable talking to anyone else about this issue—only them. I use scarcity all the time when set-ting up meetings with potential clients. Instead of telling them that my calendar is wide open and they can pick any day and time they want for our appointment, I'll give them just a couple of relatively short windows over a week-long period from which they can select. Doing so makes it appear that I'm extremely busy, and that my time (and by extension, that of my entire team) is valuable. The prospective client now wants the meeting even more. I haven't lied to my prospect—I *am* very busy. I've just chosen to offer limited flexibility in scheduling to highlight that reality.

Principle #4: Consistency

We humans love to experience consistency in our daily reality, associating it with stability, wisdom, and confidence. As research has found, behavioral consistency helps build cognitive trust (not to be confused with emotional trust).[7] In a business context, members of the consulting firm McKinsey have spoken of "the three Cs of customer satisfaction: Consistency, consistency, consistency."[8] If you have kids, you know this principle doesn't just apply to customer care. You walk into a room to find a prized glass vase lying shattered on the ground. Your son or daughter stands nearby. When you ask if they broke the vase, they say, "Nope, not me." If you observe that a ball of theirs is a couple of feet away on the floor, and that this ball wasn't there just ten minutes earlier, and that you heard them throwing something around the house, they still deny breaking the vase. "I just came into the room and it was broken," they say. Kids do this kind of thing all the time—lying to the point of ridiculousness, just to remain consistent with their original story.

You can easily mobilize our drive for consistency in your daily life. Reinforce people's inner urge to remain consistent, for example, by rewarding behavior of theirs that you like. Although I had notched a victory when my son Colin conceded to eating oatmeal for breakfast, my success was fleeting. I would have to induce him to continue eating it day after day. I did that by rewarding his behavior so as to reinforce his internal consistency drive. I made no secret that I was happy with him, and I offered to make him oatmeal any way he wanted, even adding maple syrup for sweetness. Today, Colin detests oatmeal, and that's because he wound up eating it every day for an entire year as a kid, thanks to my hacking skills and his internal drive for consistency. (Think it's easy to have a hacker as a parent? Ask Colin—it isn't!)

Companies play on the consistency principle all the time, most notably in their loyalty programs. Starbucks knows its customers naturally maintain morning coffee "habits." They reinforce those habits by giving you points every time you buy a drink and more points if you develop other habits they like, such as adding a breakfast sandwich to your order. You can develop rewards systems of your own to help people in your life behave consistently in ways you like. Want your children to stretch their artistic muscles? Praise the pictures they paint and post them on the wall. Before you know it, you'll have more paintings than you know what to do with. If you want your spouse to communicate with you more, don't just demand that behavior. When your spouse begins to tell you about their day, actively listen and ask follow-up questions, "rewarding" them with your interest. When they're done, proffer a second reward in the form of a hug. These two actions will help them create a consistent pattern.

You can also use consistency in the course of conversations to nudge people in desired directions. You stand a better chance of getting someone to agree to a request if you first pose easier questions and get them to say "yes" to those. They'll be more inclined to say yes to what you really want simply because they'll want to appear consistent to themselves and to others in the answers they give. Also, when someone has agreed to your wishes, try getting them to articulate that to you explicitly. "So to confirm," you might say to an employee, "tell me again what goals we decided on, and when you're going to complete those projects." If your employee commits voluntarily to taking an action, and verbalizes this commitment to you, they'll be more inclined to follow up and not backtrack thanks to the psychological desire to remain consistent.

Principle #5: Social Proof

People tend to regard an action or idea as "good" or acceptable if they believe others do, too. In research experiments, scholars have demonstrated the power of social proof for a range of actions, including doing good deeds, littering, and "even in deciding whether and how to commit suicide."[9] Hackers of humans use peer pressure to influence their "targets." And they also try to appear similar to their targets so that targets feel more comfortable doing their bidding. In their mind, they're helping an insider, not a stranger.

Students of mine used such techniques to obtain personal information from strangers in a Las Vegas mall. One student in a team of four sat down in the food court with an iPad in hand, posing as a successful developer of Apple Store apps. He purported to have a new game that had not yet been released (prior to arriving at the mall, he had quickly downloaded an app that allowed you to develop simple games for kids). He was in the mall, he said, asking people if they wanted to demo the app and provide feedback. To demo the app, people would need to leave their full name, place of residence, and date of birth. If this student had simply pitched passersby to demo the app, he would likely have only attracted a few takers. Instead, he had the three other students on his team stand in line pretending to be strangers who were waiting to try out the app. That alone piqued bystanders' curiosity, but then these three pretended to play the game and loudly exclaimed how "awesome" it was. When asked, the three happily provided their personal information to the supposed app developer. Seeing them do this, others in the food court began lining up and willingly handing over their personal information. Since others had done it, it seemed "safe." It was a brilliant display of the social proof principle.

Used properly, social proof can create situations in which even reluctant, cynical people concede to your requests. On one occasion, while I was trying to enter a secure building, the guard on duty handed me a clipboard to sign. Scanning the board, I noted that one of the people who had signed in earlier that morning was a man named Paul Smith. Pretending to realize that I lacked the proper identification, I handed back the clipboard, apologized profusely, and promised the attentive security guard on duty that I would return later that day with the proper ID. On my way out, I casually asked his name. I never did return with the proper ID. Instead, I returned the next day and approached a different guard. "Hey," I said, "my name is Paul Smith. I was here yesterday, and Jim checked me in. I filled out all the paperwork, and he let me in." The security guard let me in without checking my ID. For him, the social proof that I had mustered by mentioning his colleague's name was enough.

Principle #6: Authority

Most of us are socialized to respect authority figures. In a classic study reported by the psychologist Stanley Milgram and conducted at Yale University, research subjects were asked to administer electric shocks to another person under the pretext of helping experts better understand how punishment affects our ability to learn. Prodded by the researcher, subjects meted out electric shocks of varying strength as "punishment," with the shocks ostensibly growing more severe as the experiment proceeded. Milgram wanted to see how far people would go in administering pain to another person when prompted by an authority figure. Out of forty subjects, most—twenty-six—continued administering shocks until the very end of the experiment, with the voltage well above a level marked "Danger: Severe Shock." As Milgram remarked, the experiment showed "the sheer strength of obedient tendencies." "Subjects have learned from childhood," he continued "that it is a fundamental breach of moral conduct to hurt another person against his will. Yet, 26 subjects abandon this tenet in following the instructions of an authority who has no special powers to enforce his commands."[10]

Scammers use the authority principle all the time to bilk people, posing as police officers, IRS agents—you name it. Between January and May 2019, the Federal Trade Commission logged almost 65,000 reports of scammers pretending to be from the Social Security Administration, and almost 20,000 reports of scammers claiming to work for the Department of Health and Human Services.[11] Scary, isn't it? You certainly don't want to use the authority principle to cheat people in your everyday life, but you can use it in subtler ways to become more persuasive. When trying to convince a boss to hire you, you might influence them by deepening your voice slightly or using more sophisticated vocabulary appropriate to the job, since both might suggest authoritative knowledge. When trying to resolve an issue with customer service personnel, mentioning your long-standing patronage of the company and evoking your familiarity with its products might lead them to take your complaint more seriously, since you'll have established your "authority" as a valued customer.

Remember those students of mine who induced people in the Las Vegas mall to disclose their personal information? During the next class I taught, I challenged my new set of students to outdo these exploits. They sure did, this time mobilizing the authority principle. A team of students went to a bar and approached the lead singer of a band that was performing that night. One of the students told the singer that they were students working on a study and needed to get as many people as possible to fill out a survey. Most of the questions on this survey were bogus, but the last few asked for the same information as the other students sought: name, place of residence, date of birth. The lead singer agreed to help. Later that evening during the band's performance, one of the students jumped onstage with the singer's permission, grabbed the microphone, and said, "Joe, the lead singer, just helped me with a study for my graduate school project, and he's asking everyone here to help me." The lead singer chimed in, "Yeah, help this guy out!" Within a few moments, dozens of people at the bar were lined up to fill out the survey, just because the lead singer—an authority figure in this context—asked them to.

Principle #7: Liking

If people like people who are similar to them (the tribalism described in the last chapter), they *really* like people who like them.[12] If you like someone, evoking genuine concern, care, and affinity commensurate to the level of rapport that exists between you, they will in turn like you—and go to great lengths to make you happy. Of course, liking your person of interest by itself isn't enough to guarantee that they will like you back. If you show them how much you like them by paying them compliments, asking how they are, telling them how much you like them, and so on, yet you reek of body odor, are shabbily dressed in a context where you're supposed to be dapper, or hunch yourself over into an off-putting, defensive posture, your person of interest still isn't going to like you. Your body language and dress actively turned them off. So, in addition to liking someone, you have to use these elements to create a "blank canvas," if you will, that doesn't impede that person from liking you back and responding positively to your requests.

Even if you smell great, dress appropriately, avoid forbidding body language, and take other measures to make yourself likable, your person of interest still might not reciprocate your expressions of affinity. In one epic fail that occurred while I was trying to break into a building, I approached the receptionist and complimented her on one of the many framed photographs displayed on her desk. One featured her two teenage daughters in their bikinis during a beach vacation. "Wow," I said, "that's a great picture of your daughters." I had meant this as an innocent compliment to convey my affinity for her. She responded with a hostile glare, pegging me as a creepy stranger who had eyes for her scantily clad daughters. I didn't even try to request entry. Instead, I left and had someone else on my team try instead. To this day, the encounter represents one of my most cringe-worthy moments as a professional hacker.

You might studiously avoid any miscues and find that your person of interest *still* doesn't like you back. Don't worry, it might have more to do with them than you. My wife has an acquaintance who was in a horribly abusive relationship with a guy. He apparently looked quite similar to me—same height, same build, same color hair. My wife's acquaintance had been so traumatized by this man that she began to visibly shake whenever I walked within a few feet of her. I could have smiled all I wanted, tilted my head back in a way that suggested openness, smelled great, showered her with compliments, even told her outright that I liked her, and it would have made no difference—she wouldn't have liked me back. If you've tried everything and still can't get someone to like you, it might well be out of your control. Rather than continuing to frustrate yourself, you will be best off avoiding this person and seeking what you want or need from someone else.

BUILDING YOUR INFLUENCE "MUSCLES"

Now that you're familiar with the key influence principles, let's work with them. Try the following exercise:

Pick someone important in your life, such as your spouse, child, or friend. Your job is to convince them to try to eat something that they think they would never want to eat, using one or more of the principles of influence. This food item can't be too gross or bad for them—you need to leave them better off for having met you. But the food has to be strange enough to be somewhat of a challenge. What will you do to incite your person of interest's culinary boldness?

While writing this book, I used this exercise to get a friend of mine—I'll call him Joe—to try a Japanese food that clearly grossed him out: raw *uni*, the gonads of sea urchins. We were grabbing dinner at a sushi restaurant, and in the space of ten minutes as we were sitting down, ordering, and waiting for our food I blasted him with multiple influence techniques, just for fun. Having known one another for a while, we had already built a certain amount of rapport, which I enhanced slightly as we entered the restaurant by talking up how great it was, knowing that Joe likes a good meal.

From there, I left the impression that I had expert knowledge of sushi and of this restaurant in particular (authority principle), throwing around sushi terms, describing in detail why this restaurant had the freshest possible sushi, and chatting with the waitresses as a regular would (they also clearly recognized me, which further established my authority). For good measure, I also tossed in some social proof, telling Joe about several people he knew who had previously eaten *uni* at this restaurant and loved it. Joe tentatively agreed to try the dish, so we included it in our order. I was halfway there.

When the food came out, it was every bit as fresh as I promised, which further buttressed my credibility (consistency principle). Since

I had induced Joe to promise to try *uni*, his innate tendency toward consistency also impelled him to want to deliver on that promise. Fellow diners of Japanese descent, I alerted him, were also enjoying *uni* (social proof) and so should Joe, given the high esteem in which I held him for being an adventurous eater (liking). Staring long and hard at his *uni*, Joe finally put it in his mouth, chewed slowly, and swallowed. He didn't like it very much. He told me he would never order it again. Still, he felt better off for having tried something new. He could at least brag to his friends and family that he had tried sea urchin gonads.

Try this exercise with a few people, testing out the seven influence principles. Use only one if you like during an encounter or mix and match them. Experiment. Have fun. Make note of what *doesn't* work. From there, look for other opportunities in your daily life where you might profitably exercise influence. If you have conversations coming up where you'll have to make a request of someone, plan these out in advance. Start with your pretext and from there list influence tactics that might match. If your pretext involves presenting yourself as the "newbie work colleague," you probably won't want to use the authority principle. If your pretext involves playing the role of the "stern boss," avoid the liking principle. Also pay attention to your own emotions. If you're feeling nervous about the encounter, you might want to avoid using the authority principle, as you might lack persuasiveness. If you're feeling sad or depressed, it might feel harder to deploy the liking principle—you might not feel affinity for much of anything.

Once you've narrowed down your list of possible influence principles to deploy, don't cling to it unduly. As you start to execute tactics in the moment, abandon or modify them as necessary on the fly. Whatever you do, don't overdo these tactics. Otherwise, your person of interest will start to become aware of them and their critical faculties will kick in—they'll become suspicious and might even come to dislike you. Take the liking principle too far, and you risk coming off as obsequious. Take authority too far, and you'll seem arrogant and smug. Take reciprocity too far, and you'll seem inappropriate. In each of these cases, your person of interest will feel much less inclined to help you and might even move to end the conversation.

In the course of these encounters, you might find you don't need to mobilize influence principles as you'd planned, since your rapport building (which you've also been practicing all along) proved sufficient. In that case, stop! Cease and desist. If you don't, it could prove fatal, as it once was for me and my colleague Ryan. We were breaking into a building posing as, you guessed it, pest control guys. It was eleven thirty at night, and the site was empty. As we were making our way around the building, we got lucky: a lone member of the staff was leaving the building and heading to the nearby parking lot. Before the door could close behind her, I stuck my foot in to catch it. The woman hadn't seen us as she'd exited, but she'd heard me. She turned around, startled, and asked who we were. Pointing to our outfits, I said, "Pest control, ma'am. We're inspecting for spiders and scorpions. Just a quick inspection, and then we'll be spraying tonight while nobody is around."

"Oh, okay," she said, and continued on her way. That was it—I had won. In just a few seconds, I had built rapport. She clearly believed me and was leaving the premises. I should have shut up and continued on my way. Instead, I kept yapping. "Yeah," I said as she was walking away, "this time of year, spiders are really bad. We decided to come late at night because it can be scary when you spray. They come out and die slow." Ryan glared at me as if to say, *Dude, what are you doing?* Without thinking much about it, I was trying to mobilize the consistency principle, showing this woman that our actions were consistent with the pretext we had established of being pest control guys. Despite Ryan's glare, I couldn't stop myself—I blathered on in this vein, talking about spiders and the chemicals we were using, digging an even deeper hole for myself. The woman turned back to face us. "You know what," she said, "I don't know if I feel comfortable with you here."

"No, no," I said, "we'll be in and out. Don't worry, you can go on your way."

She shook her head. "No, I don't feel comfortable. I need you to leave before I call the police." She backed away and walked quickly to her car. We had been so close—I had my foot in the door. And yet, now we had to leave, all because I had tried to deploy an influence principle when it wasn't necessary. Once you've already got your person of interest helping you, let them do it and leave it at that! When it comes to hacking humans, less is usually more.

Each day for the next week, pick a different influence principle, and challenge yourself to use it during minor interactions you have. Take a moment at the start of each day to brainstorm multiple ways you might deploy it as a tactic. If you're trying to use the authority principle, make a list of how you might project a modest amount of authority in different social contexts—by picking a piece of clothing that you think exudes authority, dropping bits of expert knowledge, and so on. If you're trying to use the liking principle, maybe you'll challenge yourself to approach a colleague at work with whom you frequently clash and use compliments and other means to learn more about them. The possibilities are endless!

THE ULTIMATE SECURITY GUARD

As you gain more experience with these influence principles and apply them alongside the other strategies in this book, you'll be astonished

how easy it is to get people to do your bidding or to think as you do—
not because they have to, but because they *want* to. Influence is your
ticket to getting free stuff, getting hired, getting your colleagues to support your decisions, enticing your kids to eat their breakfast, and so
much more. In fact, as you become more adept at influence, the risk is
that you'll become overly confident in your new super power, assuming it can get you *anything* you want. In that case, you're in for a rude
awakening. Judicious deployment of these principles never guaran-
tees success. Truly masterful hackers of humans hope for the best but
know their super powers have limits. Some people are so psycholog-
ically adept and alert to the workings of influence that they just can't
be swayed, no matter what you do. There aren't many of these people,
but they're out there.

I once met the ultimate security guard in the course of our hacking
work. As part of this assignment, we had to compromise three separate
buildings on a corporate campus, this time posing as repairmen from
the Big Blue Repair Company who had come to fix something in several of the company's server rooms. We nailed the first two buildings
no problem, bypassing security even though we were not on their list of
authorized visitors. At the third building, we encountered a young guard
who from his stiff demeanor, crew cut, and athletic build seemed to be
ex-military. "You're not on the list," he said when I told him my name.

"That's odd," I said, "because we were just in some of your other
buildings, and the security there let us in no problem."

He shook his head. "I'm not security for those two buildings. I'm
security for this one. Sorry, but you need to be on the list."

Fishing for information, I asked, "Who was it, John, who was supposed to put us on the list?"

"No," he said, "Fred Smith, the director of IT."

"Yeah, I could swear our office said he did. Let me call and find out
what happened."

We left the guard with a fake business card and went out to our car to do some quick online research on this Fred Smith guy. We found out who he was and obtained his contact information. Spoofing his phone number, I called the security desk where I'd just been denied. "Hi, this is Fred Smith," I said to the young security guard. "Did you just turn away two repair people? Well, they were supposed to come up here on fifteen to do some repairs. So, I'm going to call their office and have them come back. Please add their names to the list."

"Sure thing," the guard said.

Bingo, I thought, problem solved. We were in.

About forty minutes later, I strolled back over to the security desk. "Hey," I said, "I got a call from my office saying we're back on the list. I guess we can go in now, right?"

"Uh-uh," the security guard said, frowning. "Before you do, let me ask you a question. I took your business card and looked up your company name. I can't find the Big Blue Repair Company in this state anywhere. Where are you from?"

"Oh," I said, "that's because we're new to the area. We just moved in here."

"That's odd," he said, "your card said you were family owned for twenty years."

I was flustered now and stuttered a bit. "Well, we are, but in a different state."

"What state? I'd like to look you up. Just because you're on the list doesn't mean I'm letting you through."

We never did compromise this last building. This guy was too good, resisting any influence tactic we threw at him. We'd tried authority by impersonating the IT director. We used the consistency principle, in that my business card and outfit perfectly matched my pretext. We used social proof, informing the security guard that we had been in the other two buildings and his colleagues there had let us in. None of that worked—the security guard's invisible "force field" was too strong. He was a born gatekeeper, which was why we later advised his company to put him in charge of training all of their security guards.

If guards everywhere were as good as this guy, and if employees of companies everywhere were as alert to the influence tricks criminals might try, my team and I would be out on the street looking for work. Sadly for organizations but fortunately for us, most people have personal force fields that are far weaker than this guard's. They're vulnerable to the influence principles, far more so than they realize. That spells opportunity for those of us who understand these principles and know how to mobilize them. Practice influence tactics to get what you want and win others over to your cause. As you improve, you'll have the satisfaction of knowing you've left people better off for having met you, even as you get more of what you want. Further, you'll spot influence tactics instantly in the interactions you have with others. The more conscious of them you are, the less you'll be swayed, and the more control you'll have over your decisions. Do you *really* want to donate money when you're solicited? Do you *really* want to let a stranger into your home? Do you *really* want to bring on someone to your team who makes a seemingly strong pitch? Maybe, but maybe not.

On some occasions, you might find yourself giving out information you don't need to give. The people who solicited the information might be hackers, and some of that information might be quite sensitive. Chances are, these strangers deployed some specific influence techniques that short-circuited your inhibitions and got you talking. By mastering these techniques yourself, you can use them not to hurt people, but to develop more intimacy in your relationships and to help keep your loved ones safe, healthy, and thriving. How might you get your doctor to tell you what your diagnosis really means? How might you induce your boss to tell you what she really thinks of your performance? Turn the page and find out.

CHAPTER 5

MAKE THEM WANT TO TELL YOU

*Get people to open up and tell you what
you want without even asking.*

The previous chapter described how to get people to do your bidding. Now we focus on a specific form of influence in which you prompt people to divulge information they might otherwise keep secret. You'll be astonished not just by what you'll learn by using this form of influence but by how confident you become in social situations and how much your relationships improve. If you've ever struggled at a cocktail party to make casual conversation, read this chapter.

Here's a challenge: approach a perfect stranger, start a conversation, and within a reasonable length of time get them to tell you something personal they've never told anyone else in their life, ever. Could you do it? How? If that task seems intimidating, try seeing if you can simply get the person's full name, date of birth, or the city in which they reside.

My students tackle these and similar challenges as homework

assignments. With a little practice, they succeed brilliantly. Bear in mind, many of these students aren't social butterflies. Some are shy and introverted. For them, the idea of approaching a stranger and starting *any* conversation seems daunting. By the end of the week-long class, however, almost all of them blossom, becoming adept at gathering information and more comfortable than they'd ever imagined in all kinds of social situations. With a bit more practice over the following weeks or months, they become master conversationalists who know how to draw out anyone they meet.

The media often paint hackers as pasty-faced nerds who stare at computer screens all day long and barely know how to interact with a fellow human. Anyone who has seen the American drama series *Mr. Robot* knows exactly what I'm talking about. I'm sure some hackers resemble that stereotype, but in general, successful scammers, con artists, and spies are some of the friendliest, most approachable, most engaging people you'll ever meet. They not only know how to start a conversation through pretexting and rapport building, and how to influence people to take a desired action once the conversation is going. They also know how to conduct a conversation deliberately to obtain sensitive information they're seeking. They're such smooth talkers, in fact, that they obtain this information without their "targets" even realizing that they had ulterior motives. From their targets' standpoint, they were just having an enjoyable, interesting, and "safe" conversation with a fellow human being.

A decade ago, when radio-frequency identification technology (RFID) was becoming popular, I attended a cocktail party for a company I was targeting. My goal: learn about the new security technology it had recently installed. As I stood at the crowded bar, an employee from the company approached. We had been introduced to one another before but were basically strangers. I gave him a classic, "Hey, bro" greeting and asked if he wanted a drink. We started making small talk—I asked whether he liked coming to these kinds of events, or whether he did so because his boss insisted. He said he enjoyed these parties. After several more minutes of banter, I mentioned that I worked at a company—I'll say Xerox—and that we had just installed this brand-new technology. "I don't know what it is," I said, "but it's these weird cards." I went on: "I'm not supposed to talk about it, but you know, it just seems so weird. Call me old-fashioned, but I just like having a regular key in my pocket."

My new drinking buddy leaned in. "Hey," he said, "you want to hear something even better? There's this project at our company that's top secret. It's a brand-new system and you use the card to get through the front door, then you use it again to get through the metal man-trap thingy." We continued chatting, and within a few more minutes, I learned all about the plastic key card system (RFID cards) the company had installed, where it had installed it, and what its key vulnerabilities were. Cha-ching!

It had seemed to my drinking buddy that we were having a friendly, "safe" conversation, but in fact I was relying on a principle called "trusted confidence knowledge." Human nature dictates that it's okay to discuss private information—even very personal matters—if the person you're talking to has divulged private information as well. Psychologists have offered different interpretations of this phenomenon. Some believe we reciprocate when someone has divulged private information in order to maintain a sense of equilibrium in the relationship. The so-called social attraction–trust hypothesis holds that we return the favor of sharing privileged information because we want to build trust and connection with others.[1] Whatever the case, my drinking buddy felt "safe" divulging secret information to me because, like him, I appeared willing to talk about my company's security. I couldn't have possibly been a hacker or someone else with another motive.

Except I was.

GET ANYONE TO TELL YOU ANYTHING

People in my business have a word for the act of obtaining information without asking for it overtly. We call it *elicitation*. Bad guys use this all the time. Social media sites are crawling with spies from various countries who create fake profiles, connect with unsuspecting users, and engage them in seemingly innocent conversation. With relatively little risk and effort, they obtain valuable information that helps them recruit these users to share secrets or target others.[2] Spies also use elicitation in person in attempts to gain access to sensitive information, whether it's classified government information or corporate secrets. That friendly stranger at the airport who spots you using a brand of government-issued pen or wearing a corporate badge and inquires what agency or department you work for might be just making small talk. Or they might be a spy trying to shake out sensitive intel.[3] Terrorists also rely on elicitation to help plan attacks, conducting seemingly innocent conversations with employees to learn which doors on certain buildings are locked, how security is deployed, the times of day in which the facility is busiest, and so on. In 2019, the Michigan State Police warned members of the public to look out for "attempts to gain information about military operations, capabilities, or people."[4] Other law enforcement agencies have put out similar alerts.

Although it's important that we all stay vigilant, we're never really safe. In the hands of a skilled practitioner, elicitation is so powerful it's difficult to defend against. If you think of a piece of information you'd *never* want to give out, the PIN for your bank accounts is surely near the top of the list. When we create these codes, we expressly choose numbers others won't know but we'll remember. ATMs have special shields around their keypads, reinforcing the message: don't let anyone see your PIN. And yet, a friend and I once got total strangers in a restaurant to voluntarily reveal their PIN. We did it without manipulating or coercing them, and while leaving them better off for having met us.

We weren't trying to steal their money—we were just doing it for fun to see if we could. We were in a quaint Italian restaurant in Washington, D.C.—the kind where the tables are packed close together. Couples were enjoying their meals on either side of us. "Hey," my friend said to me, as per our previously arranged plan, "did you read that article in *USA Today* that said that sixty-eight percent of people surveyed use their birthday as their bank PIN?[5]

"Well, I totally believe that," I said, taking a bite of spaghetti pomodoro. "I mean, my PIN is zero-seven-seven-four." Of course, that wasn't my birthday or my PIN number, but the people around us didn't know that.

My friend wiped tomato sauce from his mouth. "Man, that's so stupid. People can guess that. I don't use that. I use a combination of my wife's and my birthday—it's one-two-zero-four."

A guy next to us couldn't help but overhear. Nodding at his wife, he said, "I told you using your date of birth was a stupid idea."

"Yeah," she said, "but it's really easy to remember: one-zero-one-eight."

I almost choked on my food. I couldn't believe it. This woman had just given us and everyone else sitting around us her PIN. But it got better. The woman said to her husband, "No one can remember your number: two-four-three-seven-one-four."

"That's not it, Julia," the man said. "It's two-four-three-seven-*nine*-four."

The waitress, who was refilling our water glasses, chimed in. "Well, I use Bank of America, and they let us use words or numbers, so I just used the name of my daughter's favorite stuffed toy, and that's 'Panda.'"

This conversation went on a little longer—we got another two or three PINs. If I'd said to the couple next to us, "Excuse me, but can both of you please give me your PINs? I'm curious what they are," they never would have divulged them. The question would have activated the critical thinking parts of their brain and aroused their suspicion. But in the context of the conversation as it unfolded, they felt perfectly comfortable blurting out those numbers. We obtained the information we'd sought, while in a small way the encounter left them better off for having met us. They'd engaged in some light banter and learned a factoid they'd found interesting.

Remember William Moulton Marston, the psychologist whose work gave rise to the DISC assessment described in chapter 1? Turns out he was also the guy who invented the Wonder Woman superhero character. You'll recall that Wonder Woman can get bad guys to disclose information by wrapping them in her "lasso of truth." Mastery of elicitation skills is like having a magic lasso in your back pocket. You can get people to reveal almost anything. And then some.

My students and I were in a busy Las Vegas mall, and for fun I told them they could pick any "target" they wanted, and I would get them to tell me their full name, place of employment, and hometown. They picked an absolutely gorgeous woman in her late twenties who was standing in the food court waiting for her salad. This woman was scantily dressed in short shorts, cowboy boots, and a flannel shirt. My students reasoned that an attractive young woman would probably be an especially difficult target for me because she'd be used to brushing off men's advances. Because I was a male stranger, she'd react defensively or protectively when I approached. "Oh, come on," I said, "pick someone else." But they insisted.

I had no clue how I was going to approach this woman. What could I possibly say that would ingratiate me with her and prompt her to tell me what I wanted? Noting her appearance, I focused on her boots as my best hope for making a quick connection.

I walked over to where she was standing, grabbed a tray, and took a spot behind her in line. After a brief pause, I said, "Excuse me, can I bother you for a minute with a question?"

She turned and said, "Sure, what can I do for you?" But her body language indicated that she was indeed defensive. She gave me a quick roll of the eye, as if to say, "What pickup line will you use now?"

She was in for a pleasant surprise. "I'm in town on business," I said, "and it's my anniversary this coming week. My wife loves cowboy boots, but I'm not a fan. I wouldn't even know how to buy a cowboy boot. I saw yours and thought they were really nice. Could you tell me where you got them? If it's in this mall, maybe I could buy a pair."

Her whole attitude changed. Her eyes brightened, and she cracked a big smile. "Sure. It is in the mall, and I work there myself." She proceeded to tell me all about the boots, as the salesperson she probably was, and to direct me to the store. "Where are you from?" she asked. When I told her I lived in Florida, she said, "Oh, I'm from the Atlanta area, not too far."

"Wow, what are you doing working all the way out here in Vegas?"

She told me a bit more about her life, and then I repeated the directions to her store back to her to make sure I got them. I accidentally got them wrong, prompting her to say, "No, silly. Here, let me show you." Taking me by the hand, she led me about fifty feet away. Pointing down a corridor of the mall, she repeated the directions.

I thanked her warmly and told her I would head right over to buy my wife a pair. Leaving the tray on a nearby table, I pretended to start walking. After a step or two, I turned and said, "Hey, you know what? Maybe I should wait until you're on duty."

"No, no. Just tell them Samantha sent you. They'll give you a discount."

"Thanks, I will," I said, smiling. "Man, you're a lifesaver." I glanced at my students, who were all watching, and then back at her. "Hey, my name's Chris, Chris Hadnagy. I'd love to tell my wife who helped me out. You said your name's Samantha. What's your last name."

"Cooper," she said (not her real name).

"Fantastic," I said. "Thanks again for all of your help, Samantha."

I turned to go, reveling in my victory. And then, to top it off, she called after me. "Hey, you might not know what kind of boots to buy. You should probably take a picture of my boots and send them to your wife so that she at least sees them and knows if she likes them. Since you're not from around here, you'll have trouble returning them if she doesn't."

My students couldn't hear our conversation, but the next thing they knew, this beautiful woman was modeling her boots for me, a perfect stranger, so I could take her picture. Full name, hometown, place of employment—I got everything, *plus* pictures of her boots. With the exception of her last name, I didn't ask for any of this information. I just crafted the conversation in a way that led her naturally to want to tell me.

EVERYONE NEEDS A MAGIC LASSO

Having a "magic lasso" might make for a neat parlor trick, but will it help your everyday life? Um, yes. If you're on a first date, you could play the twenty questions game and ask your date directly: "Do you want kids?"; "Are you gainfully employed?"; "Do you share any of my hobbies and interests?"; "Do you have any weird habits or quirks I should know about?"; and so on. Maybe they'd answer truthfully, maybe not. Almost certainly, the conversation would become more tense or awkward. If you used elicitation techniques, you could glean all of this information about the other person and more while keeping the conversation light and enjoyable. Let's say you're looking to marry someone who wants only one or two kids. To learn your date's perspective on this question, you could say something like: "You know, my siblings all have large families—four or five kids. I just don't know if I could handle that many. Seems so stressful." A statement like this will likely invite a revealing response, without you having posed a direct question. Of course, if you don't actually have siblings with large families, you'll want to slightly alter this statement to avoid lying. Maybe say something like: "When I grew up, we lived next to a family with four kids. I don't know how the parents did it. That might be too much for me."

Elicitation also works well in business settings. Let's say you sell software that helps companies manage part of their human resources function, and you're meeting prospective customers at a networking event. You're not interested in selling your software to small companies with fewer than two thousand employees. You could explain this to people you meet, asking them point-blank how big their companies are. If they're from large companies, you could follow up by inquiring whether they'd be interested in learning about your software. Such questions might not be out of line or offensive, but they're not especially fun or engaging. If you get an answer you don't want, you might give off negative vibes by unconsciously frowning or ending the conversation too quickly.

As an alternative, you might simply start a conversation, asking friendly questions about the kind of company they work for and trying your best to establish common ground. If the person revealed they worked for an insurance company, and you happened to have done a stint selling insurance earlier in your life, you might say, "Oh, cool. I don't know much about insurance, but I did sell it for six months during college. That's a hard business. I don't know how you guys do it." The person might respond by saying they don't actually sell insurance but run the IT department. "Well," you could say, "you must be pretty big if you have a whole IT department." The person might then tell you they've been growing rapidly and are up to five thousand people. Perfect—now you know this could be a potential client. So, you continue the conversation further to find out if they might want or need your product. You could probe to see if they are experiencing the kinds of problems your software is designed to solve. "At my last company," you could say, "we had a really hard time keeping employees happy. I heard that insurance companies are struggling with this, too." Whether or not you wind up landing a new prospect, you will have had a pleasant conversation and come off as friendly, interesting, and engaging.

With elicitation, you're approaching conversations purposefully, interacting more smoothly and patiently than you otherwise would. You're doing this out of self-interest, recognizing that most people don't respond well to being pummeled by direct questions. But you're also being kinder. All of us have some agenda we're pursuing when interacting with another person, whether we recognize it or not. You might seek information about how someone is feeling, or whether they like you or not, or whom they've spoken with, or whether they'll be a good partner on an upcoming endeavor. With elicitation, you're clear about your agenda but you don't just pursue it single-mindedly and at all costs. You take the time to *talk* with others, to get to know them, to connect with them, to hear what they have to say. You engage with others on their terms, not just yours. You put some thought into what you're saying, so that people feel more comfortable opening up to you.

In my experience, most people don't know how to elicit information from others. When they're not aggressively posing questions to extract information, they pursue conversations in clumsy ways that reveal their agendas and alienate others. I suspect this is because when most of us grew up our parents tended to interrogate us when they wanted information. They didn't often sit down to speak with us in a kinder, more neutral way. So, we never learned how to do this. We grew up assuming people were naturally defensive and the only way to get information was to squeeze it out of them. In truth, our business associates, bosses, children, elderly parents, friends, and neighbors are a lot more willing to divulge information than we might realize. They just have to feel comfortable. To ingratiate ourselves with them, we have to suspend our own needs and desires for a moment. Taking a deep breath, we have to understand where others are coming from and slow down enough to have a richer, more fulfilling interaction. We have to make the conversation about *them*, not us.

SEVEN STEPS TO EFFECTIVE ELICITATION

There's an easy process for making conversation about someone else, so that you can elicit information and leave the other person better off for having met you. First, *frame an intended goal*. What information do you seek from a conversation? The clearer your goal is in your mind, the more thoughtfully you can steer an encounter. But beware: you can't choose *any* goal. The information you seek must roughly align with the pretext and level of rapport you have with your target of interest. If we call people at a company when conducting a vishing (voice phishing) attack, say we're from the IT department, and request their Social Security number, they'll get suspicious and won't give it to us. But if we tell them we're calling from the HR department, they're more inclined to open up. They understand why someone from HR would need a Social Security number, since HR handles withholdings and other tax-related matters. An IT guy? It's possible but we have to work harder at the pretext to make it fit.

Second, with your goal in mind, *observe your person of interest*. This step is critical. Whether it's a total stranger or someone close to you, watch them for twenty to thirty seconds if possible—long enough to notice key details but not so long that you come across as creepy. Observing them can clue you in to whether you're catching them at an opportune time. Do they seem in a hurry to leave? Are they already in the middle of a conversation with someone else? Are they wearing headphones and ensconced in their own, private world? If the signs don't seem promising, postpone the conversation. If a conversation seems possible, scrutinize their body language for clues on how to approach. If they seem confused about something, perhaps there might be a way for you to help. If they seem frustrated, perhaps you can commiserate. If they're accompanied by others, think about whether their "tribe" will be an asset or a hindrance in your task.

If you fail to observe properly, you might screw up the next step: *frame an "invitational" question and an exit strategy*. When you're approaching a stranger, your opening question—the one you hope will "invite" a conversation—is critical, since if you can't build rapport in the first three seconds, the conversation won't continue. I learned this the hard way. On one occasion, several of my students challenged me to demonstrate elicitation in a hotel bar. Brimming with confidence, I approached a guy sitting in an adjacent lobby. Without observing or thinking about my question, I walked too briskly up to this guy, got in too close, and said loudly, "Hey. Can I ask you a question?" He turned out to be an older gentleman and physically much smaller than me. My unsubtle approach startled him—so much so that his chair tipped backward, sending him sprawling onto the floor. Mortified, I ran around to the back of the chair and tried to tip it back up. The chair was much lighter than I thought, so I wound up launching this guy several feet, sending him into a face plant on a nearby couch. Hotel staff ran up, thinking I was attacking the guy. Not good. Did I extract his full name, date of birth, and city of residence? I did not. Pro tip: don't do what I did here.

When framing an "invitational question," first ask if you can approach and enter their personal space. "Hello there," you might say, "can I borrow a minute of your time?" Let them lower their force field just a little. Then make sure your more substantive, follow-up question will likely spark further conversation. The biggest mistake people make is to pose a closed-ended question that doesn't lead anywhere. If you try to start a conversation by saying, "Hey, I'm looking for a good restaurant around here. Do you have any suggestions," your person of interest might say, "No, sorry, I'm not from around here." Or they might say, "Yeah, there's a great Peruvian place about a mile down the road." Either way, it's hard to continue the conversation. They'll expect you to thank them and be on your way. If instead you pummel them with additional questions, you'll arouse their suspicion.

Implicit in your opening question should be an exit strategy. If possible, you want to answer one of those four key questions that everyone wonders at the outset of an interaction: How long will it take? So, say something like, "Hey, can you help me with something quick? I just need a minute." Or, "I'm about to run, but I just had to ask . . . ." Such an opening indicates that the conversation really will be quick. And be sure to keep it quick. If you want more time, you need an invitation from the other person. Run the clock past your allotted time in their mind and you risk alienating them and jeopardizing your elicitation efforts.

Once you've delivered your invitational question, *drive the conversation forward* (step #4) by posing more questions. Most people think of conversations primarily as opportunities for *them* to talk. In an elicitation conversation, you pose questions to steer the conversation and allow the other person to do more of the talking. It's essential that you continue to make these questions open-ended, since you want to keep the conversation going long enough to obtain your desired information. Of course, posing questions so that the person of interest can talk means you'll be spending most of the conversation *actively listening* (step #5). Most people struggle to listen actively. While someone else is talking, they're thinking about the next point they're going to make. If you aren't actively listening to what your person of interest is saying, you won't position yourself to ask the next follow-up question.

To improve your ability to listen actively, challenge yourself to pose more reflective questions during your conversations. To frame a reflective question, repeat back the last three or four words your person of interest says, posing it as a question. If you're talking about travel and your person of interest says, "Yeah, Peru is the coolest country I've ever visited," your reflective follow-up question would be: "Really, Peru is the coolest country you ever visited?" Reflective questions will keep your person of interest talking about the topic at hand. But challenging yourself to pose these questions can get you in the habit of engaging more deeply in the conversation and listening actively. With a reflective question, you also signal to the other person that you're truly paying attention.

Poor listening will also prevent you from succeeding at the sixth step, *remembering the detail.* You can do a fantastic job conducting a conversation, subtly inducing your person of interest to divulge important information. But if you aren't adept at remembering detail, your elicitation efforts won't amount to anything. I can't tell you how many students of mine have conducted the homework assignments described at the beginning of this chapter, obtained the desired information, and yet couldn't remember it well enough to repeat it back to me. You might claim you don't have a great memory so you just won't record details like a professional hacker. Don't believe that! I used to have a terrible memory, but with practice I've reached the point where I not only remember what people tell me in fine detail, but also numerous environmental details, such as body language and clothing. Posing reflective questions can improve your memory for detail, since you're forcing yourself to repeat information. Of course, you don't want to overdo that, since you risk boring your audience or sounding like an idiot. Here's a little game to play with yourself to help improve your memory for detail:

When you venture into a café, hotel lobby, or other public place, select a specific demographic group beforehand on which to focus (Caucasian women, African American men, elderly people, Asian women, and so on). Challenge yourself to remember the shirt or blouse color of the first person in that demographic group whom you see. When you spot someone in that group who, say, is wearing a gray shirt, repeat "gray shirt" to yourself several times and see if you still remember it after you've left. Once you get good at this, challenge yourself to focus on multiple demographic groups and to remember other details. For example, when walking into a Starbucks you might challenge yourself to remember the first Caucasian woman's sweater color, the first African American male's shirt color, and the name of at least one person behind the counter. Do this for a month or two and you'll be shocked at how much your memory improves!

The final step when eliciting information is to *end the conversation in a way and at a time that leaves people better off for having met you.* Much of the time, your initial setup ("Do you have a minute for a quick conversation?") will naturally lead the conversation to end at a certain time. But be careful. Your elicitation efforts might prove more successful than you think, leading your person of interest to become immersed in an extended story. If you quickly break off the conversation because you've obtained the information you sought, you'll reveal yourself to be rude and overly concerned with your own objectives. The other person will feel disrespected and worse off for having met you. Be patient with the conversation and continue to listen actively and respond kindly even after you've gotten what you want. The conversation isn't only about you.

As with the other strategies described in this book, elicitation will feel more natural the more you practice it. Try it every day with the people in your life, total strangers as well as friends, family, and colleagues. Try at first to obtain relatively innocuous information, like the full name of a fellow Starbucks patron or what your teenager did during their school day. As you become more confident, use elicitation to induce people in your life to divulge meaningful information. What does your significant other *really* think about your relationship prospects? Is your boss as happy about your performance as they seem to be? Is your best customer planning to increase their orders for next year, or cut them back? What happened at the party your teenager attended last weekend? You're about to find out!

TAKING ELICITATION TO THE NEXT LEVEL

As you feel more comfortable pursuing conversations more purposefully, you can improve your results by working in some additional techniques. We encountered one of these techniques—"Trusted confidence"—at the beginning of the chapter. In collaboration with Robin Dreeke, former head of the FBI's Behavioral Analysis Program (BAP), I've developed five additional elicitation techniques that will help you draw people out and get them to "leak" information to you.

1) Make obviously untrue or illogical statements

If you try nothing else in this book, make it this technique. People have a natural inclination to correct statements that seem incorrect, especially if they harbor strong beliefs about the topic at hand.[6] If you're in the grocery store and you hear someone utter a complete falsehood about your favorite football team, you're going to feel a strong impulse to correct them. At the very least, your mind will stir and you'll think, "These people don't know what they're talking about!" You can use this tendency to your advantage when eliciting information. To find out if someone is really interested in a topic, purposely saying something untrue will usually prompt them to correct you, in the process giving you information you didn't have before. You can even throw out ridiculous or nonsensical statements and people will correct them with the right information. A student of mine would get people to give him their birthdays by approaching them as they ate their lunches. "Hey," he'd say to one of them, "you're eating strawberries. That must mean your birthday is in February."

Obviously, there was no connection between eating strawberries and having a February birthday, but they would correct him anyway. "No, it's in July."

"Oh, the fourth?"

"No, the twenty-first."

"Oh, cool," he'd say, and move on.

2) Give people a bracket

If you're trying to get someone to reveal an exact number to you, try providing them with high and low estimates. Chances are your person of interest will confirm whether the quantity at issue is in range, and even tell you exactly what it is.[7] People adept at buying cars do this all the time to discern how much room for negotiation there is. "Tell me," they might say, "if I wanted to get this car, and I needed a discount, could I get somewhere between $5,000 and $10,000 off the sticker price?" If the salesman is interested in negotiating, they might come back and say, "Any discount would probably be closer to $4,500." Now you have a better idea of how far you could take this negotiation. If you had just come out and said, "I need $4,000 off the sticker price for me to buy it," the salespeople will usually say they can't do it, since they're trying to lowball you. But if you come in with a bracket that's both realistic and slightly advantageous to you, you've either established a viable starting point from which to negotiate further, or you've learned that the dealer won't be able to meet you at a viable price point.

3) Help them to assume you know something or someone

If you claim to know something or to know others "in the know," you can make people feel more comfortable to talk. On one occasion when I was breaking into a building, I changed one of my colleague's names on my phone to the name of the vice president of the company we were breaking into. I asked this colleague to wait for me in the car and watch my interaction with security through the building's front windows. At a certain point, he would see me get into a tussle, and he was then to text me the following: "Where the hell are you? We've been waiting fifteen minutes."

From researching the company on Glassdoor, I knew that this vice president had a horrible reputation. People raged about how brutal it was to work for her. Knowing this, I walked boldly into the lobby carrying a big file of papers. Rather than slow down as I neared security, I quickened my pace, looking like I was going to blow right through it. "Whoa, whoa," the guards on duty said. "Stop. You can't just come in here like that."

"Really?" I said. "You didn't see me walk out just a few minutes ago to go to my car and get my papers?"

"I don't know what you're talking about," one of the guards said.

"Look," I said, "I don't have time. I'm sorry if you're falling asleep on the job, but I have a meeting in a few minutes and I just walked out to get these papers."

The guard shook his head. "I need to see your badge."

Just as he said that, the text from my colleague came in—again, showing up on my phone as if it came from the vice president.

"Really," I said, turning the phone so that he could see who texted me. "You want me to hit dial so I can tell her why I'm not up there?"

He waved me off. "No, it's okay. You're good."

In this case, I was telling a lie, making it seem like I knew something (or in this case, someone) that I didn't. In everyday life, you want to confine yourself to the truth. Not only is lying unethical but you might get called on it, and then what? On another occasion, when I was trying to elicit information from a physics professor, I approached him under the pretext of claiming to love a paper he had published on quantum physics. I knew nothing about quantum physics (still don't). When he asked me what parts of the article I liked and what questions about it I had, I struggled to answer. He knew I'd lied and wasn't happy. "Come back when you've read it," he said, walking off. A big, fat failure.

4) Feign incredulity

If you indicate you don't believe something your person of interest has said, you will likely prompt them to defend themselves, revealing information in the process. Be careful here, since you don't want to offend your person of interest by questioning their veracity. If you're chatting with someone and they tell you they just wrote a novel, don't blurt out, "I don't believe you could do that." Soften it by saying, "Wow, you wrote a book? Really?" This second response isn't saying "I don't believe you" but rather something like, "What you're saying is surprising on its face, so tell me more." Quite often, they will tell you more, revealing details not just about their novel or their writing process, but about other parts of their lives that you might find interesting.

5) Quote reported facts

I got that whole restaurant of people to give me their PIN by quoting an intriguing fact about behavior, prompting them to want to "test it out" by revealing their private information. The statistic we quoted was a real data point we'd found—we didn't make it up. If you're going to use this technique, educate yourself beforehand, identifying facts that might prove helpful in a conversation. In general, the more relevant information you can amass before embarking on a conversation, the better. If you're going to an industry conference on a particular topic to establish a presence for your company, read up on the topic while also collecting some interesting facts that might help you generate a conversation.

Start a conversation with someone at the grocery store. Your challenge during the course of conversation is to use one or more of the above tools to find out the month in which this person was born. Bonus points if you can do this in one line when you first approach the person. If you only choose to try one technique, make a deliberate false statement. It's scary how well it works!

As you practice these techniques and notch some early successes, you'll start to feel more confident in your abilities as an elicitor. But don't get too cocky. My students fail all the time because they seek out information beyond what they'd intended simply because they feel they can. The greedier you are, the more prone you'll be to overreaching. The moment your person of interest realizes you're pressing them for information, they'll feel used and clam up. They'll also feel worse for having met you, which is *not* what we want. Facial expressions and body language can help you spot when techniques you're deploying aren't working. If necessary, back away. Not everyone will provide you with the information you seek, nor will they do it every time. A person of interest might be in a bad mood or in a hurry, or the particular question you posed might not have struck a chord.

Above all, do what you can to stay focused on the other person and to meet them on their level. This goes beyond what you say to include how you say it. I can't remember where I discovered this little device, but I tell my students to stay alert to the RSVP—the rhythm, speed, volume, and pitch with which their person of interest is speaking. On the one hand, changes in these four conversational elements suggest when you're failing to connect with your person of interest and distrust is mounting. On the other, you can mirror their RSVP and generally connect better. If you meet someone and try to replicate their accent, you'll probably look like a fraud or leave the impression that you're mocking them. But you can move closer to their RSVP— volume and speed especially—without causing offense. Speaking just a bit more quickly and loudly, say, to someone from a big city can allow the conversation to feel more natural to them. Without even being aware of it, they'll feel that much more inclined to open up.

HACK YOUR WAY TO A DEEPER CONNECTION

People call alcohol a social lubricant—and it is. But so are the techniques discussed in this chapter. Some of us are born with the "gift of gab." Others of us have to work at it. Whether master or novice, you, too, can ace the art of conversation and deploy it to your advantage. The payback isn't just more control over conversations, more information coming your way, and the ability to get more people to enjoy your company and find you affable. It's the chance to connect more deeply with people, sometimes unexpectedly and even with total strangers.

Remember the exercise I mentioned at the beginning of the chapter, the one about asking a total stranger to tell you a secret they hadn't told anyone before? Two young students of mine—a male and female—pursued this challenge at a Las Vegas hotel (we were holding a training in that city, as we often do). My students were circulating among the betting tables and slot machines when they met a couple in their sixties, a husband and wife, and initiated a conversation. The two quickly established some rapport, and soon the group were chatting about their lives, their families, even some of their dearly held beliefs. About twenty minutes into this pleasant but fairly unremarkable conversation, the male student decided that the rapport between them had grown sufficiently strong that he could ask just about anything and obtain a serious reply. So, he popped the question. "I've been walking around tonight just trying to meet some strangers and build relationships," he said, "and I find that one of the best ways of doing that is to just throw out a really deep question like, 'Tell me something you've never told anyone.' So, what do you say?"

The husband and wife looked at one another and tears welled up in both of their eyes. The wife began to sob.

The male student felt terrible—what had he done?

The husband looked at him and said, "A year ago, our son committed suicide. It has been an awful, awful year. Two weeks ago, we made a pact with one another. I was going to kill her, and then turn the gun on myself."

My students were speechless.

The husband wiped his eyes with his sleeve while his wife struggled to compose herself. "We had everything planned, but at the last minute, we couldn't go through with it. What was the point? We decided to devote our lives to helping other young people struggling with depression and suicidal thoughts. We're here in Vegas one last time to have fun. Then we're going to take our entire life savings and pursue our mission."

My students gave this couple a hug and for the next half hour they continued to talk and laugh and cry together. Then they went to dinner together and exchanged numbers. When our training was over and the students went home, they continued to stay in touch with this couple. I don't know if their relationship blossomed further and they're still in touch, but I do know that the application of elicitation techniques led to a very special moment of intimacy and the forging of a meaningful relationship.

My students didn't simply go up to this couple and ask them to tell them something they'd never told anyone else. They "earned" the chance to pose this question by building rapport. They approached the couple in a friendly way, showed an innocuous interest in their lives, listened to what they were saying, asked thoughtful follow-up questions, and paid attention to how this couple appeared to be reacting to the conversation moment by moment, adjusting accordingly. These students had an agenda of their own, but pursuing it prompted them to think far more carefully about what they were saying and how they were saying it than they otherwise might have. Elicitation really is a super power, one that when ethically applied allows you not to dominate people and command them to divulge information but to build real (if often short-lived) relationships, so that they'll naturally want to open up. The more you practice elicitation and the other strategies described in this book, the better you get at them. All of your relationships shift for the better.

The topics we've covered so far—pretexting, rapport, elicitation, and influence—all belong to the positive, pro-social side of social engineering. Although bad guys use them to cause harm, the rest of us can deploy them to help others while also pursuing our own goals. But there are tools in the hacker's toolbox that should remain off-limits in everyday life. These tools are extraordinarily powerful but it's impossible to use them without causing harm that in some cases is quite severe. I'm speaking of the dark arts of manipulation. If you've ever been strong-armed into parting with your money or something else of value, you know how hurtful manipulation can be. In the next chapter, I'll teach you how manipulation works, not so you can deploy it to your advantage but so you can be on the alert against conmen, crooks, spies, and other bad guys. There are devious people out there in the world. The best protection is to know how they operate.

CHAPTER 6

STOP DEVIOUSNESS IN ITS TRACKS

Protect yourself against would-be manipulators
by understanding and recognizing their tricks.

Many people think of hacking humans as "manipulating" people. I beg to differ. When you exert influence using techniques presented in the past several chapters, people want to comply with your wishes—they're happy to help you out. Manipulation is different—and much darker. When you manipulate people, you deviously trick or even force people to comply against their wishes, often causing considerable harm in the process. My team rarely uses manipulation techniques, and I urge you to avoid them entirely. You do have to know about them, however, so that you can protect yourself from nefarious, would-be manipulators.

Years ago, after I was booted out of college but before I became a chef, I used my human hacker skills to get a job selling disability insurance to a customer base composed primarily of farmers. I knew as much about farming and rural life as the next twenty-year-old surfer dude from Florida's west coast. I knew even less about insurance. But the company took a chance on me, assigning our local office's top salesman to school me in the art and science of selling disability policies to small, struggling farmers.

What an education that was. The top salesman, whom I'll call Gregg, lied shamelessly to get farmers to buy much pricier insurance than they actually needed. During a typical sales call, Gregg might have encountered a farmer who, given the value of his farm and the level of income he derived from it, needed $175,000 in disability insurance in case he was injured on the job. Gregg would convince that farmer to buy $1 million worth of coverage, at a much higher monthly premium, by painting a horrifying picture of what would happen if the farmer ever got injured without that kind of coverage. "Your family will lose your farm," Gregg said, breezing through some numbers he'd come up with. "You'll be destitute. None of your kids would go to college. Your life will be ruined."

To lend credence to this scenario, Gregg would invent a supposedly real-life story about a farmer in a neighboring county whose family was now destitute after he'd lost his legs to a piece of machinery. The farmer's wife was now working at Walmart for six dollars an hour. His kids had dropped out of school; some were working long hours at thankless jobs, others were meth addicts. The farmer was forced to borrow money from his elderly parents just to pay monthly expenses. The family couldn't even afford health insurance. All because the farmer had signed up for tens of thousands or perhaps a hundred thousand dollars of coverage as opposed to $1 million. If the customer asked to verify the story, Gregg demurred, invoking client confidentiality. "I'm sure you read about it in the paper eight or nine months ago," he'd say, prompting most customers to nod their heads in agreement.

As we've seen, exerting influence entails inducing others to think similarly to you so that compliance with your wishes becomes their idea and in their best interest. Manipulation, by contrast, involves preying on people's emotions to *compel* compliance, regardless of how it affects the other person. As Gregg taught me and as I've seen countless times since, manipulation is both easy and frighteningly effective (although it isn't always outright fraudulent, as in the case of Gregg's behavior). When we experience fear, pain, lust, or other strong feelings, our rational faculties short-circuit and that tiny, walnut-sized chunk of gray matter known as our amygdala takes over—what Daniel Goleman has called "emotional hijack."[1] Gregg mastered this dynamic and applied it shamelessly, triggering an emotional hijacking response at will. His targets went into "fight or flight" mode, making quick, unreasoned decisions. Although a few customers managed to extricate themselves from this trap, asking critical questions and showing Gregg the door, most did exactly as Gregg advised. He notched the sale. They got an onerous monthly insurance bill.

Manipulators like Gregg are everywhere. Although I'd like to think that most salespeople, politicians, attorneys, journalists, and religious figures behave ethically, it's not hard to find those who fire up our fears, hatreds, lusts, and so on to achieve their goals. Manipulation is also endemic in the corporate world, from Las Vegas casinos that ban clocks and cut off natural light so we'll lose ourselves at the black-jack table,[2] to stores that pump out seductive odors so that we'll linger and buy more,[3] to the billions of dollars in advertising that impel us to buy products and services we don't need by preying on our emotions. This is to say nothing of the criminal manipulators out there—the countless unsolicited phone calls, emails, and texts that threaten you with various kinds of scary legal action, the loss of your job, or some other disastrous outcome if you don't provide certain information, pay a fee, or take other action. In addition to generating trillions each year in ill-gotten gains, manipulative scams inflict severe emotional damage on victims. In one horrific case, a man fell prey to a ransomware hack that informed him he had been caught downloading porn and needed to pay over $20,000 in fines. Unable to afford such a large fine, he became so distraught that he committed suicide and killed his four-year-old son.[4]

As a social engineer, I use manipulation all the time to hack into IT systems and buildings, but only at our clients' request and within parameters that they set. Although these efforts often don't leave our targets better off for having met me, the minor emotional stress they cause serves an important purpose: helping companies protect themselves from criminal hackers. In this chapter, I'll help you protect yourself and stay safe by describing the key forms of psychological manipulation hackers and others use to get what they want, often criminally and at your expense.

STOP MANIPULATING

There's another reason to understand manipulation techniques: so that you can stop yourself from inadvertently applying them. It isn't just unscrupulous individuals and companies who deploy the dark arts to get what they want. All of us do it from time to time, often in small or subtle ways and without thinking much of it. I'm a pretty big dude, and when I fly, it's a pain sitting by the window and having someone scrunched next to me in the middle seat. If I'm one of the first to board and its unreserved seating, I keep an anxious eye on the passengers filtering in, praying nobody else sits next to me. I hate to admit this, but I've sometimes done more than pray. I've put my jacket or another personal belonging in the seat, making it seem like it's taken. I've done a little manspreading of my legs and arms, suggesting that anyone with the temerity to sit next to me will enjoy no personal space of their own. And I've donned headphones, pretending to listen to music so that passengers will be less inclined to ask me if the seat is taken.

If I were deploying influence to get my fellow passengers to sit elsewhere, I would have engaged them in polite conversation and asked them kindly to sit elsewhere. But on these occasions, I forced them to make a decision on false pretenses by triggering unpleasant emotions: fear of "breaking the rules" or appearing rude if someone has indeed already claimed that seat; or distaste at sitting next to a big, sweaty guy who is seemingly aloof and disrespectful of others' personal space. My manipulation was selfish, inconsiderate, and disrespectful. Although it didn't cause grievous harm, it did serve to make my fellow passengers' days just a little bit harder.

Behavior like this is common in situations when strangers are competing with one another for space or some other scarce commodity. But we also resort to manipulation in small ways when dealing with friends, relatives, and other important people in our lives. When you want your partner to behave in a certain way, do you always approach them in a straightforward and kind manner? Or do you sometimes push them into it by arousing their emotions, suggesting how frightening it might be if they *don't* behave as you wish, and how wonderful it would be if they do?

One afternoon, I really felt like eating steak for dinner, and my wife was on a "no-meat" kick. While we were driving somewhere together, I planted images in her mind of delicious meat dishes. "Did you smell that barbecue last night? Man, it smelled amazing!" I talked on and on about grilling and reminded her of some of our favorite grilled meats. Later, I asked casually what she felt like having for dinner. "I don't know," she said, "but I'm craving a steak." We did in fact eat steak for dinner that night—I had manipulated her into setting aside her desire to eat vegetarian. She didn't suffer negative consequences, but if the situation were different (for instance, if she had heart problems and were avoiding animal protein on doctor's orders), she might have. Either way, I was behaving selfishly, exploiting her emotional vulnerabilities to comply with my wishes, with no thought of her needs or desires.

If you're a parent, you probably resort to manipulation to keep your kids in check. When our kids aren't going to bed on time, doing their homework, or performing their chores, we could engage them in conversation, encouraging them to *want* to comply with the rules. But it's hard to do that when we're stressed or tired. So, we remind them of all that we do for them and make them feel guilty for failing to comply with our simple wishes. We threaten to take away privileges if they don't comply, arousing fear. We bribe them with the prospect of dessert if they do as we wish. All of these standard parenting hacks are forms of manipulation, however trivial they might seem. Instead of leading with compassion, we strong-arm our way to compliance.

Avoiding manipulation can improve your relationships. It takes more thought and effort, but by choosing to exercise influence in your daily life instead of imposing your will, you'll become kinder and more compassionate. You'll listen more, understand others better, deliver to them more of what they want and need, and cultivate rapport and trust. How much rapport and trust do you build with your spouse by subtly eroding her ability to exercise free will when making joint decisions? How much do you build with your kids by promising them candy if they do their homework? I certainly wasn't doing anything to build a relationship with my fellow travelers by donning my headphones and manspreading. If I had instead explained my situation and kindly asked them to sit elsewhere, I would have given them the opportunity to perform an act of kindness and me the opportunity to feel and express gratitude.

In his book *Changeable*, the psychologist J. Stuart Ablon describes an approach to relationships called Collaborative Problem Solving (CPS), in which parents, teachers, and others in positions of power don't force others to comply simply because they can, but instead are "nicer," engaging in an empathetic conversation with them to arrive at a collaborative solution. As Ablon relates, schools, mental hospitals, and juvenile prisons have seen dramatic improvements in behavior after setting aside traditional discipline and employing CPS. At one psychiatric setting for kids, staff were often forced to physically restrain kids because of poor behavior—in one year, they did so 263 times. A year after introducing CPS, they did so only seven times. The influence techniques described in this book are not the same as CPS, which is a very specific, structured approach. But the success of CPS shows that we need not compel others with less power to behave as we like, whether by manipulation techniques or through disciplinary means. Other options exist that allow us to treat people with respect and build strong, trusting, empathetic relationships with them.[5]

Although manipulation techniques are quite powerful in social engineering, so, too, are influence techniques. In many situations, they're often more effective than outright manipulation. Remember Gregg, the lying insurance salesman who trained me? When I started working with him, he was the company's top-ranked salesperson globally. During my year tenure at the company, I dethroned him, achieving the highest ranking for a full six months. Although I learned a lot from Gregg, I decided early on to adopt an ethical approach. I spoke honestly with customers about their insurance needs and told truthful, verifiable stories about other local farmers who had purchased policies and filed claims with us. The policies I sold were often smaller than Gregg's, but I sold many more of them. Best of all, I could sleep at night knowing I was helping to fulfill a real need for people and improve their lives.

I can certainly imagine extreme, life-or-death situations where it might prove necessary to manipulate people to compel them quickly to take a desired action. If I were in a hostage situation and I needed the attacker to drop his weapon, I would have few scruples about arousing intense fear in him by describing the SWAT team marksmen and their deadly accuracy. But short of that, you're *so* much better off pursuing your own goals and the welfare of others concurrently, while also staying alert to others who might try to use manipulation techniques against you.

THE SUSCEPTIBILITY PRINCIPLE

You might think you're pretty good at spotting would-be manipulators. You encounter scams every day on your phone and in your email inbox, and you see right through them. You know enough to take a cynical eye toward advertising and shifty salespeople. Nothing can get by you! Ah, but it can. The sheer pervasiveness of manipulation can make us complacent and hence more vulnerable. We wouldn't think of responding to a robotized voice message warning us in halting English that we'll go to jail for some vague reason if we don't call a certain number and pay an exorbitant fee. But scammers are always upping their game, surprising us with schemes that are increasingly well wrought and believable.

In 2019, the British bank Barclays warned of a scam in which criminals online purported to own a beautiful vacation villa available for rent. The criminals lured unsuspecting vacationers by offering the properties at a steeply discounted rate. They used real pictures stolen from other sites and sported a logo from the United Kingdom's professional association of travel agents. Dazzled by the prospect of an amazing and seemingly genuine deal, victims unthinkingly forked over money to reserve the property, losing thousands of dollars. Surveying two thousand consumers, Barclays found them to be shockingly vulnerable, with a majority admitting that they would book a property even if it seemed "too good to be true."[6]

In another increasingly common scam, criminals call people and claim to have kidnapped a family member, demanding immediate payment of a ransom. They use spoofing technology that allows them to make it seem that the call is coming from the loved one's phone.[7] "Unlike traditional abductions," the FBI has said, "virtual kidnappers have not actually kidnapped anyone. Instead, through deceptions and threats, they coerce victims to pay a quick ransom before the scheme falls apart."[8] If you didn't know about these scams, but someone called you up and claimed they would kill your daughter if you didn't pay them $2,000 in one hour, and if that call seemed to come from her smartphone, you'd probably be terrified and perhaps even pay the ransom.

Unless you're in the security business or law enforcement, you won't be familiar with every new scam that pops up. But you can still reduce your chances of becoming a victim by understanding more deeply how scammers manipulate people regardless of their specific scheme.

Criminals use manipulation to induce stress, anxiety, or discomfort so that the victims will make decisions that contravene their best interests. In my teaching, I call this the *susceptibility principle*. The ransomware hack described earlier that resulted in a man and child's death deployed this principle. So too do any number of scams that threaten some kind of awful consequence for incompliance. In one especially common scam targeted at the elderly, hackers purporting to be from the Internal Revenue Service call claiming that your Social Security number has been disabled and you won't be receiving any further checks until it's reenabled. That, of course, requires payment of a fee. These scammers are sophisticated. They'll address victims by name and confirm their address and other personal information, using profiles they bought off the dark web. Their victims will hear background noises, as if the scammer is calling from a busy government office, and the call will come from a spoofed, Washington, D.C., area phone number. An elderly person receiving such a call might be so terrified that they'll pay the fee, dependent as they are on their Social Security check for their monthly expenses.

> Spend a half hour watching commercials. Analyze how they use manipulative tactics to obtain their objectives.

Susceptibility can also work via more positive emotions, as in the vacation rental scam described above, or in the attempts of parents to bribe kids to do their homework, or in all those emails, texts, and phone calls that claim you won a prize and just need to click on this link in order to claim it. Another example is the classic "honeypot" technique, in which a manipulator arouses lust in their target to achieve some selfish objective. Television advertising deploys this approach, manipulating viewers to buy by featuring attractive announcers and dressing them in revealing ways. We've all heard the adage that "sex sells"—companies peddling fast food, beauty products, alcohol, and lowbrow entertainment routinely feature sexually provocative imagery, hoping to entice viewers.[9] Such pitches seem effective for companies selling products that people buy on impulse and that don't carry much risk. For products that are more complex and expensive, research has found that sexually provocative advertising actually doesn't work as well. In our era of #MeToo, provocative ads might also be losing their effectiveness for product categories like fast food, where they had formerly delivered for companies.[10]

Some advertising arouses both positive and negative emotions in the course of delivering their pitch. You're watching television, and an ad comes on that depicts a starving dog lying in filth. Some sad music comes on and you hear, "Won't you please give just a few pennies a day to help animals like this?" Then you hear happy music and see pictures of healthy, playful dogs that the organization has saved thanks to generous donations from people like you. Feeling this incredible urge to help that dying dog and transform it into that wonderfully healthy dog, you call the number on your screen and donate. But like sex, this tactic is now proving less effective for a savvy viewership craving authenticity and real-world impact.[11] According to some experts, leading with creativity, humor, and emphasizing results—that is, drawing on influence-building techniques instead of emotional manipulation—does more to create sympathy for important charitable causes.[12]

FOUR PATHWAYS TO SUSCEPTIBILITY

Deft manipulators increase their odds of success by playing on various aspects of human psychology. Here are four pathways to the susceptibility principle that I encounter all the time and that you should remain mindful of in everyday life:

Pathway #1: Environmental Control

As researchers have shown, our physical environments exercise a powerful hold on us. The Harvard psychologist Ellen Langer, dubbed the mother of positive psychology, was in the forefront of such academic scholarship.[13] In 1981, she conducted a pathbreaking and unprecedented experiment, testing whether germs and genes alone accounted for the aging process, or whether other psychological factors could also exercise an impact. That year, Langer, a young scholar at the time, gathered eight septuagenarians in New Hampshire. Upon entering a converted monastery, these men, suffering the usual aches and pains of advanced age, were transported to the year 1959—more than two decades prior, when they were young and vital. Their clothing, entertainment choices, discussion of current events, and home furnishings all reflected their midcentury youth. They spoke about these historical topics using the present tense and were even treated like younger men, ordered to march their belongings up the stairs by themselves after entering the premises.

After only five days, these men's biomarkers improved dramatically—miraculously even. Everything from their posture to their eyesight to their impromptu decision to ditch their canes and compete with one another in a touch football match! Unfortunately, this now classic experiment, thereafter known as the "counterclockwise study," was too expensive, difficult to replicate, and ahead of its time to make much of an impact in academia and popular consciousness. It wasn't until decades later, after a 2010 collaboration with the BBC, that Langer, by then the coauthor and author of numerous studies, gained broader recognition for her extraordinary contributions to our understanding of the mind/body relationship.[14]

If Langer's research suggests how we might organize our environments to benefit ourselves and others, hackers, con men, and others modify environments to compel targets to do their bidding, often to their own detriment. At an extreme, intelligence agencies use environmental control techniques bordering on torture to compel terrorists to divulge information. After terrorists attacked the United States on September 11, 2001, the George W. Bush administration helped inaugurate the enhanced interrogation program, subjecting terror suspects to environmental techniques such as incessant noise, waterboarding, placement in small, dark "confinement boxes," and sleep deprivation (via forced contortion of the body into painful positions using restraints).[15] Such treatment is controversial—some insist torture is barbaric and ineffective, not inspiring targets to divulge sensitive information, while others insist that "torture works" and that authorities should revive even more punishing techniques than enhanced interrogation to combat terrorism.[16] At the other end of the emotional spectrum, we have the environmental control techniques deployed at Las Vegas casinos. Not only do these places rob customers of their sense of time; the loud noises and bright lights from the slot machines assault their senses, prefiguring the excitement they'd experience by winning. Free-flowing alcohol provided by casinos and scantily clad hostesses intensify the sensory overload and further suspend customers' critical-thinking capacity, leaving them inclined to gamble far more than they should.

Some Devious Ways That Casinos and Amusement Spaces Manipulate You into Parting with Your Money...

- Loud, constant noise from winning slot machines leaves the impression that everyone around you is winning.
- The use of red colored lighting might prompt people to spend more money.
- Dim lighting might cause people to focus more on gambling than on social interactions.
- Pleasant odors might cause people to gamble more.
- Signage avoids the word "gambling," which carries stigma, opting instead for "guilt-reducing statements referring to leisure," such as "Test your skill!"
- Placement of ATMs inside casinos induces people to gamble more, as do comfortable seats, free alcoholic beverages, pretty hostesses, and the presence of nearby bathrooms.
- Casinos put restaurants in the middle of gambling areas so that hungry customers have to pass through them.

Source: Mark Griffiths and Jonathan Parke, "The Environmental Psychology of Gambling," Gambling: Who Wins? Who Loses?, ed. Gerda Reith (New York: Prometheus Books, 2003): 277–92.

The social dimensions of our environments often figure prominently in attempts by manipulators to compel our actions. Why do pledges willingly submit to obscene and painful hazing rituals in order to join fraternities? Yes, they're usually drunk off their rockers, but they're also operating in an environment in which the social pressure to submit is overwhelming. Picture a room filled with dozens of other rowdy brothers who are also behaving in uninhibited ways. The music is loud, the alcohol is flowing, and no authority figures are around. Other pledges are submitting to hazing, allowing themselves to be beaten and physically abused in ways too gross to mention here. The implication is clear: if you don't submit like they are, you're both a loser and out of the frat. In such a circumstance, the individual pledge's rational faculties are severely undercut, and it's almost impossible for him not to "go with the flow." Upon awakening the next day, when he's done being sick, a pledge will likely be thinking, "How could I possibly have done that?" Simple. His fraternity brothers made him more susceptible to persuasion by using his social context against him.

Pathway #2: Forced Reevaluation

Another pathway to susceptibility is what is called forced reevaluation, the technique of making people doubt what they have been taught or what they think they know by confronting them with contradictory facts. You might have heard of gaslighting, in which a person prompts a person of interest to doubt not just a particular fact or idea, but their own sanity. That is forced reevaluation taken to an extreme. The experience of contradiction causes tremendous uncertainty: you thought the world worked in a certain way, and all of a sudden you discover that your basic understanding doesn't hold. That uncertainty in turn leads to anxiety or even panic, which prompts you to behave in ways that might prove counter to your own best interest.

Research has confirmed that the prospect of an uncertain future stresses us out even more than the knowledge of something bad looming ahead. In 1994, a group of Canadian scholars developed the Intolerance of Uncertainty Scale (IUS), demonstrating how an inability to cope with uncertainty represented a "cognitive vulnerability" and was associated with negative outcomes like anxiety or eating disorders.[17] But in 2016, scholars published the results of what one journalist has called "the most sophisticated experiment ever conceived on the relationship between uncertainty and stress."[18] Many gamers out there would just love it if their gaming experience became more lifelike and "experiential." How's this for experiential: Researchers asked participants to play a video game in which they had to flip over a series of rocks. Sometimes a snake lingered underneath those rocks, and when it did, researchers jolted participants with a powerful electric shock.

Researchers tracked the presence of risk (or "irreducible uncertainty," as it's termed in the study), comparing it to the volunteers' self-reports of stress and physiological indicators like pupil dilation and the presence of sweat.[19] You guessed it: stress and uncertainty were positively correlated, with stress levels peaking when uncertainty of a shock reached 50 percent (that is, as close as possible to perfect uncertainty).[20] It turns out that the part of the brain associated with dopamine activation goes on high alert when we can't predict the outcome of an event.[21]

We don't need statisticians and brain scientists to tell us that uncertainty is stressful—we've all experienced it. Did you ever take a tough exam in high school without preparing very well for it? When you know with certainty that you got a D−, you'll probably stop worrying (or at least worry less) and instead focus on managing the situation (by getting extra help, say, or thinking of a way to break the news to your parents). But before you find out your grade, you'll feel more anxious, rehearsing in your mind scenarios in which you sit down triumphantly at the dinner table and tell your parents you managed a B+, or in which you slump down and incur their disappointment by announcing that you failed.[22]

When a skilled manipulator is prompting you to question your previously strong beliefs (forced reevaluation), the resulting uncertainty can be so strong that to ease the anxiety you feel, you'll comply with wishes that you ordinarily wouldn't have. Let's say it's a Tuesday night in October, and you think your college-age daughter is safe in her college dorm. Then you get a call informing you that she's been kidnapped, and the criminals will rape and kill her if you fail to transfer $2,000 in Apple gift cards in the next ten minutes. The image of your daughter being threatened might strike terror in you, but so does the shock of discovering that your daughter is not safe in her dorm as you had assumed, but in some unknown and unsafe place. The apparent revelation forces you to reevaluate everything else you think you know about your daughter, her circumstances, and maybe even life itself. You might suspect that the call is a scam, but in that moment, the prospect of uncertainty is so strong that you don't quite know what to believe. So rather than chance it, you send the money.

We see forced reevaluation at work in corporate settings. Let's say you work in IT at a company with very strict rules about disclosing information. If someone calls you and says that the CEO asked you to give out information because there have been two hundred security breaches over the past two days, and some heads are about to roll, you might give out the information, reasoning that the company didn't really want you to keep to corporate policy about information disclosure in such a dire situation. The contradiction unsettles you—again, you now don't know what to believe. So rather than risk ticking off the CEO, you give in to your anxiety and make an exception.

Sometimes companies deploy forced reevaluation on their own employees to make them work harder. Rather than simply lay people off, companies will announce months in advance that they will be laying off a certain number of people, without naming who those people are. Think of the impact such a move has on individual workers. Until the announcement, they might have assumed that the company was doing fine and their jobs were secure. Then they hear that the company isn't fine and layoffs are coming. Even if their own performance has been strong, a seed of doubt is sown in their minds. Something important they thought they knew about the company turns out to be untrue. What else is untrue? With their anxiety rising, they're going to work harder just in case—quite possibly the company's intended result in giving advance warning about layoffs.

Pathway #3: Increased Powerlessness

A third, extremely effective route to susceptibility is to take away a person's power. People want to feel in control. At some deep, primal level our species has equated control with power, and power with survival.[23] And at the heart of control is choice. Human beings and animals alike prefer having choices, even if they won't improve an outcome.[24] As one research study, aptly called "Born to Choose," put it, "Belief in one's ability to exert control over the environment and to produce desired results is essential for an individual's well being."[25] Successful companies understand this, and have extended autonomy to their employees, increasing their productivity, happiness, and performance.[26] As Professor Ranjay Gulati of the Harvard Business School has observed, "Leaders know they need to give people room to be their best, to pursue unconventional ideas, and to make smart decisions in the moment. It's been said so often that it's a cliché." In particular, decades of research have shown that employees "want some form of choice and voice in what they do at work, and that this can spark greater commitment and improve performance."[27]

If someone can take away your (oftentimes illusory) sense of choice and therefore control, the fear and outright distress you feel might be overwhelming, to the point that you'll make rash decisions you otherwise wouldn't. Over time, if your loss of control persists, you might give in simply because you've become habituated to it. The result is what Martin Seligman and his colleague Steven F. Maier termed "learned helplessness."[28] In the mid-1960s, Seligman, a graduate student at the University of Pennsylvania, was studying avoidance learning in canines. Seligman and his team applied electric shocks to dogs, who either chose to endure the abuse or escape their fate by scaling a barrier. Following repeated abuse, some of the dogs stopped attempting escape and, dejected, submitted to the torture. The researchers modified the experiments, readministering shocks and offering escape routes to the dogs, but the results were the same: a large subset of the animals remained defeated. Seligman was no monster: he wanted to reverse learned helplessness among humans and canines alike and has devoted the rest of his distinguished career to trying to overcome learned helplessness through learned optimism.

Pathway #4: Punishment

Manipulators will sometimes punish others or levy the threat of punishment to elicit strong emotion (namely, fear or even terror), making their targets more susceptible to persuasion. The most obvious example of this is torture. Studies have shown that torture is stunningly effective at eliciting confessions but terrible at eliciting truthful information. "We've Known for 400 Years That Torture Doesn't Work," declares an article in *Scientific American*. Citing inquisitors inflicting torture from the European witch craze, the article demonstrates what we all know to be true intuitively: people will confess to just about anything to stop the pain.[29] But belief in the magic of judiciously applied torture persists. In the hit television series *24*, Kiefer Sutherland plays the no-nonsense interrogator Jack Bauer, who uses any means necessary to extract intelligence from terrorists and thereby save major metropolitan areas from misery and mayhem. "It's a Hollywood fantasy," concludes *Scientific American*. "In reality, the person in captivity may or may not be a terrorist, may or may not have accurate information about a terrorist attack, and may or may not cough up useful intelligence, particularly if his or her motivation is to terminate the torture."[30]

Criminals mobilize the punishment pathway to a lesser but frightful extent through any number of scams, whether it's ransomware that seals off your computer and demands a payment, or the countless scams that claim you committed a crime and threaten you with imprisonment if you don't pay a penalty. It was precisely such a threat that led that poor Romanian man to kill himself and his child.

The threat of punishment doesn't have to be especially severe or dramatic to compel a response. Remember that bank I mentioned earlier that asked us to try manipulation to extract sensitive account information from their employees? We succeeded in that assignment by having one of our female team members call up an account specialist purporting to be an assistant who worked for one of the bank's customers. The assistant explained that her boss, who was pregnant, was going into labor and yet desperately needed the account information to handle a last-minute work matter. The account specialist asked the usual verification questions to establish the boss's identity, but every time he did, the boss went into a little bit of labor, moaning and groaning audibly into the phone.

The account specialist was empathetic, but he explained that he simply couldn't give out the information. Finally, after about twenty-five minutes of buildup, we had the "boss" go into full-blown labor and scream to her assistant: "Don't you dare hang up that phone until you get that account information. Payroll isn't going to go out unless you do!" Pretending to be panicked and overwhelmed, the assistant pleaded one last time with the account specialist to give her the sensitive banking information she sought. The guy finally caved. Clearly, he sympathized with the boss and her panicked assistant. The "punishment" we were implicitly threatening was the guilt he'd feel once he'd hung up the phone at not helping these two people in dire need of assistance. Firing up his fear of feeling guilty and the psychic pain that would entail, we got what we wanted.

The four pathways I've described often overlap with one another, and we frequently find instances of manipulation that deploy all of them at once to varying degrees. Consider the situation in which a company announces pending layoffs. That move doesn't merely compel employees to work extra hard because of forced reevaluation, as I discussed. The threat of "punishment" implicit in the layoffs—future job loss and unemployment—also manipulates employees to redouble their efforts. There is as well the increased powerlessness that comes with uncertainty about your professional destiny: some senior leader high up on the executive floor has made a decision that might change everything for you. Aspects of the workplace environment might also change, exacerbating your fears and prompting you to work even harder. At the same time as your company announces future layoffs, they might also cut back on office luxuries and travel. All of a sudden, everyone around you is bringing their own snacks to work and staying late, eager not to be one of the unlucky few to lose their jobs. Sitting at your desk every day and taking this in, it's easy to see how you might give in to the prevailing fear and work late yourself.

Think of a request you will have to make of someone in the days or weeks ahead. Take a sheet of paper and draw a line down the middle. On one side, jot down some ideas as to how you might use influence tactics to achieve your objectives. On the other side, think about the pathways to susceptibility described here and how those might apply. Commit yourself to taking the higher road and deploying influence. If you're a parent with children who don't want to do their homework, what manipulation tactics do you typically use and how might you avoid them while still getting what you want?

MY TRANSFORMATIONAL MOMENT

Years ago, just after I had put up my shingle as a professional hacker of humans, a very large company hired me to throw everything we had at them—phishing, vishing, attempted break-ins to their physical facilities, you name it. We did, and their security was so good we just couldn't break through. I was at wit's end, and at that point I should have stopped and admitted defeat. But instead, I let my ego get the better of me and hatched a plan to manipulate our way in.

A female colleague of mine and I sat down in the company's cafeteria atrium, which was outdoors, unsecured, and easy to access. We were posing as members of the company's HR department, and as a pretext we were there to ask employees to fill out information forms regarding their health care policies. The forms contained information we secretly wanted—employees' full names, date of birth, and employee ID. We could in turn use that information to compromise the company's computer system.

As per our preset plan, my colleague announced to me that she had failed to meet a deadline I'd given her, I stood up, pushed back her stack of forms, and in a fairly loud voice appeared to blow up at her for screwing up our work project. "You worthless wench," I said. "No wonder you can't keep a job. If you don't get this fixed by tonight, you're fired." I stormed off, and two guys who had been sitting nearby and heard the whole thing jumped up to run after me, intending, I thought, to beat me up.

I pretended not to see them, and my colleague stopped them and defended me. "No, no," she said, "please, guys, please. He's under a lot of stress. He and his wife are having problems at home. I was supposed to get this project done, and it was all my fault. He had every right to yell at me." Her voice trailed off as she said this, giving way to tears and slumped shoulders. It was mock Stockholm syndrome.

"No one has a right to yell at you," one of the men said. "Nobody should treat you this way."

Another bystander, who appeared to be a senior manager at the company, came over to ask what happened.

"Her boss just yelled at her," one of the Good Samaritans said. "He's going to fire her today."

"Nobody's getting fired today," this bystander said. He took the forms and ordered everyone in the cafeteria to fill them out. Within ten minutes, we had seventy forms filled out, with more than enough information to break into the computer system.

Big victory, right? Not at all. We had manipulated our way in. The employees didn't comply because they wanted to, but because of negative feelings we had aroused. We used the punishment pathway, confronting our targets with the psychically painful prospect of seeing someone else humiliated and fired. To some extent, we used forced reevaluation as well, creating a boss-employee interaction that directly challenged the norms of professional conduct. Our actions left our targets disgusted at what they'd witnessed. They felt bad for my colleague and were angry at me. They didn't feel better for having met us. They felt worse. No coincidence that the company never called us back to work for them again.

What we should have done, once we had determined that all of our ordinary techniques had failed, was call off the test and congratulate the company on their effective security. We could have then proposed using manipulative techniques such as this, justified for the sake of protecting them against the most unscrupulous plotters, and gotten them to agree to it. Then, and only then, would I have felt good about using such techniques.

This episode, which took place early in my career, represented a lapse of ethics on my part, and one I continue to deeply regret. I'm happy to say, though, that it was a turning point for me. Until then, I had tried to minimize harm to others and do the right thing, but I hadn't given much thought to the ethical standards I would uphold. I hadn't asked myself what kind of hacker I really wanted to be—what my purpose was. Was I in it for the money? Or would I dedicate my career to doing good and trying to make a difference in others' lives? If all I wanted was money, then exploits like this were probably fine—I hadn't caused that much damage. If I wanted to do good, then with a few exceptions I had to avoid exploits like this, even if I knew they would work.

In the wake of that episode, I reflected on my core beliefs, and I thought a great deal about my kids. If they ever came to work at my company, I wouldn't want them to see me manipulating people as a daily practice, much less engaging in that behavior themselves. Even if they never did work for me, I wasn't sure what kind of role model I could be if I routinely treated others around me so callously. Such thoughts proved immensely clarifying. I now knew I wanted to do good. I understood how lousy it felt to win by manipulation, and I wanted to avoid that as much as possible.

I proceeded to fundamentally change everything about how we ran our company—how we designed our exploits, how we trained our team, how we dealt with clients. To keep us focused, we adopted Robin Dreeke's mantra—"Leave them better off for having met you"—as our "north star." I also became keenly focused on ethics in my personal life, staying alert to times when I might be inadvertently manipulating and changing or avoiding that behavior. I looked for new ways in which I could use human hacking techniques for good. In 2017, I created a nonprofit, the Innocent Lives Foundation (ILF), that uses hacking techniques to help catch and convict child pornographers. To date, ILF has assisted in over 250 cases. I'm not perfect, but I've gotten a whole lot better. My relationships have deepened, and I've become happier. You can keep your conduct firmly on the side of light, while also staying attuned enough to manipulation to protect yourself. You'll be both better off and safer for it, and you'll *still* get much more of what you want from people.

To increase the odds that you'll get more of what you want while avoiding manipulation, I'd like to share some additional techniques that when skillfully deployed can boost the effectiveness of influence techniques. A bit later, I'll discuss how to get the details of your social interactions right so that you come across as authentic and natural. But first, let's explore how you can use a basic understanding of body language to dramatically improve your interactions with others. Criminals and professional hackers can quickly and accurately interpret your body language to glean your inner emotional state. They also know how to use their body language to evoke emotions in helpful ways. By becoming more attuned to body language yourself, you can become far more sensitive to what others are experiencing and aware of your own presence, qualities that help you build relationships and induce others to want to help you.

CHAPTER 7

LET YOUR BODY DO THE TALKING

Improve your relationships by going beyond words.

Professional hackers of humans are masters at noticing others' nonverbal communications, including how they move their hands, their facial expressions, and so on. And well they should be, because as psychologists have shown, most of what we communicate comes through nonverbally. This chapter introduces some essentials of nonverbal communication, drawing on research by the renowned body language expert Paul Ekman as well as my own work in this area.

A number of years ago I was hired to break into a highly secure office building owned by a government contractor. To protect against malware, the company strictly forbade employees from inserting foreign USBs into the computers it issued. Every computer in this office sported a little "No Foreign USBs!" sticker. My goal was to see if I could induce the front desk receptionist to insert a USB with malicious code on it that would direct the computer to communicate with one of ours (what is called a "reverse shell").

I pulled into the parking lot, and as I got out of my car, I took out a folder containing copies of a fake personal résumé and purposely dumped steaming hot coffee on it. With this folder in hand, I walked into the front door. "Hi, how can I help you?" the receptionist asked with a smile. But I wasn't smiling. I had a look on my face that evoked a mixture of sadness, dejection, stress, and irritation. "Oh no," she said, upon glancing in my direction. "What happened to you?"

I scanned the pictures on her desk, spotting one of some kids, a man who was probably her husband, and a Labrador retriever. "Well," I said, "I was driving here because I have an interview in like ten minutes with HR, and I was really hoping to get the job, and this *dog* runs out in front of my car. I love dogs so much, I didn't want to kill it. So, I slammed on my brakes, and my coffee fell out of the coffee holder, all over my car, and it soaked copies of my résumé. And I have an interview here in ten minutes."

"Oh, that's awful," she said. "What can I do to help?"

"I don't know," I said. "I've been out of work for six months, and I really need this job. I've been going from interview to interview, and it just seems like I'm not winning anything today. I guess the universe is against me."

"Well, there's a Kinko's down the road. Maybe you can run over there and print one and come back."

I shook my head. "I don't have time. They're very strict about these interviews. They said to be on time, and to come prepared. I don't want to make a bad first impression by being late."

She nodded. "Yeah, you're right."

I pulled a USB out of my pocket. "Hey, could you maybe help me? Could you print out just one copy of my résumé? It's on this USB key. Then I'd be all set."

I handed her my USB key, and as she took it, I could tell she was thinking about whether to break her company's rule. So, at that exact moment, before an awkward pause ensued, I brought the inner edges of my eyebrows together and up, while also bringing the corners of my lips down into a frown—a facial expression indicating that I'm experiencing sadness. In doing this, I hoped to spark a decisive bit of empathy in her. Sure enough, she bent down to insert the USB, looked at the "No foreign USBs" sign, paused for a full second, and just inserted it. "Oh, there's two folders here," she said.

There were indeed two. The top one was the malicious file, and the bottom my résumé.

"The top one is probably the most current, so click that," I said. She did. A second later, my phone dinged loudly with a text from my team saying they had gained access to her computer.

I glanced down at my phone. "Oh, that's my reminder that I'm almost late for my interview."

"Well, we better hurry up," she said. "This file isn't working."

"Try the bottom one," I said, which she did. She printed out my résumé, put it in a nice, new folder for me, and offered to take me over to Mrs. Henry in HR.

"Wait," I said. "Is this ABC company?"

"No," she said. "That's next door. We're XYZ company."

"Are you kidding me," I said. "Oh, gosh. How embarrassing."

"You really are having a bad day."

I huffed out of the office, claiming that I was headed over to the neighboring company. Mission accomplished.

A number of techniques figured in this story, but the pivotal one was the frazzled, overwrought expression I wore on my face upon first arriving. That one look said a thousand words and set up everything else that was to come. It inspired the receptionist to want to help me, with the story I told only confirming the truth that seemed to have been written on my face.

If you can master the art of nonverbal communication, you'll have a far easier time getting others to do your bidding than if you rely on words alone. And you'll also be able to detect others' states of mind through facial expressions, small tics, shoulder posture, and so on. FBI interrogators, spies, and others in the security field receive extensive training on body language. The best of them, like my friend Joe Navarro, are so good they can almost immediately spot emotions in total strangers and then track subtle but important changes in how these individuals are feeling as conversations proceed.

I wish this chapter could bestow a similar level of ninja mastery, but alas, it can't. Nonverbal communication is an immense topic (and one that incidentally dates back to the writings of Charles Darwin).[1] Many parts of your body convey emotions or ideas—including your head, face, hands, limbs, torso—and you can use each of these in myriad ways to communicate. A range of other elements also convey emotion nonverbally, such as the clothes and jewelry you wear, whether and how you make eye contact, your tone of voice, the precise ways you choose to make bodily contact with others (or don't), how your body smells, and so on. Factor in cultural differences in the meaning of bodily signs and signals, and you've got quite a complex picture indeed. It can take years of practice to reach the level of mastery that top security professionals possess.

If such mastery is your goal, your first step is to consult a number of books on this and related subjects, most notably the works of Navarro and Dr. Paul Ekman.[2] You should also start practicing nonverbals and observing people in social settings. But you don't need to master facial gestures, hand movements, and the like in order to up your game as a human hacker. Developing just a bit of extra awareness of how our bodies "talk" can greatly improve your ability to influence others. Let's examine a few basic techniques you can use right now to spot and elicit emotions, focusing primarily on facial expressions. Spend a few hours practicing these techniques, and you'll become more emotionally sensitive during social encounters and behave more deliberately. Your ability to execute the strategies described in other chapters of this book will improve in turn.

A LITTLE TRICK THAT HELPS A LOT

To get us started, I just *have* to share a powerful technique you can use right now to improve your social interactions, with virtually no practice. When you're conversing with someone, it can help to keep track of whether they generally feel comfortable or uncomfortable with what's transpiring. You can do that by observing subtle quirks in their body language. For example, if a person tends to tilt their hips and belly toward you, a phenomenon Joe Navarro has termed "ventral fronting,"[3] this can indicate comfort. The word "ventral" refers to the underside of a person or animal. When a friendly dog rolls onto his or her backside, exposing his or her soft underbelly for you to scratch, that's a ventral display. It's a powerful indication of openness, vulnerability, interest in you, and eagerness to make a connection. Humans offer up other kinds of ventral displays. For instance, we show the underside of our wrists and hands as opposed to keeping our palms facing down. If I ask you to have lunch with me and make the underside of my hand visible, I'm inviting you in a softer, more passive way, suggesting my eagerness to get to know you. If I keep my palms facing down, I'm projecting a stronger, more commanding, more formal presence. Tilts of the head that expose our neck and smiles are other great displays of comfort.

When I enter into a social situation, I cue in immediately to these nonverbals. Spotting open ventrals, I know that the people I meet are either genuinely open to engaging with me or are purposely trying to ingratiate themselves with me so that I'll open up to them and go along with their desires. You do have to beware of the deliberate use of open ventrals. Some of history's most notorious con men and criminals were charmers who cynically displayed friendliness to lure in unsuspecting victims. Most of the time, open ventrals will indicate a genuine comfort and willingness to engage, information that together with the squaring of the hips might prompt you to fire up your rapport-building efforts. And when during the course of a conversation you notice a person abandon open ventrals and adopt more protective gestures, this indicates that the conversation might have taken a turn for the worse. Take a different approach or abandon the conversation altogether.

IT PAYS TO KNOW THE "BIG SEVEN"

With this rough understanding of body language in place, let's review how humans express specific emotions, most notably on the face. Scientists have distinguished two kinds of facial expressions: *macroexpressions*, gestures we consciously make to evoke how we're feeling, and *micro-expressions*, involuntary muscle movements that we make, usually without realizing it, when we experience an emotion. Macro-expressions persist for a few seconds or longer, while micro-expressions are extremely quick, lasting only a fraction of a second. Let's say you're walking down the hallway in your office building and a colleague who hates your guts rounds the corner up ahead. The moment he spots you, a flash of contempt passes over his face. His cheek or a corner of his mouth on one side of his face rises ever so slightly—just a hint of a smirk. That's the micro-expression. A moment or two later, as the two of you approach, he flashes a fake-looking smile, offers a brief nod of the head, and says, "Hi there, nice to see you." The smile and head nod are macro-expressions.[4]

Micro-expressions are extremely important to security professionals and human hackers alike. Mastering those, an operator can instantly gauge someone else's emotional state before *they* even recognize how they're feeling. But micro-expressions are difficult for an untrained eye to spot. If you're new to facial expressions, you're better off learning first how to read and deploy macro-expressions. Even those might seem to pose a formidable challenge. We experience so many feelings including lust, love, hatred, complacency, melancholy, frustration, excitement, dismay, friendliness, amusement, discontent, disillusionment, apprehension, ecstasy, remorse, and the list goes on and on. How can we become more emotionally aware without having to catalog all these emotions and study their precise manifestations on the human face?

Simple—focus in on the Big Seven. Researchers have discovered that the profusion of human emotions boil down to a small group of "base" or constituent emotions, just as the many hues on a painter's palette in theory resolve down to just three primary colors (yellow, red, and blue). Scientists differ as to the precise number of base emotions, but many, including Dr. Ekman, believe there are just seven: anger, fear, surprise, disgust, contempt, sadness, and joy. Think how much better you'd be at communicating if you could instantly spot these key emotions on people's faces. You'd avoid a great deal of confusion about how other people are feeling, and you'd be able to build rapport more effectively—not jumping in with a self-interested request when another person is angry or cracking a joke when someone is sad.

By learning how to display the base emotions yourself, you'd also be able to nudge people to feel emotions that work to your advantage while deploying influence tactics. Let's say I'm breaking into a building and I've kicked off a conversation with the receptionist. When it comes time to make a request of her, I would probably do well to get her to feel a mild sadness, which is linked to the feeling of empathy. If she empathizes with me, she'll be more likely to grant my request. But how do I get her to do that? Simple: I express sadness by lowering the corner of my lips as a speak. Venturing beyond facial expressions, I would further express sadness by putting my hands in my pocket, slumping my shoulders, and lowering my voice.

Research has found that we can purposely arouse emotions in others by displaying those emotions on our faces, a phenomenon scientists call "mirroring."[5] This ability of ours derives from the presence in our brains of so-called mirror neurons, special cells that, in the words of one pair of researchers, "respond to actions that we observe in others" and "fire in the same way when we actually recreate that action ourselves."[6] Interestingly, we can arouse emotions within ourselves just by expressing them on our faces. In one fascinating study, scientists found that people who walk outside in sunny weather without wearing sunglasses experience anger more frequently because of all the squinting they do. We tend to squint when we're angry, so when we squint from some other cause, our brains pick that up and actually trigger the subjective experience of anger.[7] Do you tend to experience road rage more when you leave your sunglasses at home? Now you know why. The next time you need to make a request of someone, be sure not to squint, and try instead to convey sadness via your facial expressions. It really works!

A third reason to understand expressions of the Big Seven emotions is to become more aware of your own habits, particularly those that might not be working for you. The notion of so-called resting bitch face (RBF) has become widespread in popular culture, with some critics regarding it as sexist.[8] Researchers have determined that RBF in fact is a "thing," and contrary to the terminology, not at all limited to women. In one study, researchers used facial recognition technology to distinguish between an emotionally neutral face and RBF. They found that RBF seemed to convey hints of contempt, a highly negative emotion defined as "a feeling that someone or something is not worthy of any respect or approval."[9] RBF is subtle but it conveys enough contempt for viewers to pick up on it.[10] When they do, the implications in social situations can be quite negative.

Contempt isn't the only negative emotion we might unintentionally display. One student of mine, Ramona, was a friendly, highly attractive, young German woman who worked as a Zumba instructor. Upon first meeting her, I thought she would have no problem with the homework assignments I gave the class. I was wrong: every time she tried to start a conversation and achieve some objective, she failed. Ramona had no clue why and asked me to observe her as she spoke with strangers in a public place. It took me only a few minutes to diagnose the problem. Without realizing it, Ramona was expressing what appeared to be anger via her facial expressions, alienating others and prompting them to react negatively.

Debriefing with her, we discovered she felt nervous about the assignments because she was determined to do well, and this intensity was manifesting itself on her face as anger. Once Ramona began to purposely evoke happiness on her face instead of anger, others warmed up to her and she nailed the assignments. After finishing our class, she transferred this adjustment to her everyday life, to great effect. For years after the class ended, Ramona wrote me raving about the differences she was seeing in her relationships. For so long, she had been conveying a sense of anger and also disgust without knowing it or even feeling that emotion subjectively. Now that she had made a habit of conveying happiness, everyone was seeing her as a warm, friendly, approachable person.

SPOTTING AND EXPRESSING THE BIG SEVEN

To further familiarize you with the Big Seven, let's run through them one by one. In each case, I'll describe how the emotion in question comes to life on our faces, weaving in some descriptions of additional, nonfacial body language that further conveys the emotion. My discussion here draws heavily on the work of Dr. Ekman, who collaborated with me on my earlier book about nonverbals, *Unmasking the Social*

Engineer. Drawing on my own experiences, I'll also offer some advice on how to work with these emotions in everyday hacking situations.

Emotion #1: Anger

When a person feels angry, their facial muscles tend to tense up. Their eyebrows become furrowed, their lips tighten without puckering, and they glare at the object of their anger. Other parts of their bodies tighten as well, notably the fists, which become clenched, and the jaw. Their chest puffs out, and their head and chin push forward. If they're really angry and aggressive, they will lower their chin. Their voice becomes harsher and usually louder.

Mark Twain likened anger to an acid, noting that it "can do more harm to the vessel in which it is stored than to anything on which it is poured."[11] Ralph Waldo Emerson noted, "For every minute you remain angry, you give up sixty seconds of peace of mind."[12] Fortunately, human hackers have no great need to appear—or become—angry. Although you might wish to evoke other emotions strategically, it's best to avoid projecting anger, as this emotion often serves as a gateway to physical violence or harsh speech. If you spot anger in others, you might try to ease that anger, readying yourself to make your escape if you can't deescalate the situation. "Wow," you might say, backing up and lowering your shoulders and hands, "you seem really upset. Is something wrong?" Express concern, but don't call someone out on their anger in a hostile or aggressive way, as that might embarrass and further anger them. Check yourself to ensure that you're not inadvertently or unconsciously appearing angry, since even small nonverbal expressions could serve to accelerate the situation. If you see a person lower their chin, it might be too late for escape. That's usually a sign not just of anger but of imminent violence on the other person's part—a punch about to be thrown, or something worse. In that case, if you're trapped and can't make an immediate escape, strike first and get away quick.

Emotion #2: Fear

When confronted with a stimulus we perceive to be threatening, we tend to freeze our bodies in place. Our eyebrows move upward and we open our eyes super-wide to take in the scene. Our mouths open and our lips pull pack toward our ears, almost as if we're saying, "Eeeeek!" Often, we'll audibly gasp, taking in oxygen. Our muscles in our neck, upper face, and hands tense, forcing blood into them. Adrenaline pumps into our bloodstreams. All of this is a biological response to fear, one that primes us to either flee or fight.

As hackers of humans, we might often find it helpful to instill mild fear in others. If you're trying to convince a sibling to help you out with

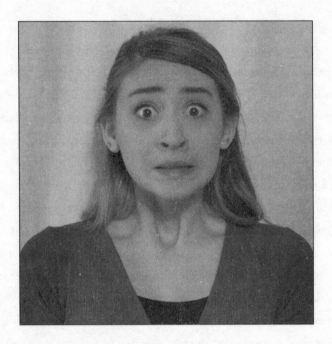

Mom's medical bills, evoking sadness (as the route to empathy) might be the best approach, but you might also wish to evoke a bit of worry as well about Mom's condition, saying something like, "I want the best for Mom, and I worry about her quality of life if we don't get her the best care." Arouse too much fear, however (by saying something like, "Mom will die within three months if you don't write me a check for ten thousand dollars"), and you risk manipulating your sibling. You're putting them in a state of great discomfort, knowing they will take almost any action—even one that runs contrary to their own best interest—just to ease the pain.

In many other situations, you'll perform better if you try *not* to convey fear. If you walk into your boss's office requesting a three-week vacation, any nervousness you feel might come across on your face as fear, which in turn might evoke fear in your boss. They'll begin to focus on their own concerns, such as the impact your vacation will have on your clients and colleagues. Fear will shape their decision making, possibly leading to a negative response.

Bear in mind, if you're actually afraid, your best move is probably not to hide it, even if conveying fear otherwise wouldn't be ideal. In a fascinating body of research, scientists have discovered that people around us actually *sense* when we're afraid or "emotionally stressed," whether we acknowledge our fear openly or not. Our bodies give off chemical markers in our sweat, and as researchers have documented, parts of the brain in people around us perk up in response, alert to possible threats.[13] If you feel afraid when trying to influence someone and you pretend you're not, you'll erode your credibility with them because on some (possibly nonconscious) level they'll *know* you're afraid.

You're better off acknowledging how you feel, doing so in a way that doesn't break with your pretext and elicit a defensive response. If you're asking your sibling to help with Mom's medical bills and adopting the pretext of the concerned and empathetic family member, don't say, "I want to talk to you about Mom, but to be honest, I'm really nervous, because you often blow your top and I don't know how you'll react." Rather, say something like, "I want to talk to you about Mom, but I'm nervous about it—it's just a difficult subject for me and I'm super emotional."

If you approach someone with a request and detect fear, rethink your approach or take action to reduce the fear. Years ago, I stood in a supermarket parking lot and watched as a wad of money dropped from the pocket of an elderly woman as she walked to her car. I jogged over, picked up the money, and then walked over to the woman to return it to her. She had her back to me as I approached and was loading her groceries in her trunk. With no warning, I tapped her on the shoulder and blurted out, "Excuse me, ma'am." When she turned, she saw this much larger man standing right in her face and was shocked. Not only did her face show fear, she screamed, "I'm being mugged! I'm being mugged!"

Three burly guys in hunting jackets heard her and ran over to confront me. I in turn was terrified—I had no idea if these three were armed. Another guy in my position might have felt tempted to react defensively. He might have confronted the three men and aggressively said, "Hey, back the hell up, guys." I chose instead to deescalate the situation. Instead of facing the men, I remained focused on the woman and tried to diminish her fear via my speech and nonverbals. Taking a big step back, slumping my shoulders slightly to indicate submissiveness, I said, "Okay, please just calm down." I held out the cash at eye level while keeping my other hand visible. Lowering my voice, I said, "Ma'am, I'm really sorry I startled you. You dropped this as you were leaving the store. I was just returning it to you." Feeling in her pocket, she realized she had lost her money. Retrieving it from me, she thanked me profusely. Only then did I turn to the three men and say, "See? No mugging. I'm walking away slowly." It was a close call, but my awareness of nonverbals allowed me to resolve a potentially dangerous misunderstanding.

Emotion #3: Surprise

To express surprise, we raise our eyebrows, open our eyes super-wide, and gasp, as we do with fear. But whereas we pull our lips back toward our ears to convey fear, we evoke surprise by forming our mouth into an O-shape. Initially when we're surprised, we have a tendency to lean back. If we experience a happy surprise, such as people jumping out at us and shouting, "SURPRISE!," we tend to lean back in and smile. Otherwise, we continue to lean out. People who feel surprised also put their hands up at the ready, cover their chest with their hands, or cover the back of their neck (suprasternal notch).

Surprise can often work to a human hacker's advantage. I was breaking into a building and encountered a receptionist who, judging from her red, puffy eyes, appeared to have been crying. When she inquired how she could help me, I asked if she was okay. That evoked a pained sigh, so I stepped out of hacker mode and asked what was wrong. She recounted that she and her husband had just celebrated their twentieth anniversary, and her husband had given her an expensive pair of diamond earrings. "He'd been saving two years for them," she said, "and I wore them into work today to show them off. I lost one of them." At that, she broke out into sobs, her shoulders heaving and shaking.

"Well," I said, "let's look for it." I got down on my hands and knees and scoured the area around her desk.

"I already looked there," she said.

"Sure, but maybe a second set of eyes will make a difference."

She joined me on the floor and looked as well. After several minutes, a ray of light happened to catch her body, and I saw something glimmer. "Hey," I said, "I don't want to be too forward and touch you,

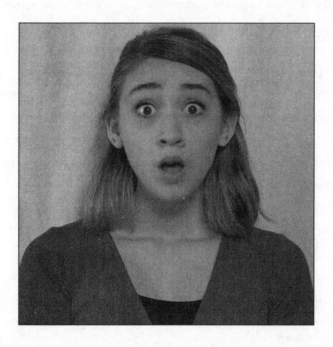

but have you checked your sweater? I just saw something glimmer on the back of your shoulder." She gave me permission to reach over and touch her shoulder, and sure enough, there was the earring, stuck in a fold of fabric. I pulled it out and presented it to her. Her mouth made a classic O of intense surprise mingled with delight and then sheer elation.

She gave me a big hug, and we both stood up. "Wow," she said, as she handled the earring, "we've just spent fifteen minutes looking for this." At that, I couldn't help but go back into hacker mode. Judging from the look of surprise, I had just given her an incredible gift. I could ask for anything and probably receive a positive response. "Oh, crap," I said, glancing at my watch. "I'm late for my meeting at HR." I grabbed my stuff and made for the door, praying that she'd just buzz me in without bothering to check my ID and issue me a badge, as she was supposed to do. Sure enough, she did.

If you find someone in your life reacting with surprise, it could represent an opportunity for you, assuming that the surprise is a positive one. If it's a negative surprise and you caused it, reassess your approach to see if you're prompting fear in some way. You can also project your own feelings of surprise to good effect. If someone shares an interesting fact and you wish them to feel validated, you might feel an inclination (as many people do) to top that fact with an even better one. Fight that urge, and instead flash a look of surprise while saying something like, "Oh, wow, I didn't know that. How cool!" Their sense of validation might boost your efforts to build rapport and, eventually, obtain something that you desire.

Emotion #4: Disgust

To convey disgust, we wrinkle our noses by tightening the muscles on either side of it. In extreme cases we might also pull our eyebrows down and loosen our mouths while pulling up our upper lips. Sometimes people squint in an effort to evoke disgust, but it's really about those muscles on the sides of your nose. When you flex those muscles, you'll find that you have a hard time breathing. That's because your body is blocking offensive odors from coming into contact with your olfactory receptors. People expressing disgust also turn their heads away, block their eyes, and cover their mouth or nose with their hands.

Be cautious about evoking disgust in others. It's an extremely strong emotion—so strong, in fact, that it can stay with us for years afterward. Usually, evoking disgust won't help you, but on occasion it can. If you're trying to get your mother to help you change your infant son's diaper while you're helping your other small child get dressed, you might evoke how unpleasant it will be for your son to sit there in a dirty diaper, flashing disgust on your face. Then transition to a smile as you evoke how sweet smelling and cuddly your son will be once his diaper is changed. You will have outlined the positive impact your mother can have in a stark, emotionally powerful way, leaving her more likely to want to change that diaper and help you out.

Emotion #5: Contempt

Many people confuse disgust with contempt. Whereas we usually feel disgust toward an action or object, we always feel contempt toward a person. Unlike disgust, contempt implies a moral judgment and a feeling of superiority over the contemptible object. Research by relationships expert Dr. John Gottman found that contempt was the single most important factor predicting whether a married couple got divorced. A couple might feel angry, resentful, or frustrated with one another—that's bad enough. But if a couple feels revulsion rooted in moral superiority toward one another, the marriage is doomed. It makes sense when you think about it. How can you remain happily married to someone who feels morally superior to you, or vice versa, and who is probably treating you accordingly? As a posting on the Gottman Institute's website proclaimed, "Contempt is the most poisonous of all relationship killers. We cannot emphasize that enough. Contempt destroys psychological, emotional, and physical health."[14]

Contempt is the only one of the Big Seven emotions that gives rise to a so-called unilateral facial expression. When we feel contempt, we tend to evoke it very subtly by raising the cheek on one side of our face. Our chin also tilts upward, and we appear to be "looking down our nose" at another person. Meanwhile, our bodies tend to become puffed up, our postures more erect and domineering.

Contempt is so negative that I can't think of a scenario in everyday life when a hacker of humans would want to evoke it. It would be virtually impossible to do so and still leave people better off for having met you. And if someone flashes contempt at you, beware: like anger,

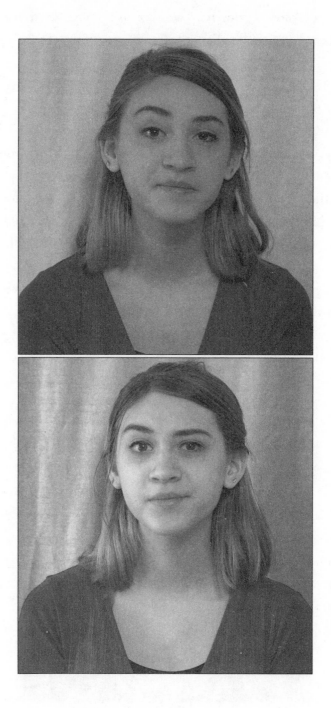

contempt is often a gateway to violence, as we often see in relation to xenophobia, racism, anti-Semitism, and other forms of tribal hatred.

Emotion #6: Sadness

Compared with emotions like anger and fear, which involve a tightening of facial muscles, sadness entails a slackening or softening. We evoke mild forms of it (and relatedly, of anxiety or worry) by causing our eyelids to droop and the corners of our mouths to turn down. Meanwhile, we pull the inner corners of our eyebrows in and up. As for the rest of our bodies, sadness tends to diminish us physically, make us smaller. We lower our heads, droop our shoulders, fold our arms together, or even seem to hug ourselves, rendering our overall postures softer and quieter.

    As we've seen, we can deploy sadness to our advantage during human hacking exploits, but it's vital that we restrict ourselves to evoking

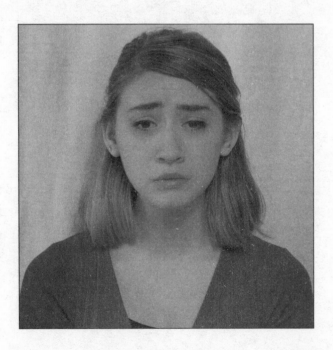

mild sadness or worry for the sake of triggering empathy in others. Extreme sadness evoked through frowning, tearing of the eyes, or audible sobbing will cause discomfort in others and make it harder for us to leave them better off for having met us. If you perceive sadness in someone else, try to mirror it yourself. Lower your voice, slump your shoulders, speak more slowly, as all of this helps show care and concern. You also can't go wrong, both from a humanitarian *and* a human hacking standpoint, in trying to determine the cause and whether you can help. At the very least, you'll build a bit of rapport with someone and show them that you care. You might put yourself in a position to impact that person's life for the better, which you might then parlay (if you're in hacker mode) into something you want.

Emotion #7: Happiness

We end our quick survey of the Big Seven with the most positive emotion of them all, happiness. We express happiness by smiling, of course, moving the corners of our lips up toward our temples. While our cheeks are rising, our eyes trigger what appears to be crow's-feet. Further, we tend to inflate or expand our bodies, standing taller, moving our chins higher, puffing out our chests, and increasing the rhythm, speed, volume, and pitch of our voices. Everything about our physical presence appears to be on an upward swing when we're happy. The world is fantastic! We're fantastic!

In many situations when you're trying to realize an objective while leaving people better off for having met you, evoking happiness will serve you well. However, if you encounter someone who is sad and you seem jovial and upbeat, you risk coming across as insensitive. A person who has just lost a beloved parent and is grieving likely won't feel comforted by a cheerful exhortation to "look on the bright side," accompanied by a well-meaning assertion such as, "I know how you're feeling."

Do you really know how that person is feeling? Is that person in the moment going to feel prepared emotionally to look on the bright side?

Instead of projecting happiness, ask questions that prompt the grieving person to remember happy memories themselves, such as "What was your dad's favorite hobby?" or "What kinds of movies did your mom like?" Sometimes a person is so sad that even this tactic won't help. In that case, forget about trying to nudge the person toward more happiness. Just sit with them. If appropriate given your level of rapport, put your arm around them to comfort them as they sob or cry. In a soft voice, you might explain what you're doing, saying something like, "I'm just going to sit here with you because there's probably nothing that I can say that's going to comfort you right now."

If you're seeking a favor from someone and that person's nonverbals are communicating happiness, evoke happiness yourself to build a connection. A person who is feeling happy will usually feel confident in the moment and less empathetic to others' needs. If you evoke mild sadness and empathy in the course of making a request, you'll come across as a killjoy. Engage with the happy person for a while, asking them questions and getting them to evoke all of the wonderful things that have happened to them. Share their joy, taking genuine pleasure in it. After a while, when the person asks how you're doing, you can begin to move the conversation toward your request. You're trying to leave them better off for having met you, and if you can't help them sustain the happy feelings they had upon first encountering you, they won't feel better off at all.

WORKING WITH THE BIG SEVEN

To build facility with the Big Seven, you have to practice. Begin by watching people, paying special attention to how they use their bodies and particularly their faces to express themselves. Start first with the ventrals described earlier:

> Go to a public place where a large number of people are milling around—a food court in a mall, for instance, a public park, or a busy Starbucks. Before paying attention to facial gestures, notice how people have placed their bodies relative to one another. When people are interested in one another (sexually or otherwise), they tend to align their feet and hips so they're directly facing that person, and they tend to lean toward that person. Can you spot instances of such behavior? How about instances in which people are not squarely facing those with whom they're speaking?

Once you've got that down, move on to facial expressions:

Observe people at a distance, so that you can see them but not quite make out what they're saying. Watch how they move their mouths. Are they pursing their lips? Licking them? Puckering them? If you had to guess, what do you suppose they're talking about? What emotions are they expressing? When you feel like you're pretty adept at noticing facial expressions, try to observe a conversation that is within earshot. Were your interpretations of facial expressions accurate? They might not be at first—a lip puckering that you perceive as an expression of annoyance might simply be the gesture a person makes when they're thinking seriously about something. Careful observation over time can help you distinguish nonverbal expressions of emotion more accurately.

Then practice signaling the Big Seven yourself:

Each day this week, spend fifteen minutes or so practicing one of the Big Seven emotions in the mirror. Choose a different emotion each day so that by the end of the week you'll have practiced all seven. As you make the expressions, notice how you're feeling inside. Do you feel a sudden pang of sadness after spending a few minutes evoking sadness with your face and the rest of your body? How about when you evoke anger? As you become more aware of the connection between your nonverbals and your emotions, you'll be able to "train" yourself to perform better in specific situations. For instance, knowing that you're feeling nervous when going on a date, you might make a point of evoking happiness just before the encounter.

If you're going to give a presentation or anticipate some other encounter where you'll need to speak at length on a given subject (a sales pitch, for instance, or a job interview), try the following:

A week or two before the encounter, video yourself beforehand to observe and correct nonverbals that might not convey your desired emotions. Are your shoulders slumped? Are your fists clenched? Do you appear angry or contemptuous? How do you really feel about the upcoming encounter, the people you'll be presenting to, and the ideas you're delivering? If you film yourself beforehand, you might be surprised at what you find. You'll be equally surprised at how much better your presentations go once you start adjusting for these emotional nuances.

As you become more familiar with nonverbals, remain mindful of the limits of this knowledge. As adept as you might become at spotting emotions, you can't *really* read another person's mind. Nonverbals can tell you that people are feeling a certain way, but they can't tell you *why* they are. If you lose sight of this reality, you'll start to make some pretty significant errors in interpretation.

On one occasion while I was teaching my class, a student named Mike kept grimacing at me. I interpreted it as anger and was at wit's end trying to figure out what I was doing to offend him. Finally during a break in the class I asked Mike about it. It turned out he wasn't angry. Rather, he was in pain because he had tweaked his back. I had registered Mike's emotions more or less correctly in that I knew he was upset about something. But I had no clue what the problem was without asking him about it. My own assumptions were completely wrong.

If someone in your life is communicating one of the Big Seven and it would help you to know why, ask them about it rather than simply making assumptions. But ask in a sensitive and respectful way. If I had called out Mike publicly in front of the class, I might have embarrassed him. Our feelings are very private, and I would have been exposing his to the outside world. Find a private place and pose your questions in a way that is curious and empathetic rather than aggressive or accusatory.

If we're tempted to jump to conclusions, we must also recognize that individuals can deploy nonverbals in idiosyncratic ways and for their own disparate reasons. The general rules I provided for the Big Seven are simply that—rules. Exceptions also exist. If you spot a man at a distance walking quickly toward you with his arms folded across his body and sporting a pronounced resting bitch face expression, you might presume he's angry or otherwise unhappy. But what if he's simply cold? What if he's feeling tired or under the weather? What if he injured his shoulder and it feels more comfortable to walk that way? What if the sleeves on his shirt are too short and he's self-conscious about how that might look, so he's folding his arms to hide it?

There's a simple trick you can use with anyone to ensure that your reading of facial expressions or other body language is more accurate. When you first meet someone, suspend judgment about their emotional state and simply observe their behavior, including their facial expressions, how they carry their body, and their tone of voice (rhythm, speed, volume, pitch). This becomes your baseline observation. As you begin an encounter with them, notice changes that depart from the baseline. In the case of the man walking briskly toward you, if he spots a woman nearby, stops, and turns his hips toward her, you can be fairly sure that she's succeeded in arousing his (sexual or nonsexual) interest and attention. If he doesn't stop walking, he's not interested. If he stops walking but turns to her only briefly, he's mildly interested.

The baseline technique helps not just with strangers but with people we know well. Let's say I come home from work to find my wife sitting at the table. She's staring at her computer screen with her arms crossed and her brows furrowed. These nonverbals might indicate that she's angry or otherwise upset, but on the other hand, she might simply be engaged with what she's reading. Noting her baseline, I can quickly determine how my speech or action is resonating with her by observing changes. Let's say I charge in and say, "Hey! I had a great day today! Everything was awesome!" If she's angry or upset, my joviality might have only annoyed her. I can expect to see her brows furrow more. Maybe her arms will clench. Note to self: "I just screwed up. She's not happy." On the other hand, if I approach more calmly, lower my voice, and ask her about her day, I might see her arms unfold and her brows evoke sadness instead of anger. Note to self: "Uh-oh. Something bad has happened today." That might prompt me to ask a follow-up question or two to identify the problem.

If you get in the habit of noticing people's baselines, you might also be in a better position to spot potential falsehoods, simply because you're now observing people more closely. Let's say you and I are facing one another, and I ask if you liked the fancy box of chocolates I bought for you. If you shake your head slightly no as you say, "Yeah, they were fantastic. Some of the best I've ever had," your nonverbals are at odds with your speech. Did you lie? The apparent discrepancy is a warning sign, but I don't know for sure. Maybe you liked most of the chocolates, but you couldn't stand the one filled with orange liqueur, and that accounts for the ambiguous signals. To get a better sense if you are lying, I'd want to follow up with more conversation about the orange liqueur. If I hear you say, "Yeah, I gave my kids the orange ones, I'm just not into those," I might have a better sense of what might have accounted for the incongruency. If despite sufficient questioning I still can't explain the incongruency, it may well be that you're lying.

Practice observing others, develop that skill, but don't overinterpret what their body language seems to be saying. So much rides on the follow-up questions you ask. If you fail to ask them, you'll quite often interpret incorrectly, compromising your ability to influence others.

A MORE SENSITIVE YOU

Nonverbals are straightforward conceptually, but you might find their practical application quite challenging relative to other techniques in this book. Most of us have at least some sense of how to influence people, yet few of us in my experience are tuned into nonverbals. As children, we don't receive much training on nonverbals at home or during our formal schooling. As we enter adulthood, the proliferation of smartphones and other devices leads many of us to spend a lot more time staring at screens and a lot less time observing others and cuing into their emotions. Further, many of us are so overwhelmed by the demands of daily life that we're out of tune with our own bodies and emotions, and we don't think much about the connection between the two.

If working with nonverbals feels strange to you, try to stick with it anyway. Anybody can learn this stuff—it just takes practice and a desire to improve.

To underscore this point, let me leave you with one of my favorite stories. Years ago, when my daughter Amaya was eight years old, she had a chance to meet Dr. Ekman in person. Intrigued by his work, she read his book *Emotions Revealed* and informally practiced her skills. At the time, I had no idea that these skills were sticking—after all, she was only eight. Boy, did I have a surprise in store for me.

We were driving together one day, traveling about forty miles per hour, when Amaya tapped me on the shoulder. "Dad," she said, "did you see that woman we just passed on the side of the road? She looked sad." I hadn't noticed the woman, so my first inclination was to keep going. "Dad," Amaya said, "you always tell me we have to help people if we see them in trouble. You've got to go back and see what's going on."

How could I say no to her? I turned around and headed back the way we came. Sure enough, I spotted a woman who appeared to be in her early sixties sitting on a bench. I hadn't really noticed her before, focused as I'd been on other parts of the road. Judging from the clean T-shirt, sweater, and jeans she was wearing, she didn't appear to be homeless, but her face bore all the classic signs of serious sadness, including red and puffy eyes. There was no blood or anything else to indicate that she was in physical distress. "I need to go talk to her," Amaya said. I tried to dissuade her, fearing that this woman was unstable or posed some kind of danger, but again, Amaya insisted.

I pulled over and was getting out when Amaya said, "Dad, I'm going over alone. Let me do it, okay? Please?" I stood back as she approached the woman, watching vigilantly and readying myself to jump in at any sign of trouble. Amaya approached the woman and explained that we had driven by and noticed that she seemed sad. "Is everything okay?" she asked.

The woman looked up at her and burst out crying. When she had calmed down a bit, she recounted how her husband had left her and kicked her out of the house. She had no money of her own and was going through bankruptcy. She was trying to obtain housing at an assisted living facility, but that wasn't going well. She was sitting there on the side of the road because she just didn't know what else to do—her life seemed totally hopeless.

We asked if there was anything we could do, but she said there wasn't—she needed to work through her problems on her own. She did have one request: Could she give Amaya a hug? I nodded that it was okay, and the two embraced. "Thank you," she said to Amaya. "Thanks for noticing me and for being so kind. You made my day just a little bit happier, and that's a pretty big deal."

If an eight-year-old can master nonverbals enough to notice a woman by the side of the road as we drove past at forty miles per hour, you can make progress, too. As Amaya's story also suggests, mastering nonverbals can help any of us become not just more adept at influencing others, but more sensitive and compassionate. Amaya approached this woman without wanting anything from her. She walked away feeling great. By taking time out to notice another person's feelings and by then acting on what she'd noticed, she'd made that person's day just a bit brighter.

As important as nonverbals are, we need still other skills if we are to stand the best chance of connecting with others and influencing them as we desire. You know the basic principles for influencing others and leaving them better off for having met you, but do you attend to the details in your speech and behavior? Doing so makes the difference between an encounter that feels real and compelling to others, and one that feels contrived, awkward, or self-serving. Mess the details up, and you might wish you had skipped the social encounter altogether. Get them right, and you're well on your way to obtaining what you desire while also leaving others in better shape too. Let's take a look.

CHAPTER 8

POLISH YOUR PRESENTATION

Keep social encounters "real"
by fine-tuning your approach.

Even with the most logical pretext, you can still fail in your social interactions because subtle details of your dress, speech, or demeanor render your behavior inauthentic or unbelievable. To maximize your chances of success, keep authenticity foremost in your mind, avoiding a number of key hacking "fails." A well-told story seems "real" and believable at every turn. Your social encounters should, too.

Not long ago, my team and I traveled to a developing country to break into the headquarters of a large bank. They do things differently over there than we do in the United States. As part of the bank's security measures, they had burly, tough-looking men with automatic weapons riding around the parking lot on motorbikes. Fortunately, we had human hacking techniques on our side. We discovered that the bank was undergoing a bunch of technical tests to ensure that it complied with international standards. With a bit more probing, we learned which company was conducting the tests and created professional-looking shirts embroidered with the company's logo. We hired a local to stroll into the headquarters before us and start a conversation with the security guards, saying he had come to do some work, and asking what documentation he would need to bring to gain access.

While that conversation was taking place, a colleague and I were going to walk up wearing the shirts we had made. I would talk on my cell phone, and both of us would carry official-looking clipboards.

I strolled up as planned with the phone to my ear, nodding my head and saying, "Yeah, yeah, I'm coming up now. We'll complete the test in a second." We strolled right past security, and they didn't say a word. Inside the headquarters, we walked around, quickly orienting ourselves. Time was short—we didn't want to get caught. Spotting a door marked "ATM Testing Center," we approached it just as a woman was walking in. She unlocked the door with her badge and we followed her in. "Excuse me," she said,

"Oh, yeah," we said, "We're doing a PCI [payment card industry] compliance test."

"Oh, okay," she said.

She did what she had come to do, and a minute later left the room. And that was it. Over the next fifteen minutes, we compromised the entire bank.

This job went off so smoothly, despite those guards with automatic weapons, because we had created a suitable pretext for ourselves, as described earlier in the book. But *how* we executed on that pretext mattered, too. We got the details of our presentation exactly right, tweaking them so they supported our pretext and framed meaning in desirable ways. There were the uniforms and the clipboards, but that was just the beginning. If I had seemed nervous upon approaching security, or if I had spent too much time describing who I was and arguing that I was legit, the guards would have become suspicious. If I didn't seem like I knew where I was going or that I understood what a testing technician did, or if I had asked security personnel directly where the server room was, they again might have doubted us. Something about us would have seemed off or false.

Understanding these nuances, I took a carefully calibrated, minimalist approach. Rather than speaking more than necessary, I *acted* like I belonged, talking on the phone, seemingly busy and directed, while the guards were distracted by the local. I did say that I was coming upstairs loud enough for the guards to hear—this suggested that I belonged, as did the fact that I just strolled past security, as if I had done so numerous times before. Having two people instead of one worked to our advantage—it made sense that a company performing extensive testing would send in multiple people. All of these details worked together to create a frame of meaning that said, "These guys are supposed to be here, let them in." So, the security guards did.

Skillful storytellers attend to the details of their narratives with an eye toward making them consistently believable and natural. Filmmakers and novelists know that a single mistake risks alienating audience members, causing them to become aware of the story's artifice. In that case, the entire experience loses its magic. To succeed with the human hacking techniques presented in this book, you must adopt the mindset of a storyteller, attending to the details of social interactions with authenticity in mind. You must know your "audience" in sufficient depth and anticipate what will appear real and natural to them as you execute on your pretexts and apply elicitation and general influence techniques.

I've touched on authenticity throughout this book, but the subject is so important that we must also address it in a more methodical and focused way. I can't provide you with a rulebook for rendering your human hacking efforts perfectly natural every time. Social interactions are too complex and varied. What I can do is focus on the biggest mistakes hackers make that prompt their targets to "wake up" and become alert to their cons. Remember these mistakes and steer clear of them, and your efforts to influence others will become far more real, believable, and compelling.

FIVE BIG AUTHENTICITY "FAILS"

In my experience, five key "fails" account for the vast majority of ill-fated attempts to influence other parties. Committing any of these errors will prompt your person of interest to become alert to your hidden motivations and techniques. They might not understand exactly what your goal is, but they'll sense that such motives exist and are shaping your behavior. That alone will prompt them to raise their guard, interfering with your efforts to steer the conversation advantageously. People make these mistakes *all the time* in everyday discourse, breaking the spell they otherwise might have had on others.

Hacking Fail #1: You're Too Direct

"Show, don't tell" is an old adage in storytelling. The idea is to portray a theme or moral via characters' actions rather than to have them or the narrator relate the theme overtly. If you're ploddingly explicit about delivering a message, the audience might recognize it as a message they are intended to consume, and the entire presentation will lose its power. To borrow a term from the linguist George Lakoff, you'll draw their attention to the "frame" of meaning you're trying to create. Frames, Lakoff writes, "are mental structures that shape the way we see the world. As a result, they shape the goals we seek, the plans we make, the way we act, and what counts as a good or bad outcome of our actions."[1] But frames often work on us because we aren't aware of them. We just think we're seeing reality as it is. When we do perceive a frame, it might still work on us, so long as we don't sense that it is being used against us or others. When we do perceive a hostile intent, our critical minds go to work and these frames lose their power.

Think back to that example I developed in which you're trying to get your sister to help you out financially with your elderly mother's care. As I advised, one way to proceed using influence techniques might be to hold the conversation over dinner at a restaurant you know your sister likes and at a time when she won't be tired or feel stressed from work. Order your sister's favorite appetizer or bottle of wine, and then start the conversation by building rapport. Later, when it comes to delivering your pretext, you might say something like: "Listen, I wanted to have dinner with you because I need your help. Mom's condition is declining. She can't take care of herself any longer. I'm not quite sure how to handle it. But I value your opinion, so I thought I'd ask what we should do here."

From there, you might use influence techniques to nudge your sister toward the notion that she should contribute toward your mother's care. You might deploy social proof, observing that another trusted relative or friend contributed to their mother's care. Or you might use the liking principle, expressing your esteem for what a great daughter your sister has always been. What you *shouldn't* do is say or do anything that makes your sister aware of all you have been doing to influence her. As the waiter serves your sister's favorite wine, you shouldn't say, "Oh, look, I ordered your favorite wine." Later, as the waiter serves the main course, you shouldn't say, "I know you love that dish. I wanted to eat here because I know it's your favorite restaurant." Such seemingly harmless comments risk taking your sister out of the experience and focusing her attention where it doesn't belong—on you and your possible motives. You're practically saying to her, "Look, the reason I thought about doing something nice for you was because I wanted you to comply with some request of mine." Not so smooth.

When I sneak into buildings posing as an elevator repairman, I don't blurt out to the security guards, "Hey, here's my repairman outfit, and these are my repair tools. I'm an elevator repairman." The guards know I'm a repairman from my outfit and the tools I carry. I'm not suggesting you should never openly acknowledge your pretext or actions you've taken to influence others' behavior. Let's say I'm posing as a repairman from Otis Elevators and wearing a shirt emblazoned with that company's logo. If the security guard, seeking to make casual conversation, exclaims, "Oh, you work for Otis?" then acknowledging I do becomes a natural part of the conversation. But if the question hasn't been posed, there's no logical reason in my target's mind for me to point out my job description to them. That I'm doing so will prompt the guards to notice and scrutinize me.

Hacking Fail #2: You Negate the "Frame"

Some unsuccessful human hackers are even more cringe-worthy in their ham-handedness. Not content to spell out what they're doing for their person of interest, they go a step further and pointedly reassure that person that they're not doing anything nefarious. I've heard students trying to sneak into a secure facility hold up their fake ID badge and say: "Look, see? I'm an employee. It says so right here." And then they say, in what they take to be an offhanded way, "I mean, it's not like I'm a hacker or something."

What?? Don't say that! A competent narrator of a story interested in making a point, say, about the meaninglessness of life would never blurt out: "It's not like I fabricated this whole story just to convince you that life has no meaning." Such a move would blow up any authenticity the narrator had managed to establish. As Lakoff has famously observed in the context of political discourse, "when we negate a frame, we evoke the frame."[2] The very words we use in negating an idea perpetuate that idea by bringing it to others' minds.

If you were to remark to your sister, "It's not like I asked you to dinner tonight just to hit you up for money for Mom," what is she more likely to think? The idea that you might have an agenda of your own might never have occurred to her. But now you've planted the seed of an idea. That seed might sprout during your conversation and grow into a nasty weed of skepticism and doubt—the very opposite of what you intended. Don't *ever* negate the "frame" or narrative you're creating via your pretexting and rapport-building efforts and your mobilization of influence techniques. Not even a little bit.

Hacking Fail #3: You're Too Perfect

Any story you might tell requires details. Otherwise it seems vague, overly abstract, meaningless. Moreover, you have to reinforce the frame of meaning when delivering a pretext by offering multiple, affirming details. When I pose as a pest control guy, I have the uniform, the spray canisters, and a clipboard with a fake work order on it all working together to establish that my pretext is legitimate. But that's enough. I don't then have to go on to give the security guards a lecture about the insects I'm there to spray for, nor do I divulge the particular pesticide I'm using, nor do I tell them how many other facilities I've sprayed that week. Pile on too many details in an attempt to be "perfect," and I'll leave my target thinking about all these details and how many there are. They'll become aware of the story as a story they are meant to consume and believe it less. I'm liable to come off seeming anxious, jittery—and potentially fake.

When my team and I broke into the bank mentioned above, we marshaled a number of relevant details. I knew what my purported name was, our company's name, why we were there, what a compliance test was, what parts of the bank were being tested. But I didn't walk into that bank and announce that my manager, a man named Rafik

Ghalili from our Chicago office, had told me during a meeting we held on June 17 to come to this country to finish a PCI compliance test, which was performed initially on September 13. I didn't inform the guards that I'd been doing compliance tests for my company for the past six and a half years and that I received my training at our Baltimore, Maryland, facility. Nobody cares about all that detail. That I had somehow felt inclined to spout all of it would have seemed odd to the guards.

Hackers often don't deliver too many details but rather make the few they do deliver too extreme. Sometimes they tell lies in an effort to produce the "perfect," killer detail that will win over a target. I recently scheduled a meeting with a business associate who knew that my favorite band was the rock-and-roll band Clutch. When this associate, who didn't know me well, picked me up in his car to head to the meeting, he had a Clutch album that he'd downloaded playing in an effort to build rapport with me. When I remarked on the choice of music, he said, "Oh, yeah, I heard you talking the other day about how much you loved them, so I thought I'd download an album and put it on for you."

My associate didn't claim to have become a rabid fan of Clutch overnight, nor did he purport to know every last song or album the band had released. If he had, I might have wondered about his truthfulness, as nothing he had said or done indicated that he had any particular affinity for Clutch or their style of music. If I had gone on to inquire casually what his favorite song was on the album we were listening to, or if I had asked some other follow-up question that required knowledge of the band to answer, he might have reacted awkwardly, scrambling for what to say. In his effort to lend authenticity to his rapport building, he'd have eroded it.

If you're inclined to try to make a social interaction "perfect," bear in mind an observation that the Roman emperor Marcus Aurelius made thousands of years ago. "When bread is baked," he said, "some parts are split at the surface, and these . . . have a certain fashion contrary to the purpose of the baker's art, are beautiful . . . and in a peculiar way excite a desire for eating."[3] Most of us value imperfection. We find it not only beautiful and enticing, but also desirably authentic—what one researcher has spoken of as "aspirational realness."[4] This holds true when it comes to bread and many other consumer goods, and it holds true for social interactions as well. So, don't feel compelled to get everything about your presentation absolutely right. An ethic of "good enough" works best.

Hacking Fail #4: You're Tone Deaf

Unsuccessful hackers don't simply take details too far. They get details *wrong*, speaking or acting in ways that distract from their pretext or even contradict it. If your pretext has you playing the role of a kind or compassionate sibling, say, or of the dignified, respectable authority figure, or of the upstanding professional, and you drop multiple f-bombs in the course of conversation, your pretext will seem less believable. This is a huge problem in my industry. Since social engineering is traditionally male dominated, many operators unthinkingly use horrifically sexist language. You'll often hear security professionals who had succeeded in breaking into a company's computer system say, "I just raped that server!" What kind of image does that convey? If you're trying to influence others yet you speak like a jackass, you can expect failure. Likewise, if you're a newlywed trying to forge a relationship with your spouse's family, none of whom are native English speakers, and you load down your conversation with fancy English words that your spouse's relatives are unlikely to understand, like "confabulated" or "irascible," you probably won't make much headway in your pretext of being "the welcoming and accommodating new family member."

Besides language, other aspects of your presentation might wind up offending your person of interest if you're not careful. As we saw in the last chapter, our body language sends subtle cues to others. If I'm a large-bodied male trying to interact with a woman who is physically much smaller than me, and my hips are facing square in her direction, she might subconsciously perceive that as threatening. If I'm a male of any size trying to build rapport with a new female student who is wearing a hijab, and I offer a handshake, I might also inadvertently cause offense, since strict Islamic cultures forbid any touching between strangers of different genders. If I'm addressing an elderly person who is hard of hearing and I speak quickly and softly, I might unintentionally put that person in an uncomfortable position, compromising my efforts to influence them, especially if I were playing the attentive and compassionate grandson/neighbor/friend. If I'm playing the role of the attentive father and I'm constantly glancing at my phone while my son or daughter is speaking, I again compromise my authenticity. My efforts to exert influence will suffer.

We must consider, too, our general appearance and how it might come across to others, particularly strangers who don't know us and who have only stereotypical impressions of us to go on. If I'm a tall, bald male, many people will perceive me as angry or aggressive. I could be the world's sweetest, most empathetic person, but that's the stereotype. When attempting to influence others, I must bear that stereotype in mind and correct for it in my speech and behavior, perhaps by going out of my way to smile warmly and speak softly or by giving my person of interest the chair at the table that sits a bit higher (thus putting them in a position of authority or power). Similarly, if I'm a buxom female trying to influence a roomful of men, I should think about how long my sleeves are, how low my blouse is cut, and similar elements of my presentation, and what my audience might infer, rightly or wrongly, about my motives. No matter my gender, I should bear in mind the socioeconomic dimensions of my presentation. If I'm wealthy but interacting with someone of limited means, will my Gucci bag or Rolex watch support my rapport building or will it cause others to regard me as a snob?

We might dislike the stereotypes people deploy and the biased judgments they make about categories of people—I know I do. But we can't ignore others' perceptions, as flawed and hurtful as they might be, and hope to influence these individuals. Week in and week out, I play on these biases in order to induce people to click on a link or admit past a security barrier. I detest these stereotypes, but they're real and deeply entrenched. To a critic who would fault me for playing on these unfortunate stereotypes rather than challenging them at every turn, I'd point out that criminals don't hesitate to exploit biases people have, and since my job is to help organizations improve security and make society safer, I have to as well.

Nonprofessionals can't afford to simply steamroll over those perceptions, either. Some might argue that we should call out our friends, relatives, and neighbors on their biases in an effort to bring about change. At times, that might be necessary. As I've said throughout this book, it's important not to compromise our deeply felt moral principles when interacting with others. But most of the time, if our goal is to influence others, we're better off showing a bit more humility, meeting people where they are to the extent we can. We can't change the way the world thinks in our everyday interactions. What we can do is change the way *the next person we interact with* thinks. The best way of accomplishing that is by making that person feel as comfortable as possible and then leaving them better off for having met us, in the process potentially challenging stereotypes about us they might have had. We also have to accept that some pretexts might not work for us because of others' racist, sexist, or ageist biases. Elements of our appearance might clash too strongly with the meaning we're trying to evoke in others' minds.

Hacking Fail #5: You're Too Aggressive in the "Ask"

"Last night, when I was getting ready to turn out the lights at my office and go home, I noticed that in the corner of my office a bug was hanging from a thread and wrapping another insect in a web." As you read that sentence, what image pops to mind? Most likely, you thought of a spider. I didn't have to actually use the word "spider" to evoke that particular insect.

Whenever you have a frame of meaning, words or objects defined within the frame (the web, an insect being wrapped up) evoke the frame (the idea of a spider doing its work in the corner of a room). This principle explains why we don't need to be overly explicit in our hacking efforts (Hacking Fail #1). Just one or two elements of a frame suffice to do the work for us. But as a corollary of this principle, we also don't need to ask directly for what we want. Moreover, being too overt about our requests can backfire by causing others to become alert to the frame of meaning we seek to create.

Let's say my neighbor—I'll call her Barb—has a big golden retriever who barks incessantly and loudly when Barb lets her out in the morning and evening. This barking occurs as early as six in the morning, jarring my two small children awake at least an hour before their usual wake-up time. I want Barb to wait until at least 8:00 a.m. to let her dog out, or to make some alternate arrangement so our family isn't disturbed. If I approach Barb in her driveway one evening as she is stepping out of her car and ask her point-blank not to let her dog out until eight o'clock, she might react defensively, especially if she is tired and stressed after a long day's work. If I'm trying to play the role of the "friendly neighbor asking for help," my boldness will possibly clash with and undermine that pretext.

A better solution is to approach Barb on a Sunday morning when I'm out for a walk and she's relaxed and puttering around her garden with her dog, Max, sunning himself by her side. Even then, directly asking her to keep Max quiet in the early mornings might not help my case. As an alternative, I can approach Barb and say, "I love these new rosebushes you put in—they're beautiful. Max looks like he loves them, too. Hey, while I'm thinking of it, I wonder if you could help me out with a problem I've been having. We've been talking and we're not sure what to do about our kids. They keep waking up early in the morning because they hear Max barking. We've tried keeping the windows closed, but it's not working. I know Max has to go out, but what do you think we could do about this?"

This kind of query might start a conversation that would lead Barb to offer to wait until 8:00 a.m. to let Max out, or to come up with some other solution, such as taking him for a walk early instead of letting him out so that if he barks the kids wouldn't hear him. In that case, I would have gotten exactly what I wanted without asking her directly. Of course, she might not offer anything but instead say something like, "I'm sorry to hear that. Maybe you could put on a sound machine near their room to muffle the barking." That reaction might cause me to become frustrated at her apparent selfishness. Rather than blow my top, my best move is to try again, saying something like: "No, the kids don't like sound machines—we tried that about a year ago when the youngest was just born. Is there anything else we might do?"

If at this point Barb offers up your desired solution, great. I've been patient in my attempts to influence her, I've maintained my pretext in a believable way, and it has paid off. If she hasn't come forth with the solution, and if after another iteration this situation remains unchanged, then at that point I might decide to ask her directly to keep her dogs in until 8:00 a.m. No pretext is guaranteed to work, but at least I'll know that I've pushed mine as far as it could go, keeping it real and believable in my neighbor's eyes.

If I do have to ask her directly, I will try to do so without accusing her of anything or casting judgment. A huge difference exists between a stern statement like "Barb, listen, I tried to be a good neighbor and ask nicely, but I need you to understand that you and your noisy dog are irritating and if you don't keep it inside till eight a.m. I am calling the pound," and a more sensitive request like "Barb, I know we have gone back and forth on some ideas to try, but I just have to ask if you can keep Max in till eight o'clock. Saturday is the only day of the week I get to sleep in and it would help me and my mental health. Can you please help me out here?" Keep in mind, I don't know why she is behaving inconsiderately toward me. Maybe she's being selfish, but maybe she has other, more legitimate reasons. My goal at all times is to leave her better off for having met me while also meeting my desires. Lashing out probably won't lead me to that result.

Think about an interaction you recently had with someone that didn't go as well as you would have liked. Analyze your execution of the conversation. How did you begin? How did you build rapport? How did you lay out your pretext? What was your body language like? How were you dressed? Did you consider your person of interest and how they might perceive you? Think of three or four details in your speech or behavior that you might have done differently and try these modifications in your next, similar encounter.

KNOW YOUR TARGETS, BUT DON'T OBSESS

Stepping back from these five "fails," we find that unsuccessful hackers commit them because of a poorly calibrated relationship with their targets. These would-be hackers either spend too little time trying to understand the people they're trying to influence, or too much. They ignore their targets and take their perspectives, emotions, and needs for granted, or they become overly obsessed with how their targets might perceive them. Either of these imbalances lead hackers to deliver the wrong details, become too plodding or direct, present too many details, or even tell outright lies in an attempt to "nail down" the pretext and control their targets' perception. It isn't just novice hackers who fail to think about their targets in a balanced way. Novices might underestimate the level of understanding they'll need to be successful and then go overboard in a misguided and misinformed effort to control the situation. But seasoned pros might also take any previous success they've had for granted, wrongly assuming their current targets will resemble previous ones, and that what worked before will work again. If these pros are conscientious C-types, they might be further inclined to overplan and strive for a "perfect" interaction.

Although I'm not a "C," I've been guilty of overconfidence at times. Several years ago, we phished a manufacturing company with large government and military contracts. At the time, foreign governments were beginning to use LinkedIn to recruit spies and obtain privileged information. Posing as an attractive young woman, we sent an email to all 7,500 employees at this company inviting them to join a special LinkedIn group. We wanted as many employees as possible to click on the link; doing so would allow us to compromise their computers.

When we first started phishing at the company, about 50 to 60 percent of targets fell for a given exploit. After about eighteen months of working with this company, employees were getting better at recognizing phishing emails—our hit rate was down to about 25 to 40 percent. And yet, this LinkedIn exploit was a rocking success: 79 percent of employees clicked to join the group.

For someone in my business, that kind of success is thrilling. And it went to my head. A few months later, a second company—a big retailer with 10,000 employees—hired us to phish them. "We really need you guys to blow it out of the water with your first phish," our new client said.

"No problem," I said, "we've got just the thing."

We used the same exploit that had worked so well for us at the manufacturing company. On the day we sent it out, I eagerly awaited the results. To my shock, barely 1 percent of employees fell for our exploit within the first twenty-four hours. By the end of day two, only 2 percent had. By the end of day three, still 2 percent. By the end of the week, only about 7 percent of employees had clicked—nowhere near the 79 percent at the other company. What was going on here?

I suspected the company's spam filters might have picked out our email, but we checked and that wasn't it. We also checked for technical problems that might have prevented many employees from getting the email. Nothing.

Disheartened, I ended the phish and asked our client to have managers inside the company connect with employees who had received the email and inquire why they hadn't clicked on it. As it turned out, employees at this company weren't interested in LinkedIn. At the manufacturing company, the workforce had been composed largely of men in their forties and fifties. These employees loved LinkedIn and used it all the time. As males sitting around in their cubicles all day, many of them also had a weakness for a message from an attractive woman. At this retailer, most employees were in their twenties and thirties, and a much higher percentage were women. This generation of employees saw LinkedIn as a site for "old people," preferring instead networks like Snapchat or Instagram. When they encountered an email offering a LinkedIn invitation, they didn't pay it much attention. The females among these employees were also less inclined to click on an invitation just because it came from an attractive woman.

We had failed because I, in my great wisdom and experience (insert sarcastic laugh here), had taken my audience for granted. By thinking about how great our previous email was, I had neglected to study our present targets. The basic knowledge I had about these targets—employees at a large company working in a corporate environment—was enough for me to know that the same pretext I had used earlier—a friendly invitation to take an action related to social media—would likely work. But it wasn't enough for me to get the details of the pretext right. For that, I would look more closely at these targets and develop a clearer (albeit still fairly superficial) sense of their basic character traits, preferences, needs, and so on. I would have adjusted our execution of the pretext accordingly, sending out an email related to activity on Facebook and asking targets to click. Three months later, we got a second chance and sent out precisely such an email. This time, our click ratio was *huge*.

Try not to take your people of interest for granted. Maintain a healthy focus on them, listening carefully to what they're saying and trying your best to understand them. But don't go overboard in your attempts to control the situation. Stay calm, check whatever inner control-freak impulses you might have, and try to be as truthful as possible. It's very difficult to appear authentic while telling lies. The more your deviate from the truth, the more mental work you have to do. You must now remember all of your falsehoods as an encounter or a relationship proceeds so that you don't contradict yourself. Even if you manage to pull that off, you'll likely come across as awkward or stilted in your presentation. Something won't seem right.

When practicing rapport building, one student of mine tried to build common ground with strangers by asking them where they were from and then always claiming to be from these same hometowns. The initial recognition of apparent common ground created a burst of excitement in the targets, but that quickly faded as they realized that this student knew nothing about their hometown and was quite likely lying. Don't let that be you. The best nonprofessional hackers I know of not only understand the people they're trying to influence but also care about and respect them enough not to lie to them. They get more of what they want, and since they leave people better off, they come away from their hacking encounters feeling great.

As you practice the techniques described in previous chapters, keep the five big fails foremost in your mind, as well as the general precepts of knowing your audience, keeping calm, and remaining truthful. If you've been working hard all along to think less about yourself and more about others, redouble those efforts. Do you really know your persons of interest as well as you think? Challenge yourself to learn three or four details about them you didn't know before—what they like or dislike, what challenges they're grappling with, what elements of their background might frame how they're seeing the world, and so on.

YOU GET MORE IF YOU ASK NICELY

Polishing your interactions with an eye toward authenticity is about developing a more refined command of the social graces. If you mind the details, your conversations become smoother, more natural, more compelling, and frankly, just easier. Over time, the important relationships in your life take on a different tenor, becoming less frustrating, more loving, and more fulfilling.

Let's say your significant other comes home after a long day. They're tired and stressed and their body just *hurts*. They plop down on the couch, heave a big sigh, and flip on the TV. You approach them with a problem or issue you need to solve, one that involves them. "Listen," you say, "you left all of your clothes around the bathroom again, and you used up all of the toilet paper and didn't put a new roll on the dispenser. What's wrong with you? I work hard all day long like you do, and I can remember these kinds of things. Have a little consideration." Yours could be the most legitimate gripe in the world, but because you raised it so aggressively and with no thought of your significant other's mind frame at this particular moment, they're not going to receive it well. If you persist, they might blow their top. Nothing will get resolved. Your relationship will only be more difficult than it was. Over time, a series of such interactions will impoverish your relationship, locking you into unhelpful patterns of behavior.

Imagine, by contrast, that you waited fifteen minutes or so until your significant other had time to relax. When you did approach them, imagine that you touched them affectionately and handed them their favorite glass of iced tea. "Wow," you say, "it looks like you had a rough day. You didn't even say hi when you came in. Is everything okay?" When your significant other describes how rough their day is, you say. "That sounds hard. Listen, when you're done chilling, can you let me know? I've got a couple of things I need to speak with you about." Maybe your significant other offers to discuss it now. "No, no," you say with a reassuring smile, "take a few minutes." When you do have the conversation, you might not get what you want—more respect on the part of your significant other, in the form of better efforts on their part to keep the bathroom tidy. But you're far more likely to achieve that outcome.

Of course, what you *really* want to do at this moment is tell your significant other how ticked off you are. But that's not going to get you closer to your goal, which is to have your significant other keep the bathroom in better shape. So you adopt the pretext of "caring and attentive spouse and partner." Further, you mind the details. That glass of iced tea is a small gesture on your part, but it validates your significant other, saying to them, "I know what you like and care about you enough to give it to you." You don't say, "Hey, look, I'm giving you your favorite drink." You just give that small gift. You don't say, "Look, I'm giving you an affectionate little rub on your shoulder because I care about you," or, "Look, I'm giving you time to relax before I rip into you"—you just do those things. You don't go overboard trying to build rapport in this situation, popping open a two-hundred-dollar bottle of wine instead of handing over the iced tea, or lying and saying, "I've been thinking all day how much I love you." Those and similar actions would be ridiculous. Reorienting yourself away from your needs and desires and thinking about your significant other's frame of mind, you execute your pretext in a simple, kind, and informed way. Even if you aren't successful this time, you haven't damaged your relationship. Chances are, you've done just a little bit to improve its quality even as you've made your wishes known.

This example is somewhat trivial, but applying human hacking techniques and getting the details right can make a huge difference when it really counts. One student of mine, Conrad, took my course to help him in his job as a consultant and spent several months practicing the techniques in this book. One day, he picked up the phone to learn that his father had been diagnosed with untreatable, late-stage lung cancer that had spread throughout his body. He had only months to live. His father was in great pain, and the local hospital where he had gone for diagnosis didn't seem to know how best to treat him. Conrad wanted to take him to a much better hospital in a different city. He arranged to pick his father up and drive him a few hours to the new hospital. Meanwhile, his father's doctors would make some calls and refer his case so that the new hospital would be ready for him.

Upon their arrival, Conrad discovered that his father's doctors hadn't made the promised calls, the hospital had no available inpatient rooms, and a long line of patients were waiting for rooms. Staff told Conrad that there was no way they could help his father, but if he wanted he could go directly to the pulmonology division that treated lung cancer patients and talk directly to one of the doctors there to see if she could help. Conrad did exactly that. Although he was deeply distraught about his father's situation, he thought back to human hacking techniques and how he might be able to apply them. And he thought specifically about how he might be able to construct a frame of meaning with the right details to help him exert influence.

"I didn't know this particular doctor," Conrad remembered, "but I reflected that doctors in general are part of a 'tribe.' As a group, they have a seriousness about them. They value intelligence. They value knowledge. They care deeply about their mission as professionals. Therefore, to maximize my effectiveness, I decided to present myself not as a doctor—because I'm not one—but as someone who values these same things." This meant he would have to dress nicely and use language befitting a well-educated person. He'd have to get to the point quickly, mindful that doctors are often overworked, stressed, and in a hurry. More subtly, he'd have to appear pleasant, respectful, and focused. He'd have to stick to the facts, remaining logical and concrete about his father's situation and what he, Conrad, wanted. He'd also have to be authentic. As Conrad noted, "I wasn't pretending in evoking these traits, but rather just bringing out these parts of who I am." As long as Conrad did that, listening and empathizing with the doctor, not pushing too hard and avoiding the five authenticity fails, he'd do okay.

The conversation went well. At first, Conrad greeted the doctor politely and gave her a brief synopsis of his father's story and desperate need for treatment at the hospital. He gave her a logical timeline that she could understand. Paying attention to the doctor's responses, he mirrored her speech and body language so as to build rapport. Without becoming emotional, he evoked his own fear and that of his father, speaking frankly but in a dignified way. When the doctor confirmed that they had no available beds, he nodded that he understood and politely asked her, "So, what can we do about this situation?" Conrad perceived that he and the doctor had established common ground, were making similar gestures, and using a common vocabulary, so it seemed reasonable at this point to pose his father's problem as a joint problem that he and the doctor could work out together. Conrad offered a suggestion: "Maybe, since we don't have any spare beds, we could put him in a hallway, and he could stay there and receive treatment until a bed opens up." The doctor thought about this, and to Conrad's great relief, agreed. In a conversation that lasted only about forty minutes, Conrad had cut through the usual bureaucracy and handled the seemingly insurmountable challenge of assuring his father's treatment at this busy hospital.

Conrad's father stayed at this hospital for several months before succumbing to his illness. During that time, Conrad spoke frequently with the medical staff, taking the same thoughtful and polished approach as he'd taken with this first doctor, and also using body language to his advantage (calm expressions, open gestures, open hands, hips directed at the person if they were facing him). "Every time I approached a doctor or nurse," Conrad noted, "I made my very best effort to leave this person better off for having met me." Conrad couldn't be sure, but he believed his awareness of human hacking techniques and his determination to attend to the details of his presentation made a difference. He noticed that his father was receiving better care than the other patients. He suspected that the medical staff were reacting well to his behavior with them, which was at once finely tuned, respectful, and authentic. In this high-pressure context, where patients and their families commonly show frustration and other negative emotions, the medical staff seemed to notice Conrad's efforts to interact with them on their terms. As grief-stricken as he was by his father's passing, Conrad could take comfort in knowing that his father had received excellent care in his final days, and that he, Conrad, had done everything in his power to make it happen.

Conrad's story suggests the power we can wield when mustering the full array of social engineering principles and techniques. By this point in the book, you're well on your way to wielding this power, too. You do have to practice the specific techniques—and practice them some more. Depending on your diligence and focus, it could take you a few months, or a few years, but if you stick with it, you'll see a profound difference. As you handle spontaneous encounters, you'll have not only a new awareness of what you and others are doing but also the sense of confidence and calm that such awareness provides. You won't be perfect every time—surprises can and will occur—but you'll be better at turning those surprises to your advantage. You'll also be in a better position to handle encounters that you can foresee and for which you can prepare. To round out the book, let's bring together the techniques we've encountered and examine how Conrad might have gone about preparing for his important conversation with the pulmonology specialist. Many people become nervous before job interviews, high-stakes sales calls, legal proceedings, important "relationship" talks, and other planned social encounters. If you apply human hacking principles systematically before an encounter, you can focus yourself, minimize your jitters, and increase the odds of a successful outcome.

CHAPTER 9

PUTTING IT ALL TOGETHER

Ace your critical conversations
by planning them in advance.

If you have an important conversation coming up, do what social engineers do: plan it out. Social engineers attempting to break into companies call this developing an "attack vector," but in everyday life we can call it a "conversation outline." This chapter explains how to create an outline step by step and provides general advice for getting important conversations right.

When my team and I prepare to break into a company or government facility, we don't just wing it. We spend weeks preparing our "attack vector." We research the facility we're targeting, tracking down information about its location, physical layout, security, leadership, workforce—you name it. Our techniques are straight out of James Bond, including dumpster diving, sophisticated online searches, physical surveillance of key individuals, phishing emails, the recording of conversations using devices that look like ordinary pens, watches, and ties, and much more. When we know enough about the target, we run through the principles described in this book to build out our plan. We sketch out our pretext and rapport-building activities, deciding who will participate and what uniforms, props, body language, and verbal strategies they'll deploy. We fine-tune the details and role-play conversations. All this effort doesn't guarantee success, but it makes it a lot likelier, in part because it helps us relax and stay calm when we're actually breaking into a building. We're confident because we've done our homework. We know what to expect.

You can improve your ability to influence others by developing detailed plans for handling important, upcoming social interactions (forgoing the sneaky spycraft, of course). I do this myself in my personal life and in running my company. Some time ago, I noticed performance problems with "Jimmy," one of my employees. He was a good guy overall, but lately he'd been slacking, putting out lower-quality work than I was used to and taking an overly laid-back attitude toward his job. If he didn't improve, his behavior would alienate some of our clients and affect morale among his teammates, who would have to pick up the slack for him. I could have called Jimmy and broached the subject without giving it much thought, saying, in effect, "I'm your boss. If you don't make some changes, I'm going to fire you." Although Jimmy might have cleaned up his act, throwing my authority around like that wouldn't have done much for our relationship, nor would it have fired up his love for his job and our company.

Instead, I did my "research" by taking stock of the situation, reviewing Jimmy's DISC profile from chapter 1 (all of my employees take DISC assessments when they start working for our company), and developing a pretext from there. Jimmy was an Influencer (I) type, a team player who liked the spotlight. I would have to tone down the negative criticisms, since people who crave the spotlight don't usually like it when others fixate on their flaws. I'd have to find a subtler way to broach his weak performance and motivate him to change. If I came across as the "angry boss," I'd risk alienating him, but if I presented myself as his "friend," I could build rapport and motivate him to *want* to change his behavior.

I cobbled together a rough plan for our upcoming quarterly check-in meeting, beginning by asking general, open-ended questions like "How has this past quarter been for you? How do you see your real strengths and weaknesses?" If the meeting went as I hoped, he'd admit to slacking this past quarter. If he didn't, I'd pose further questions to draw it out of him, like "How do you feel you did on XYZ project?" and "You took the lead with client X last month. How did the project go?" I knew the project for client X didn't go so well, and I hoped Jimmy would acknowledge that. If he did, I'd say, "Oh, really, tell me about that. What do you think could have gone better?" I hoped he'd cue me into some problem he was having. In that case, I'd ask him how he thought we could change our operations so the problem wouldn't affect our team going forward. *He* would be the one generating the solution, not me, which would make a big difference in how he perceived it, and in turn, how committed he would be to putting it into practice.

In crafting my plan according to Jimmy's DISC profile, I framed the conversation in a way that would help him shine, even as we were working to help him improve. If he had been a Conscientious (C) type, I might have focused on the details. If he had been a Dominant (D) type, I could have just told him straight out that he'd been slacking and I needed him to change. If he had been a Steady (S) type who likes to support others, I could have emphasized the impact he was having on the team. Since he was an (I) type, I chose to present the conversation to him positively, framing it as an opportunity to "help me understand how we could improve." As part of this framing, of course, I had to truly listen to understand how we could improve as a company. That way, I'd get him to buy in to make the necessary changes. We'd see improvement, and I'd be able to keep him as an employee.

My plan worked. At first, Jimmy didn't readily admit that his performance had been lacking, and instead focused on times he'd done "amazingly well." When I brought up client X, he did haltingly acknowledge the project didn't go so well, and he'd been responsible. I sweetened this moment for him by responding that I knew he was a great employee and that the team had great potential to improve. I asked him: "What do *you* think we can do to truly shine during our next engagement?" At that point, Jimmy acknowledged he had changes to make, and offered some suggestions. Over the next few months, his performance improved, and our relationship deepened.

CRAFTING A CONVERSATIONAL OUTLINE

If you have a job interview coming up, a negotiation with a customer or vendor, a difficult conversation with a colleague, family member, or friend, a big date with a romantic partner, or any encounter where you want to shine, don't even think of going in cold. Drawing together the material in this book, I've developed a powerful, ten-step framework you can use to prepare what I call a "conversational outline"—a written sketch of your upcoming conversation—for almost any kind of social interaction. As you'll find, this bit of preparation will make your encounters far crisper, cleaner, smoother, and more productive. It'll also increase your confidence, allowing you to stay in the game even when conversations turn in unexpected directions. In the sections that follow, I'll describe how best to craft a conversational outline, running quickly through the ten steps. Afterward, I'll discuss how to work with the conversation outlines you create for specific conversations, and in particular what to do if (or more realistically, when) your best-laid plans go awry.

Step #1: Map the Terrain

Your first step in outlining your upcoming conversation is to take stock of the encounter and jot down its relevant facts. With whom will you be interacting? You'll want to perform a DISC analysis or come to some ballpark guess about your person of interest's profile. If the person is a stranger, as will likely be the case in a job interview or if you're negotiating to buy a car, glean what you can from some preliminary research. If your person of interest maintains social media accounts visible to the public, what do their postings suggest about their communications profile and other aspects of their personality? Can you learn more about the person by contacting others you know who've dealt with them before? If you're buying a car, could you pay the dealership a quick, initial visit, observing the salespeople for a few minutes?

Map out facts about your person of interest's likely state of mind, as well as their needs and desires. If you're planning on entering your boss's office to ask for a raise, will they have only limited time to speak with you? What special pressures are they under, and how might you help? What concerns might your request arouse in them? How much latitude might they have to negotiate? And how much power do you have in the encounter? Who "needs" the other person more? If your person of interest refuses your request, do you have other options?

Step #2: Define Your Goal

This next step is critical. When imagining future encounters, many people start at the beginning of the conversation and work through to the end. It's far better to define your goal first and allow it to shape the encounter's many facets. Be precise in defining your objective. Not long ago, I learned that my daughter Amaya had broken our house rules, participating in a particular online chat group with other teenagers even though my wife and I had expressly forbidden it. Although we were furious, we decided our goal in confronting Amaya wasn't just to get her to admit to what she'd done and agree never to repeat it. More important, we wanted to learn why she had disobeyed and deceived us so that we could strengthen our relationship with her. With these goals clearly in mind, we knew we couldn't aggressively confront her, because she'd only become defensive and most likely refuse to confide in us. We'd have to take a gentler approach, while still making clear our disappointment with her behavior.

When defining your goal, pay attention to what you've noticed when mapping the terrain (step #1). If you're entering a car dealership, and you've acknowledged that you need a car immediately and the power differential is not in your favor, then your goal might not be "get the car of my dreams at $5,000 off the sticker price." That price might not be realistic, and you can't afford to walk away if the dealer offers only $2,000 off. In framing your goal, be mindful of your person of interest's welfare and needs. What will it take to leave them better off for having met you? In our conversation with Amaya, a stronger relationship with us would leave her better off, too, as would our ability to understand her actions. Once we did, we could take appropriate steps to address any reasonable concerns she might have had that led her to break our rules.

Step #3: Decide on Your Pretext

In most situations, clarifying your goal will lead you naturally to a pretext. In the case of our conversation with Amaya, our desire to understand what in God's name had prompted her behavior meant we couldn't adopt the pretext of the "stern, angry parents," but instead had to play the role of "concerned parents." Bam—pretext selected. If you're renting a car and want to induce the sales associate to offer you a free upgrade, you might avoid playing the role of the "dissatisfied customer" and instead play the role (assuming it's rooted in truth) of the "customer who is having a bad day and could use some help." If you're unhappy with your neighbor's dog barking at all hours yet also need to maintain a cordial relationship, you'll play the role of "sleep-deprived young parent who could use some help" rather than "angry neighbor who is about to sue you."

If you lack clarity about your goal, you'll find it harder to generate a helpful pretext. Earlier in the book, I described a failed attempt to build rapport with a physics professor I was hacking. I had feigned great interest and knowledge of a scientific paper he had published. When he asked me a substantive question about the paper, it became obvious that I hadn't read it and that my pretext was fraudulent. I hadn't spent enough time preparing and zeroing in on my objective. In the back of my mind, I thought my goal was "to look smart in front of the professor." So, I tried—and failed—to act smart. If I had thought more about it, I would have adopted a better goal: coaxing the professor to spend a few minutes walking me into the building and then, after a short conversation in which he divulged some important information, to forget all about our encounter. In hindsight, I should have adopted the pretext of the "interested student" who sought to pose a quick, innocuous question about the course the professor taught. Such a role would have made more sense to the professor, required less effort on my part, and proven more successful.

Step #4: Imagine Your Rapport Building

Now that you've nailed down your pretext, consider how you'll mobilize it to establish a helpful connection with your person of interest. Let's say you're considering a job offer from another employer, and you're going in to ask your current boss for a raise. You could adopt a more aggressive pretext such as that of the "employee who'll quit if the boss doesn't agree to a raise." Or you could go with the "employee with another job offer who'd really like to stay and who'd like to work with the boss to make that happen." In either case, your rapport building should include when and how you decide to broach the conversation. Should you charge into your boss's office unannounced on a Friday afternoon at four thirty, just as she's leaving, and knowing she has a big presentation she's giving on Monday? Or should you wait until after the presentation has gone well and then ask her to grab a sandwich with you at lunch the next day? The informality of the latter option will likely make for a more relaxed encounter, enabling you to warm up by congratulating your boss on the presentation, asking for details on how it went, and so on. Don't overdo it with the friendliness, of course, asking your boss about her spouse or kids, unless you already have that kind of friendship.

Step #5: Identify Potential Influence-Building or Elicitation Techniques

Considering the terrain and your existing relationship with your person of interest, identify your likely influence-building techniques. You need not commit to using a particular technique, but it helps to have a general sense of which to use and which to avoid.

If you're planning on asking your boss for a raise, you won't want to use the authority principle (chapter 4), since for the purposes of this conversation your boss is clearly the authority. But the liking principle might help. Assuming you like your boss and have enjoyed working together, remind them of a time when you both succeeded together at a project, and acknowledge how much you benefited from your boss's leadership and guidance. Then say something like, "The reason

I wanted to talk to you today is because I got this really attractive job offer, and it's stressing me out. I really don't want to take it because I love working for you, but the money they're throwing in front of me is so generous it would be hard for me to turn down."

You might also decide to try the reciprocity principle, reminding your boss in a tactful and nonaggressive way of what you've contributed as a prelude to requesting a pay boost. "I really like working for this company," you might say, "and I've worked on some really fun and important projects for some of our biggest clients. I've loved the challenge, and I'd love to continue doing great work for the company." Then describe the job offer you've received and explain that you'd love to collaborate with your boss to see if you can figure out a solution that will keep you at your present company.

In situations when you're seeking information from others, think through your arsenal of elicitation techniques. If you're planning on entering a car dealership to negotiate a price, and you want to understand how far they might be willing to bend, you might use the bracketing technique described in chapter 5. Suggest a possible price range and see if they'll entertain it. When confronting Amaya about her bad behavior, my wife and I nudged her to talk by affirming we had insider information about what she was doing, which in fact we did. We took care not to do this in an aggressive way—we didn't want to come across as FBI interrogators. A bit of attention to our body language (open ventrals, facial expressions that suggested mild sadness) did the trick.

Step #6: Run a Quick Manipulation Check

At this point in your planning, make sure you haven't inadvertently strayed over that all-important line between wielding influence and manipulating. Would anything you plan to say or do arouse fear in your person of interest, which in turn would compel them to take action because they feel they have to, not because they want to? If you sit down with your boss and suggest that you'll leave and mess up a key project if she doesn't agree to a raise, that's manipulative. Ditto if my wife and I were to play the guilt card with Amaya, going on and on about how much we've done for her, expressing our disappointment with her behavior, and claiming that she "owes" it to us to tell us what she was thinking. Be honest here. What impact will your actions or behavior *really* have on your person of interest? Bear in mind, too, that depending on the situation your person of interest might feel fear or some other negative emotion independently of what you say or do. As long as you haven't caused that fear or exploited it to your advantage, you can feel good about your behavior and know it isn't manipulative.

Step #7: Pump Up the Nonverbals

When planning your pretext and rapport building, you might have thought already about nonverbals, including what style of dress, tone of voice, bodily gestures, and so on you'll choose. Let's say you need to work out a dispute you're having with your best buddy, and the two of you have a classic "bro-type" relationship. If you often exchange a cool fist bump with one another as a greeting, you might have jotted that down as a small way to build some initial rapport. Or let's say you've been unhappily dating the same person for the past year and are planning on breaking it off. You might plan to start the conversation with a friendly hug—or not. Glancing back at chapter 7, list any other key nonverbals that might support your influence-building efforts and lead you toward your goal, as well as any that definitely won't. Think through as well the base emotions you will want to project at key moments. If you haven't practiced them recently, take a few minutes before your encounter to do so.

Step #8: Conduct an Authenticity Check

Now that the contours of your upcoming encounter are coming into focus, how "real" does it seem? Will your pretext, rapport building, influence building, elicitation, and body language all come across as authentic given your own personality, your person of interest's prior knowledge of your personality, and the nature of your relationship? Do any of your planned actions or statements seem out of whack, excessive, or inappropriate? Just to be sure, run your plan by a disinterested party to get their impression. Choose someone whom you trust and whose social skills you respect. If everything seems fine, consider what details, if any, you could add or tweak to make the encounter even more authentic. In setting up your pretext, is there anything more you might wish to say or do so that it is believable? Are you using props to your advantage? How might you better establish your pretext silently or implicitly through your actions rather than explicitly presenting it? And are you deploying too many details or choosing some that are deceptive? Plan for these adjustments now and you'll be happier when the big day comes.

Step #9: Prepare for Likely Contingencies

In drafting a conversation outline, you're taking stock of what you know and crafting a plan to make the most of what you can control. But quite a bit about any conversation eludes your control. You have no guarantee that the assumptions you're making about your person of interest, their state of mind, and how they are likely to respond are correct. Sometimes, for any number of reasons, they won't be, and your speech or actions will have unintended and unhelpful effects. What if your person of interest is feeling unexpectedly stressed during your conversation? What if something in your physical environment distracts you or your person of interest, or arouses an unhelpful emotion? What if you lacked important information? What if you happen to respond awkwardly in the moment or inadvertently break with your plan? What if, after all you've said and done, your person of interest simply and for whatever reason refuses to grant your request?

You can't foresee every challenge, but it does help to prepare for the most likely contingencies. If you received an attractive job offer from another company, your current boss might agree to give you a raise, but only a small one that doesn't match the other company's offer. What will you do then? If you think this through in advance, you can determine an acceptable salary threshold and use it to guide the conversation. Or you might decide that if your boss's offer falls within a certain range, you'll negotiate by asking if your boss might provide you with extra benefits, such as more time off or a more flexible work schedule, that will compensate for a lower salary.

When preparing to confront Amaya about her rule-breaking, we didn't predetermine the punishment we'd levy because we wanted to account for the possibility that extenuating circumstances had played a role and she wasn't quite so guilty as it seemed. Instead, we came up with a few possible punishment options of varying severity. When we confronted Amaya, we learned that in fact one of her friends had sneakily lured her into participating in the chat room. Once she was in, she found it extremely difficult to extricate herself without losing face with her friends. She didn't tell us because she was embarrassed and fearful of how we'd react. Although Amaya had clearly broken a rule, she hadn't willfully disobeyed us. We did have to punish her to make our displeasure clear, but a harsh punishment wasn't warranted. Instead, following one of our contingency plans, we placed more emphasis on helping her devise strategies for dealing with peer pressure in the future and for communicating better with us. If we hadn't thought about likely contingencies and had stuck to an overly simple plan that called only for her to accept responsibility and suffer the consequences, we'd have missed a chance to identify and address the underlying issue.

Thinking through contingencies in advance and how you might respond, you'll be more likely to respond well in the moment and behave in ways that serve your interests. Conversely, I've seen professional hacking encounters go bad simply because we didn't consider obvious contingencies. In one instance, we broke into one of our client's buildings posing as pest control guys. Since we had to fly to a faraway city to do the job, we couldn't bring all of the professional-grade pest-spraying equipment we usually take with us to lend credibility to our pretext. Instead, we went to Walmart and picked up some cheap spraying devices. If we had planned properly, we'd have considered the possibility that an alert security guard who had observed exterminators in action before would have noticed our subpar equipment and called us out on it. We could have generated a plan to respond in a way that might have been believable—say, by acknowledging that our equipment was crappy and explaining that we used this equipment for smaller jobs and professional-grade equipment for larger, more complicated jobs. Instead, we arrived at our target facility and couldn't answer well when confronted. The security guards became suspicious. Access *denied*.

Step #10: Solidify Your Gains

Despite all that lies beyond your control, your conversation might still proceed as planned, leading you to realize your goal. What then? In most situations, it's helpful and appropriate to follow up afterward to solidify your gains. If your boss agrees to a raise, capture her agreement in writing so you both remember the details. Don't do this in an overly legalistic way. Send a friendly email in which you run through the details, thank your boss, and invite her to correct you if you got anything wrong. If you're negotiating to buy a car, sign the contract right then and there. The last thing you want to do is leave, as that will only give the dealer a chance to reconsider and perhaps back out. In situations where you don't have a written agreement and where an email might not be appropriate, make sure you at least shake hands and repeat the agreed-upon "terms" in a positive way, as this makes it more difficult for the other party to reconsider without losing face. If you hire a landscaper for your property, say something like, "I'm so glad to have found you guys, and I think $75 per week for cutting the grass and $150 for the spring cleanup is more than fair. Thank you so much!" You might also ask the landscaper to write the agreed-upon fee down on a business card or text it to you, justifying the request by noting that you have a bad memory.

WORKING WITH YOUR CONVERSATION OUTLINE

Now that you understand what a conversation outline is, begin preparing them for your upcoming encounters. It might take you ten to fifteen minutes to map out a conversation, less after you've done it a few times. To enhance your preparation, take an extra couple of minutes and play out the encounter in your mind after you've outlined it, imagining exactly what you and your person of interest might do or say.

Don't push your planning too far. If you find yourself spending more than fifteen to twenty minutes on a conversation outline, or if you're tweaking and fine-tuning the outline repeatedly in the days before an encounter, or if you're creating a conversation outline far in advance of a conversation (several weeks as opposed to days), then you're overdoing it. Not only do you risk coming across as too scripted, stiff, and inauthentic; if you're too reliant on your plan, you might freak out and become paralyzed when your conversations take unanticipated turns. Successful hackers strike a balance between planning and attention to detail on the one hand and allowing room for improvisation and the exercise of real-time judgment on the other. If your DISC profile pegs you as a C-type, you'll want to stay especially alert to over-planning, since that is your natural inclination.

It's almost inevitable that some of your conversations will go seriously awry, even if you've taken care to plan for likely contingencies. What if you come in to ask your boss for a raise only to find that she is in tears, having just learned of a death in her family? What if you sit down for a much-anticipated, high-stakes sales call only to learn that your chief competitor has just announced a 20 percent reduction in the price of a product that's identical to yours? What if these conversations kick off as planned, but you find that despite your best efforts you simply can't nudge your person of interest to give you what you want?

Professional hackers face challenges like this all the time, and we often manage to adapt quickly and salvage the situation. Remember how we hacked into a bank in a developing country that was protected by guards on motorbikes carrying automatic weapons (chapter 8)? Our initial plan called for me and a colleague to show up ourselves to perform the hack. When we arrived in the country and scoped out the building, we were surprised to discover all of these heavily armed guards. Nobody had told us about them, and we hadn't learned about them while performing desk research from afar. The presence of that weaponry posed a whole new level of risk. If our plan backfired, we could get shot. Instead of calling off the hack, we adjusted our plan to lower the risk. In this country, most inhabitants were dark-skinned, and we stood out as Caucasian Americans. Rather than barge in aggressively and demand that security let us in so that we could conduct some technical testing, as we had initially planned, we judged that a softer, lower-key approach would be safer. Thinking creatively, we hired a local to engage security in conversation while we hustled busily past them, acting as if we were supposed to be there and had been there before.

In this instance, we had enough time to whip up a new plan in advance. Other times, I've spontaneously generated solutions midstream that allowed me to salvage encounters once they were under way. In one instance, we were trying to break into the office of the CEO of a large organization to see if we could gain access to sensitive documents. Through social media, we learned that the CEO was going away for two weeks to an exotic locale for a family vacation. While he was gone, I showed up at his office wearing a computer technician's suit and claiming I had come to fix the CEO's computer. In asking his assistant to let me into the CEO's office, I told her he had prescheduled this repair with us in advance and expected it to be completed by the time he was back.

Despite my best efforts, she refused to let me in. I was stumped. My plan hadn't worked, and it looked like I'd have to abandon it. But then I got an idea. Pulling out my clipboard, I said, "Okay, I totally understand that you can't let me in. But I'm going to get in trouble if I can't do the repair. If the answer really is no, then I'm just going to ask if you could sign this form saying that you're rejecting the repair." This move put added pressure on her. If she didn't let me in, she risked angering her boss. By asking her to sign, I was clarifying and intensifying this dilemma for her, creating a new power differential between the two of us. As a tactic it was mildly manipulative, not something I'd do in everyday life, but permissible given the parameters of my engagement with this company. The assistant didn't want to sign my clipboard, but when I insisted that either she or someone else do so, she finally caved and let me in. Thinking creatively in the moment, I had deviated slightly from my original plan but had managed to bring it to a successful conclusion.

Some people are more flexible than others when facing unforeseen challenges. But you can improve your ability to stay calm and adaptable. Typically, in stressful situations we become flustered, our "fight/ flight/freeze" response activating. The key to staying flexible is to learn to monitor your emotional state more closely than you currently might. When you feel yourself becoming fearful or flustered, do what you can to step out of it so that you can regain your composure. This might be as simple as pausing during a conversation for a few seconds and taking a deep breath or two. In other circumstances, maybe you excuse yourself to go to the bathroom, giving yourself five or ten minutes to collect yourself and to think of possible solutions. In still other circumstances, you might be able to ask for a day or two to think before continuing the conversation. When undertaking your upcoming social encounters, practice staying focused minute to minute on your emotions (remind yourself to do this just before these encounters begin). As you plan for these conversations, think in advance of possible ways you might temporarily and graciously take leave and regain your composure.

If you do have to pause the interaction, perform a quick status check-in once you're back. Is your rapport still intact or is it ruined? Ask some questions of your person of interest and observe their body language to gauge their emotional state. If your rapport is ruined, find a tactful way to end the conversation. If some rapport still exists, consider adopting new rapport-building tactics or switch to a different pretext. If you maintain your pretext, one technique you can use with an unwilling person of interest is to engage them in a mini negotiation that nudges them toward your desired goal. Earlier in the book, I described how I hacked a large warehouse even though I didn't have a government-issued ID, as requested by the security guards. When the guard correctly pointed this out, I pivoted and said, "Hey, look, I just spent ten minutes going through all the previous security checks. I've got many other stops to make after this one—I can't go all the way back to my car now. Could I just use this corporate badge?" If he were following protocol, he would have politely declined instead of motioning me through. But we had reached a middle ground that allowed me to achieve my goal of gaining entry, and him his goal of feeling like he had done some due diligence. As your planned conversations proceed and you begin to meet resistance, think of potential "compromises" you might propose, taking care not to go too far and verge into manipulation.

Some unexpected challenges are so daunting that you're better off simply abandoning your hack. On one occasion, my team and I attempted to enter a government facility by posing as photographers and asking for admittance to a secure area. Unbeknownst to us, a high-ranking political figure was visiting the facility that day, which meant that the place was crawling with every species of law enforcement officer known to humanity. There must have been 150 officers thronging the grounds. I knew it wasn't such a good idea to go through with my plan, but I dismissed those doubts and tried the hack anyway.

Approaching the security cordon, my team and I found that instead of the usual hired guards on duty, a sheriff was also present. When I handed over my fake driver's license to obtain a security badge, he immediately recognized it as a fake, whereas a hired guard probably wouldn't have. When I insisted that the driver's license was real, the sheriff became suspicious and drew his gun on me, as did a couple of other officers standing nearby. They put us in handcuffs and arrested me for trespassing and possessing a fake ID. Although they would eventually release me once they learned of our true purpose, our pretext was blown. We could try again to compromise the facility, but there was no way we could pose as photographers. We would have to develop an entirely new role to play.

Forcing an encounter greatly increases your risk of failure. You probably won't get arrested or shot as I almost did, but you might appear awkward or tone-deaf, alienate a person of interest, or receive a negative reply to your request. You're much better off being patient and giving yourself permission to achieve your goal on a different day or in a different way. If you do have to abandon your plan, remember that there's no shame in failing. The only shame is in forgetting to identify your shortcomings and remedy them. Following each failure, my team and I debrief, analyzing how and why our carefully conceived plan didn't deliver. You can debrief yourself, asking specific questions such as:

- At what point did I feel overly emotional?
- At what point did I see it spiraling out of control?
- What statements of mine did the other person fail to understand? How could I have articulated my thoughts better?
- Did I say anything mean, sarcastic, or cutting?
- What needs or desires of the other person did I fail to take into account?
- Could the other person have handled the conversation better?
- Do I need to revisit the conversation or is it best forgotten?
- What could I have done to have left the other person better off for having met me?

Debrief, too, when your plans succeed. What worked well for you? What might you have done differently? How did your performance this time stack up with your previous hacking efforts? Are you seeing progress in key areas? In what areas are you still struggling to improve? What specific skills should you work on next? Every social engagement represents a valuable opportunity to learn about yourself, to improve your grasp of hacking skills, and to register your ongoing progress. As much practice as you put in, as smooth and effective as you might become in social settings, there's always room for growth and improvement. A hacker's training is never done.

EMPATHY ROCKS

One more piece of advice: as you use conversational outlines to plot upcoming encounters, pause and reflect on what you're *really* doing with this tool and, indeed, with all of the hacking principles and tactics presented in this book. In systematically researching and planning conversations in advance, we're prompting ourselves to become more aware of other people and how we hope to interact with them. To a lesser extent and in a more informal way, we're also doing that in the moment when we spontaneously deploy hacking techniques. At bottom, hacking humans is really about training ourselves to observe others more closely, think about *them*, and behave in ways that allow them to fulfill their needs and wishes, so that they in turn will help us out with ours. Hacking isn't perfectly altruistic, but it does allow you to make a powerful difference in others' lives—all because you've become far more mindful and deliberate in your social exchanges than you otherwise would be.

Remember, so much of the turbulence we experience in our relationships with others arises because we're ignorant and uncontrolled in our actions. We might regard ourselves as kind, caring people, and perhaps we are most of the time and in important ways. But most of us still stumble blindly through many of our interactions, wholly or partially ignorant of how others are feeling, how they're experiencing us, and what they need, want, and expect from us. We crack a joke or make small talk or raise our voices or behave in a thousand other ways because it somehow feels right to *us* or makes *us* feel good in the moment, unaware that it is causing others discomfort or turning them off. Transfixed by our own emotions, we let them dictate what we say or do minute to minute.

When beginners first practice human hacking, they suddenly understand all that they have been missing in their social interactions.

They start to pay more attention to others and their experience than they had been. They become more empathetic, more sensitive to others and their feelings, and they also become more aware of their behavior and its impact. Realizing they enjoy far more control over their own behavior than they ever imagined, they begin to craft their own speech and behaviors to improve how others experience them. Over time, they train themselves to observe, empathize, and control their behavior automatically in the moment. Awareness of and empathy toward others leading to deliberate action on our part: that's the essence of the hacking super power I've presented in this book.

It's possible you'll take this super power and use it to malicious ends, like the worst criminal hackers do. But I feel pretty confident that you won't. You signed that solemn pledge at the beginning of this book. You don't want to go back on your word, do you? If you ever do, accidentally or not, I know you'll regret it and mend your ways. Once you see the damage manipulation can inflict, as I have, you'll feel awful about it (if you're not a total psychopath) and do your utmost to stay firmly on the side of good. On the other hand, as you experience how fulfilling it can be to use hacking skills to benefit others, I strongly suspect you'll seek out opportunities to do more of that. On a number of occasions, I've seen people undergo lasting transformations upon first learning hacking techniques, fundamentally reorienting their lives toward helping others.

Hacking profoundly changed my student Doug. Picture this big, scary biker dude—shaved head, big beer gut, gruff demeanor, a "colorful" vocabulary, long white beard, the whole deal. That's Doug when he first showed up in my class. If you saw him walking toward you in a dark alley, you'd probably turn around. During the first day of our week-long class, I wondered what, if anything, he'd get out of what I was teaching. He seemed to have a sneering attitude toward it, at best. It turned out I was misreading him entirely. Toward the end of the week, Doug requested a private meeting with me. He told me he had been greatly affected by learning hacking techniques—it had changed his whole perspective on his behavior and his interactions with others. "From now on," he said, "I'm going to make sure that every person I meet leaves better off for having met me. And I'm going to do something nice for at least one person every day."

Doug had already begun putting his new discipline into practice. That morning, he had been eating breakfast in his hotel's restaurant when a fellow patron began loudly berating a waitress for poor service. The waitress had done nothing to deserve this treatment and was visibly upset. Cued in to the waitress's emotions, Doug felt moved to do something about it. He might have approached the fellow patron and yelled at him, calling him a jerk and who knows what else. Or he might have approached the waitress and commiserated with her about what a big, fat [insert colorful word] that patron had been. But Doug was sensitive to the feelings of others in earshot as well, and he knew neither of those options would have left them better off for having encountered him. Rather, these negative exchanges would have disturbed them and prevented them from enjoying their breakfasts.

After thinking about it for a moment, Doug approached the waitress, smiled at her, and in a soft voice, said, "I just want you to know that I appreciate everything you do." That's it. With no selfish motive of his own, Doug offered this woman the gift of a kind word, affirming her as a professional and as a person. All week long, he had focused on amping up his emotional intelligence—to empathize with others and to take deliberate action to connect with them. He had been impressed by the super power he had gained during our class and felt called to use it for good, not evil.

As you practice and eventually master your human hacking skills, use your newfound power to leave others better off. Think about what *they* want. Cue into what *they're* feeling. Make a special effort to build rapport. Wield influence techniques to make it pleasant for them to grant your wishes. Be yourself with others and speak as truthfully as you can. React graciously when others deny your requests. Hacking isn't as uniformly malicious as the media often portrays it to be. There are good hackers out there, too, and they're making the world a better place. Join us. Helping others feel great around you is the smoothest, most effective, most fulfilling way to get what you want. It gets me inside highly secured buildings and IT systems, and it will help you advance at work, build stronger relationships at home, and deal more effectively in any situation. Always—*always*—leave them better off for having met you. Empathy rocks!

ACKNOWLEDGMENTS

I never would have had the opportunity to put my thoughts down on paper had my friend Joe Navarro not introduced me to my extraordinary agent, Steve Ross, and had Steve not decided to take a chance on me. Thank you, Joe and Steve.

I'm grateful to my collaborator, Seth Schulman, who has an uncanny ability to take words, thoughts, and emotions and bring them alive on the page. Working with Seth has been a joy, a learning experience, and a blessing.

To Hollis Heimbouch, thank you for spotting the potential of this project. Your input and partnership during the writing process was absolutely perfect and greatly appreciated. I also want to thank the members of the HarperCollins team as well as Seth's colleagues for their help with research, fact checking, copyediting, and more. Your tireless work has made this book all it could be.

A number of people have shaped the ideas in this book over the years. My profound thanks go out to Dr. Paul Ekman, Robin Dreeke, Joe Navarro, and Ryan MacDougall. All of you have challenged me and helped me to improve. I also want to thank the core group that helped me create and run the Social Engineering Village: Jim Manley, Chris Roberts, Billy Boatright, Wayne Ronaldson, Chris, Kris, and

Hannah Silvers, and the rest of the SEVillage Crew—as well as Jamison Scheeres, who planted the seeds of what would become SECOM and my company. I'm grateful as well to the many security professionals and citizens who have taken my courses over the years—you've taught me every bit as much as I've taught you.

My involvement with the Innocent Lives Foundation has deeply impacted me. Tim Maloney, thanks to you I am constantly expanding my horizons and learning to be more caring and compassionate. Neil Fallon, not only do you create some of the world's best music, but you personify the spirit of this book and remind me always to stay attuned to *people* and their feelings.

I wish to acknowledge my best friends on this planet, Nick and Claire Furneaux, Ben and Selena Barnes, Kazuyuki and Amanda Nishi, Neil and Marilyn Vitale, and Mark and Teanna Hammann. You guys have been through it all with me, giving me more than I've given you. Thank you.

Lastly but certainly not least, my profound belief in God and the amazing family I have has directly led me to this point. My family has steadfastly supported me as I started and built the world's first company focused entirely on social engineering. Areesa, Colin, and Amaya, thank you for helping me become a better husband, dad, and human. You, of all people, have left me feeling better for having met you.

APPENDIX: DISC CHEAT SHEETS

DISC CHEAT SHEET—D "THE DOMINANT"

"D"s want others to be direct, to the point, open, straightforward, and focused on results.	
How do you know you might be a "D": People describe you as pushy, harsh, aggressive, or domineering but also see you as a go-getter and someone who gets things done.	

TO IDENTIFY A "D" IN		TO COMMUNICATE WITH A "D" PROPERLY:	
WORDS	ACTIONS	Be willing to:	Prepare for:
they want to know WHAT	very task focused	be brief and to the point	bluntness
rather tell than ask	may be impatient	respect need for autonomy	lack of empathy
rather talk than listen	will be direct		lack of sensitivity
may seem rude or pushy	are willing to take risks	be clear about expectations	short conversations
use authority	conscious of time	let them be a leader	abrupt comments
talk fast	history of achievements	show you are competent	
will be blunt	rely on gut feelings	stick to topic	
start with own opinions	willing to start trouble	be independent	

IF YOU ARE MANAGING A D, HERE ARE SOME TIPS:			
To help them grow you can help them:			
to feel empathy	to ask more questions	to base decisions on logic	to relax a little
to slow down and listen	to compliment others	to soften body language	to be approachable
What they want in return:			
to be in authority	freedom from details	to have power	direct answers
large challenges	flexibility	clearly defined expectations	some prestige

ON SOCIAL MEDIA "D"S WILL OFTEN:			
be short	focus on the theme	focus on the task	be aggressive

DISC CHEAT SHEET—I "THE INFLUENCER"

"I"s like others to be emotionally honest, friendly, have a sense of humor, and most of all to recognize their accomplishments.

How do you know you might be an "I":
People describe you as outgoing, braggy, competitive, superficial, but having a great sense of humor and in need of recognition.

TO IDENTIFY AN "I" IN		TO COMMUNICATE WITH AN "I" PROPERLY:	
WORDS	ACTIONS	Be willing to:	Prepare for:
they want to know WHO	use facial expressions	try an informal approach	attempts to influence
rather tell than ask	are spontaneous	be relaxed	need for spotlight
rather talk than listen	like to laugh	let them talk about feelings	overestimations
tend to go on tangents/ exaggerate	have a short attention span	keep it light	overselling
use a lot of stories	will appear warm	provide written details	vulnerable to rejection
talk fast	may be a close talker	give public praise	attempts to persuade
like to share emotion	brag about themselves	use humor	

IF YOU ARE MANAGING AN "I," HERE ARE SOME TIPS:

To help them grow you can help them:

with time management	with organization	be more analytical	
be objective	to emphasize clear results	feel a sense of urgency	

What they want in return:

to be popular	public praise	warm relationships	
visible rewards	approval	freedom from details	

ON SOCIAL MEDIA "I"S WILL OFTEN:

talk about themselves	brag a little bit	focus on looks	take lots of selfies

DISC CHEAT SHEET—S "THE STEADY"

"S"s want you to be agreeable, cooperative, and show appreciation while being relaxed.			
How do you know you might be a "S": People describe you as apathetic, unwilling to change, slow but also very supportive, a good listener, and having a good bedside manner.			
TO IDENTIFY AN "S" IN		TO COMMUNICATE WITH AN "S" PROPERLY:	
WORDS	ACTIONS	Be willing to:	Prepare for:
they want to know WHY	ask for opinions	be logical	friendliness
rather ask than tell	like friendly environments	provide security	resistance to change
listen more, talk less	like casual environments	give time for change	difficulty prioritizing
slow and steady	patient	show them they are important	difficulty making deadlines
are reserved	service minded	take time with changes	resistance to spotlight
quiet	not flashy or seeking recognition	be sincere	
warm	tolerant of others		
IF YOU ARE MANAGING AN "S," HERE ARE SOME TIPS:			
To help them grow you can help them:			
be open to change	learn to brag	to believe in themselves and state their opinions	
with self-affirmation	learn to present		
What they want in return:			
private appreciation	calm relationships	security	time to adjust
happy relationships	standard procedure	sincerity	to be heard
ON SOCIAL MEDIA "S"S WILL OFTEN:			
talk about their teammates	be very sincere	use emotion	be steady and dependable

DISC CHEAT SHEET—C "THE CONSCIENTIOUS"

"C"s want to get to the details. They want others to be accurate, pay attention to detail, and minimize socializing.

How do you know you might be a "C":
People describe you as accurate and detailed but at times overly critical, negative, and nitpicky. Although shy, you value your few close relationships.

TO IDENTIFY A "C" IN		TO COMMUNICATE WITH A "C" PROPERLY:	
WORDS	ACTIONS	Be willing to:	Prepare for:
they want to know HOW	focus on tasks	give clear deadlines	dislike of vagueness
rather ask than tell	very orderly	show you are dependable	desire to double-check facts
listen more, talk less	very meticulous	show loyalty	doesn't need other people
doesn't overreact	precise and accurate	be tactful and reserved	lots of research
slower rate of speech	time conscious	be precise	cautiousness
talk vs. write	hard to read	value high standards	
detailed and precise	wants to be right	be focused	

IF YOU ARE MANAGING A "C," HERE ARE SOME TIPS:

To help them grow you can help them:

be tolerant	enjoy groups	accept others' limitations	
learn to seek help	accept others' ideas		

What they want in return:

clear expectations	verification of facts	chance to shine	clear task outline
professionalism	no quick changes	personal autonomy	

ON SOCIAL MEDIA "C"S WILL OFTEN:

use lots of detail	ensure pictures are perfect	have longer posts	state lots of facts

NOTES

INTRODUCTION: YOUR NEW SUPER POWER

1. Rod Scher, "Is This the Most Dangerous Man in America?," *Computer Power User*, July 2011, https://www.social-engineer.org/content/CPU-MostDangerousMan.pdf.
2. Christopher Hadnagy, *Social Engineering: The Art of Human Hacking* (Indianapolis: Wiley, 2010).
3. Simon Baron-Cohen, *The Science of Evil: On Empathy and the Origins of Cruelty* (New York: Basic Books, 2011).
4. See, for example, Shahirah Majumdar, "Why Empathy Is Bad," *Vice*, December 21, 2016, https://www.vice.com/en_us/article/78bj8a/why-empathy-is-bad; Paul Bloom, *Against Empathy: The Case for Rational Compassion* (New York: HarperCollins, 2016).

CHAPTER 1: KNOW YOURSELF, SO YOU CAN KNOW OTHERS

1. This is based on a true story: Jon Willing, "City Treasurer Was Victim of a 'Whaling' Scam, Transferred $100K to Phoney Supplier," *Ottawa Citizen*, April 8, 2019, https://ottawacitizen.com/news/local-news/city-treasurer-was-victim-to-a-whaling-scam-transferred-100k-to-phoney-supplier.
2. Andrew Duffy, "Florida Man Named as Suspect in City of Ottawa Fraud Case Faces Trial in U.S. Email Scam," *Ottawa Citizen*, April 10, 2019, https://ottawacitizen.com/news/local-news/florida-man-named-as-suspect-in-city-of-ottawa-fraud-case-faces-trial-in-u-s-email-scam/.

3. Dentists, for instance, might use DISC to motivate their patients to floss regularly and brush their teeth. See Mark Scarbecz, "Using the DISC System to Motivate Dental Patients," *Journal of the American Dental Association* 138, no. 3 (March 2007): 381–85, doi:10.14219 /jada.archive.2007.0171.

4. One study, for instance, found that using DISC when forming teams improved the creativity of teams and helped people work better to- gether. See Ioanna Lykourentzou et al., "Personality Matters: Bal- ancing for Personality Types Leads to Better Outcomes for Crowd Teams," *Proceedings of the 19th ACM Conference on Computer-Supported Cooperative Work & Social Computing* (February 2016): 260–73, https://doi.org/10.1145/2818048.2819979. For what it's worth, the commercial DISC testing service that my company uses has also pro- vided me with their own research showing that DISC is reliable and beneficial.

5. "Everything DiSC: A Wiley Brand," Everything DiSC, accessed April 3, 2020, https://www.everythingdisc.com/EverythingDiSC/media/Site Files/Assets/History/Everything-DiSC-resources-historyofdisc-time line.pdf.

6. Stan Phelps, "Five Lessons on Delivering Breakaway CX from For- rester's CXNYC Conference," *Forbes*, July 19, 2017, https://www .forbes.com/sites/stanphelps/2017/07/19/five-lessons-on-delivering -breakaway-cx-from-forresters-cxnyc-conference/#63af4dce4f9d.

7. "Avista Warns of Scammers Continuing to Target Utility Custom- ers," KHQ-TV, June 18, 2019, https://www.khq.com/news/avista -warns-of-scammers-continuing-to-target-utility-customers/article _ed857844-91df-11e9-a6f2-2b08fc7d4d40.html.

CHAPTER 2: BECOME THE PERSON YOU NEED TO BE

1. "100 Funny Jokes and Quotes about Love, Sex and Marriage," *Tele- graph*, December 14, 2018, https://www.telegraph.co.uk/comedy /comedians/100-funny-jokes-quotes-love-sex-marriage/richard-jeni/.

2. Malcolm Gladwell, *Talking to Strangers: What We Should Know about the People We Don't Know* (New York: Little, Brown, 2019), 73.

3. Ibid.

4. Brittany Taylor, "Scam Caught on Camera: Man Accused of Imperson- ating West U. Public Works Employee," KPRC-TV, January 22, 2019,

https://www.click2houston.com/news/scam-caught-on-camera-man
-accused-of-impersonating-west-u-public-works-employee.

5. Clifford Lo, "Scammers Swindle Hong Kong Man out of HK$430,000 in the Space of Four Hours on WhatsApp," *South China Morning Post*, January 17, 2019, https://www.scmp.com/news/hong-kong/law-and -crime/article/2182575/scammers-swindle-hong-kong-man-out -hk430000-space-four.

6. Kathy Bailes, "Two Parents Fall Prey to St. Lawrence College Fees Email Scam," *Isle of Thanet News*, January 8, 2019, https://theisle ofthanetnews.com/2019/01/08/two-parents-fall-prey-to-st-lawrence -college-fees-email-scam/.

7. I draw this account of Lustig from "The Most Notorious Financial Frauds in History," *Telegraph*, June 6, 2016, https://www.telegraph.co .uk/money/consumer-affairs/the-most-notorious-financial-frauds -in-history/victor-lustig/; and Jeff Maysh, "The Man Who Sold the Eiffel Tower. Twice," *Smithsonian Magazine*, March 9, 2016, https:// www.smithsonianmag.com/history/man-who-sold-eiffel-tower-twice -180958370/.

8. This reported but unconfirmed quote appears in Maysh, "The Man Who Sold the Eiffel Tower. Twice."

9. David J. Dance, "Pretexting: A Necessary Means to a Necessary End?" *Drake Law Review* 56, no. 3 (Spring 2008): 807, https://lawreview drake.files.wordpress.com/2015/06/lrvol56-3_dance.pdf.

10. William Safire, "Pretexting," *New York Times*, September 24, 2006, https://www.nytimes.com/2006/09/24/magazine/pretexting.html.

11. See Art Markman, "How Your Personality Shines Through," *Psychology Today*, August 5, 2010, https://www.psychologytoday.com/us/blog /ulterior-motives/201008/how-your-personality-shines-through. This article reports on Ryne A. Sherman, Christopher S. Nave, and David C. Funder, "Situational Similarity and Personality Predict Behavioral Consistency," *Journal of Personality and Social Psychology* 99, no. 2 (August 2010): 330–43.

12. Christopher Soto, "Personality Can Change Over a Lifetime, and Usually for the Better," NPR, June 30, 2016, https://www.npr.org/sections /health-shots/2016/06/30/484053435/personality-can-change-over -a-lifetime-and-usually-for-the-better.

13. I've changed certain details in this story to preserve confidentiality.

CHAPTER 3: NAIL THE APPROACH

1. Something that scholars refer to as "homophily." For more, please see Alessandro Di Stefano et al., "Quantifying the Role of Homophily in Human Cooperation Using Multiplex Evolutionary Game Theory," *PLOS One* 10, no. 10 (2015), doi:10.1371/journal.pone.0140646.

2. Amos Nadler and Paul J. Zak, "Hormones and Economic Decisions," in *Neuroeconomics*, ed. Martin Reuter and Christian Montag (Berlin: Springer-Verlag, 2016), 41–66. See also Jorge A. Barraza and Paul J. Zak, "Empathy toward Strangers Triggers Oxytocin Release and Subsequent Generosity," *Annals of the New York Academy of Sciences* 1667, no. 1 (June 2009): 182–89, https://doi.org/10.1111/j.1749-6632.2009.04504.x.

3. See, for example, Clint Berge, "Barron Co. Residents Scammed out of $100K as Sheriff Gives Warning," WQOW News 18, June 24, 2019, https://wqow.com/news/top-stories/2019/06/24/barron-co-residents-scammed-out-of-100k-as-sheriff-gives-warning/.

4. For social engineering's code of ethics, please see "The Social Engineering Framework," Security Through Education, accessed November 13, 2019, https://www.social-engineer.org/framework/general-discussion/code-of-ethics/.

5. Ewa Jacewicz et al., "Articulation Rate across Dialect, Age, and Gender," *Language Variation and Change* 21, no. 2 (July 2009): 233–56, doi:10.1017/S0954394509990093.

6. Yanan Wang, "These Are the States with the Fastest Talkers (New York Isn't One of Them)," *Washington Post*, February 4, 2016, https://www.washingtonpost.com/news/morning-mix/wp/2016/02/04/these-are-the-states-with-the-fastest-talkers-new-york-isnt-one-of-them/; Marchex Marketing Team, "America's Speech Patterns Uncovered," *Marchex* (blog), February 2, 2016, https://www.marchex.com/blog/talkative.

7. David Cox, "Is Your Voice Trustworthy, Engaging or Soothing to Strangers?," *Guardian*, April 16, 2015, https://www.theguardian.com/science/blog/2015/apr/16/is-your-voice-trustworthy-engaging-or-soothing-to-strangers.

8. The literature on this topic is vast. See, for example, Will Storr, "The Metamorphosis of the Western Soul," *New York Times*, August 24, 2018, https://www.nytimes.com/2018/08/24/opinion/the-metamorphosis-of-the-western-soul.html.

9. Sidney Kraus, *Televised Presidential Debates and Public Policy* (New York and London: Routledge, 2000), 66.

10. Thomas R. Zentall, "Reciprocal Altruism in Rats: Why Does It Occur?," *Learning & Behavior* 44 (March 2016): 7–8, https://doi.org/10.3758/s13420-015-0201-2.

11. Janelle Weaver, "Monkeys Go Out on a Limb to Show Gratitude," *Nature*, January 12, 2010, https://doi.org/10.1038/news.2010.9.

12. Hajo Adam and Adam D. Galinsky, "Enclothed Cognition," *Journal of Experimental Social Psychology* 48, no. 4 (July 2012): 918–25, doi: https://doi.org/10.1016/j.jesp.2012.02.008.

CHAPTER 4: MAKE THEM WANT TO HELP YOU

1. Mathukutty M. Monippally, *Business Communication: From Principles to Practice* (New Delhi: McGraw Hill Education, 2013), 137.

2. Robert B. Cialdini, *Influence: The Psychology of Persuasion* (Melbourne: Business Library, 1984.).

3. Dave Kerpen, *The Art of People: 11 Simple People Skills That Will Get You Everything You Want* (New York: Crown Business, 2016); Peter Economy, "How the Platinum Rule Trumps the Golden Rule Every Time," *Inc.*, March 17, 2016, https://www.inc.com/peter-economy/how-the-platinum-rule-trumps-the-golden-rule-every-time.html.

4. Mama Donna Henes, "The Universal Golden Rule," Huffington Post, updated December 23, 2012, https://www.huffpost.com/entry/golden-rule_b_2002245; W. Patrick Cunningham, "The Golden Rule as Universal Ethical Norm," *Journal of Business Ethics* 17, no. 1 (January 1998): 105–9.

5. Jonathan L. Freedman and Scott C. Fraser, "Compliance without Pressure: The Foot-in-the-Door Technique," *Journal of Personality and Social Psychology* 4, no. 2 (1966): 195–202, https://doi.org/10.1037/h0023552.

6. Michael Lynn, "Scarcity Effects on Value: A Quantitative Review of the Commodity Theory Literature," *Psychology & Marketing* 8, no. 1 (1991), 43–57; Luigi Mittone and Lucia Savadori, "The Scarcity Bias," *Applied Psychology* 58, no. 3 (July 2009): 453–68, https://doi.org/10.1111/j.1464-0597.2009.00401.x.

7. Paul Dunn, "The Importance of Consistency in Establishing Cognitive-Based Trust: A Laboratory Experiment," *Teaching Business Ethics* 4

(August 2000): 285–306, https://doi.org/10.1023/A:100987041
7073.

8. Alfonso Pulido, Dorian Stone, and John Strevel, "The Three Cs of Customer Satisfaction: Consistency, Consistency, Consistency," McKinsey & Company, March 2014, https://www.mckinsey.com/industries/retail/our-insights/the-three-cs-of-customer-satisfaction-consistency-consistency-consistency.

9. Robert B. Cialdini et al., "Compliance with a Request in Two Cultures: The Differential Influence of Social Proof and Commitment/Consistency on Collectivists and Individualists," Personality and Social Psychology Bulletin 25, no. 10 (October 1999): 1242–53, https://doi.org/10.1177/0146167299258006.

10. Stanley Milgram, "Behavioral Study of Obedience," Journal of Abnormal and Social Psychology 67, no. 4 (1963): 376, https://doi.org/10.1037/h0040525.

11. Brandi Vincent, "The Federal Trade Commission Warns That Criminals' 'Favorite Ruse' Is Pretending to Be from a Government Agency," Next Gov, July 2, 2019, https://www.nextgov.com/cio-briefing/2019/07/scammers-are-impersonating-government-agencies-more-ever/158165/.

12. Adam J. Hampton, Amanda N. Fisher Boyd, and Susan Sprecher, "You're Like Me and I Like You: Mediators of the Similarity-Liking Link Assessed before and after a Getting-Acquainted Social Interaction," Journal of Social and Personal Relationships 36, no. 7 (July 2019): 2221–44, https://doi.org/10.1177/0265407518790411.

CHAPTER 5: MAKE THEM WANT TO TELL YOU

1. Susan Krauss Whitbourne, professor emerita of psychological and brain sciences at the University of Massachusetts Amherst, describes the general landscape of self-disclosure in the following terms: "One theory of self-disclosure proposes that you tend to reciprocate because you assume that someone who discloses to you likes and trusts you. The more you self-disclose in turn, the more the partner likes and trusts you, and then self-discloses even more. This is the social attraction-trust hypothesis of self-disclosure reciprocity. The second hypothesis is based on social exchange theory, and proposes that we reciprocate self-disclosure in order to keep a balance in the relationship: You disclose, therefore

I disclose" (Susan Krauss Whitbourne, "The Secret to Revealing Your Secrets," *Psychology Today*, April 1, 2014, https://www.psychology today.com/us/blog/fulfillment-any-age/201404/the-secret-revealing -your-secrets).

Even more fundamentally, scholars have argued that as social creatures, human beings naturally believe others (or "default to truth"). For more on the "truth-default theory" and the consequences of human gullibility, please see Timothy R. Levine *Duped: Truth-Default Theory and the Social Science of Lying and Deception* (Tuscaloosa: University of Alabama Press, 2020) and Gladwell, *Talking to Strangers*.

2. Jeff Stone, "LinkedIn Is Becoming China's Go-to Platform for Recruiting Foreign Spies," CyberScoop, March 26, 2019, https://www .cyberscoop.com/linkedin-china-spies-kevin-mallory-ron-hansen/; Anthony Cuthbertson, "China Is Spying on the West Using LinkedIn, Intelligence Agency Claims," *Newsweek*, December 11, 2017, https:// www.newsweek.com/china-spying-west-using-linkedin-743788.

3. This scenario is envisaged in "Elicitation," National Counterintelligence and Security Center, accessed December 16, 2019, https://www .dni.gov/files/NCSC/documents/campaign/Elicitation.pdf.

4. Sharon Stone, "Michigan State Police Tweet Warning Signs for Terrorism," *Tri-County Times*, April 22, 2019, https://www.tctimes.com /news/michigan-state-police-tweet-warning-signs-for-terrorism /article_65d7c0fc-653c-11e9-904c-bb92d94c6056.html.

5. Sixty-eight percent is a made-up data point. I can't recall the exact statistic here nor the newspaper, but we did use a real statistic we'd found in an actual newspaper article. In case you're interested, in 2010 the *Guardian* reported that one in five people use a birthday for a PIN (Sceaf Berry, "One in Five Use Birthday as PIN Number," *Telegraph*, October 27, 2010, https://www.telegraph.co.uk/finance/personal finance/borrowing/creditcards/8089674/One-in-five-use-birthday -as-PIN-number.html), and in 2012 it reported that 10.7 percent of all people use 1234 (Nick Berry, "The Most Common Pin Numbers: Is Your Bank Account Vulnerable?" *Guardian*, September 28, 2012, https://www.theguardian.com/money/blog/2012/sep/28/debit -cards-currentaccounts).

6. Discussing scholarship on the topic of clarity, correctness, and competition in persuading others, Art Markman, Annabel Irion Worsham

Centennial Professor of Psychology and Marketing at the University of Texas at Austin, says: "Putting this together, then, being certain of your attitude can affect whether you try to convince other people that you are right. In particular, the more strongly you believe that your attitude is the right one, the more you will focus on convincing others" (Art Markman, "Why We Need Everyone to Believe We're Correct," *Psychology Today*, July 14, 2014, https://www.psychologytoday.com/us /blog/ulterior-motives/201407/why-we-need-everyone-believe-were -correct). Such a tendency is likely exacerbated by what scholars call the "illusion of explanatory depth" (that is, the human propensity to overestimate how much they actually understand): Leonid Rozenblit and Frank Keil, "The Misunderstood Limits of Folk Science: An Illusion of Explanatory Depth," *Cognitive Science* 26, no. 5 (September 2002): 521–62, https://doi.org/10.1207/s15516709cog2605_1.

7. One of the reasons studies and surveys employ range responses (for income, age, etc.) instead of asking for these figures specifically is that it increases response rates: Joachim K. Winter, "Bracketing Effects in Categorized Survey Questions and the Measurement of Economic Quantities," *Sonderforschungsbereich 504, Rationalitätskonzepte, Entscheidungsverhalten und Ökonomische Modellierung/Universität Mannheim*, discussion paper, 2002, 35, https://epub.ub.uni-muenchen .de/19729/.

CHAPTER 6: STOP DEVIOUSNESS IN ITS TRACKS

1. Justin Bariso, "What Is an Emotional Hijack? How Learning the Answer Made Me a Better Husband, Father, and Worker," *Inc.*, July 11, 2018, accessed April 4, 2020, https://www.inc.com/justin-bariso /what-is-an-emotional-hijack-how-emotional-intelligence-made-me -a-better-husband-father-worker.html.

2. And that's just the beginning. For more on the many ways that casinos manipulate people to gamble more, see Mark Griffiths and Jonathan Parke, "The Environmental Psychology of Gambling," in *Gambling: Who Wins? Who Loses?*, ed. Gerda Reith (New York: Prometheus Books, 2003), 277–92.

3. Humayun Khan, "How Retailers Manipulate Sight, Smell, and Sound to Trigger Purchase Behavior in Consumers," *Shopify Retail Marketing Blog*, April 25, 2016, https://www.shopify.com/retail

/119926083-how-retailers-manipulate-sight-smell-and-sound-to
-trigger-purchase-behavior-in-consumers.

4. John Leyden, "Romanian 'Ransomware Victim' Hangs Self and 4-Year-
    Old Son—Report," *Register*, March 18, 2014, https://www.theregister
    .co.uk/2014/03/18/romania_ransomware_murder_suicide/.

5. J. Stuart Ablon, *Changeable: How Collaborative Problem Solving Changes
    Lives at Home, at School, and at Work* (New York: TarcherPerigee,
    2018), 119.

6. Stephen Little, "Beware Holiday Villa Scams That Could Cost You
    £5,000," *Moneywise*, January 17, 2019, https://www.moneywise.co.uk
    /news/2019-01-17%E2%80%8C%E2%80%8C/beware-holiday-villa
    -scams-could-cost-you-ps5000.

7. For more on this scam, see "Virtual Kidnapping Ransom Scam," Na-
    tional Institutes of Health Office of Management, accessed April 4,
    2020, https://www.ors.od.nih.gov/News/Pages/Beware-of-Virtual
    -Kidnapping-Ransom-Scam.aspx.

8. "Terrifying Kidnapping Scam Targets Families with Hoax Calls from
    Loved Ones' Phones," NBC Chicago 5, March 18, 2019, https://www
    .nbcchicago.com/news/local/virtual-kidnapping-scam-reported-in
    -indiana/162372/.

9. "'Advertisers use sex because it can be very effective,' said researcher
    Tom Reichert, professor and head of the department of advertising
    and public relations in the UGA Grady College of Journalism and
    Mass Communication." But he warned: "Sex is not as effective when
    selling high-risk, informational products such as banking services,
    appliances and utility trucks" (April Reese Sorrow, "Magazine Trends
    Study Finds Increase in Advertisements Using Sex," *University of
    Georgia Today*, June 5, 2012, https://news.uga.edu/magazine-trends
    -study-finds-increase-in-advertisements-using-sex/).

10. After years of tawdry advertisements, CKE Restaurants, which con-
    trols fast-food chain Carl's Jr., decided in late 2019 to substitute sub-
    stance (in their case food) for sex in the burger chain's ads: Tiffany
    Hsu, "Carl's Jr.'s Marketing Plan: Pitch Burgers, Not Sex," *New York
    Times*, November 13, 2019, https://www.nytimes.com/2019/11/13
    /business/media/new-carls-jr-ads.html.

11. Linda Raftree, cofounder of Regarding Humanity, coined the term
    "poverty porn" and strongly believes it undermines rather than helps

bolster the aims of most charities: Aimee Meade, "Emotive Charity Advertising—Has the Public Had Enough?," *Guardian*, September 29, 2014, https://www.theguardian.com/voluntary-sector-network/2014/sep/29/poverty-porn-charity-adverts-emotional-fundraising.

12. Meade, "Emotive Charity Advertising."

13. For this profile, I am indebted to Bruce Grierson, "What if Age Is Nothing but a Mind-Set?," *New York Times Magazine*, October 22, 2014, https://www.nytimes.com/2014/10/26/magazine/what-if-age-is-nothing-but-a-mind-set.html.

14. Ellen J. Langer, *Counter Clockwise: Mindful Health and the Power of Possibility* (New York: Ballantine Books, 2009)

15. Carol Rosenberg, "What the C.I.A.'s Torture Program Looked Like to the Tortured," *New York Times*, December 4, 2019, https://www.nytimes.com/2019/12/04/us/politics/cia-torture-drawings.html.

16. Editorial Board, "Don't Look Away," *New York Times*, December 5, 2019, https://www.nytimes.com/2019/12/05/opinion/cia-torture-drawings.html; James Risen and Sheri Fink, "Trump Said 'Torture Works.' An Echo Is Feared Worldwide," *New York Times*, January 5, 2017, https://www.nytimes.com/2017/01/05/us/politics/trump-torture-guantanamo.html.

17. Though anxiety was much more strongly associated than depression and eating disorders: Julie Beck, "How Uncertainty Fuels Anxiety," *Atlantic*, March 18, 2015, https://www.theatlantic.com/health/archive/2015/03/how-uncertainty-fuels-anxiety/388066/.

18. Archy O. de Berker et al., "Computations of Uncertainty Mediate Acute Stress Responses in Humans," *Nature Communications* 7 (March 2016), https://doi.org/10.1038/ncomms10996. I take my evaluation of this research from neuroscientist Marc Lewis, who suggested this study represented "the most sophisticated experiment ever conceived on the relationship between uncertainty and stress" (Marc Lewis, "Why We're Hardwired to Hate Uncertainty," *Guardian*, April 4, 2016, https://www.theguardian.com/commentisfree/2016/apr/04/uncertainty-stressful-research-neuroscience).

19. Lewis, "Why We're Hardwired."

20. Ibid.

21. Ibid.

22. Lewis offers a similar hypothetical about the anxiety an employee feels when driving to work and faced with the possibility of arriving late. Ibid.

23. Susan Weinschenk, "Why Having Choices Makes Us Feel Powerful," *Psychology Today*, January 24, 2013, https://www.psychology today.com/us/blog/brain-wise/201301/why-having-choices-makes -us-feel-powerful.

24. Lauren A. Leotti, Sheena S. Iyengar, and Kevin N. Ochsner, "Born to Choose: The Origins and Value of the Need for Control," *Trends in Cognitive Sciences* 14, no. 10 (October 2010): 457–63, https://doi .org/10.1016/j.tics.2010.08.001.

25. Ibid.

26. Diane Hoskins, "Employees Perform Better When They Can Control Their Space," *Harvard Business Review*, January 16, 2014, https://hbr .org/2014/01/employees-perform-better-when-they-can-control -their-space.

27. Ranjay Gulati, "Structure That's Not Stifling," *Harvard Business Review*, May–June 2018, https://hbr.org/2018/05/structure-thats-not -stifling.

28. For this entire profile on Seligman I am indebted to Maria Konnikova, "Trying to Cure Depression, but Inspiring Torture," *New Yorker*, January 14, 2015, https://www.newyorker.com/science/maria-konnikova /theory-psychology-justified-torture.

29. Michael Shermer, "We've Known for 400 Years That Torture Doesn't Work," *Scientific American*, May 1, 2017, https://www.scientific american.com/article/we-rsquo-ve-known-for-400-years-that-torture -doesn-rsquo-t-work/.

30. Ibid. For an alternate perspective on the efficacy of judiciously applied torture (or "torture light"), please see Mark Bowden, "The Dark Art of Interrogation," *Atlantic*, October 2003, https://www.theatlantic.com /magazine/archive/2003/10/the-dark-art-of-interrogation/302791/.

CHAPTER 7: LET YOUR BODY DO THE TALKING

1. Charles Darwin's 1872 book, *The Expression of the Emotions in Man and Animals*, was one of the first to explore nonverbal communication.

2. Works to consult include Paul Ekman, *Telling Lies: Clues to Deceit in the Marketplace, Politics, and Marriage,* (New York and London: Norton, 2009); Paul Ekman and Wallace V. Friesen, *Unmasking the Face: A Guide to Recognizing Emotions from Facial Expressions* (Los Altos, CA: Malor Books, 2003); David Matsumoto, Mark G. Frank, and Hyi Sung Hwang, eds., *Nonverbal Communication: Science and Applications* (Los Angeles: Sage, 2013); Joe Navarro, *What Every Body Is Saying: An Ex-FBI Agent's Guide to Speed-Reading People* (New York: William Morrow Paperbacks, 2008); Joe Navarro, *The Dictionary of Body Language: A Field Guide to Human Behavior* (New York: William Morrow Paperbacks, 2018); Daniel Goleman, *Emotional Intelligence: 10th Anniversary Edition; Why It Can Matter More Than IQ* (New York: Bantam, 2006); Paul J. Zak, *The Moral Molecule: The Source of Love and Prosperity* (New York: Dutton, 2012); and Amy Cuddy, *Presence: Bringing Your Boldest Self to Your Biggest Challenges* (New York: Little, Brown Spark, 2015). You might also consult my own title *Unmasking the Social Engineer: The Human Element of Security* (Indianapolis: Wiley, 2014).

3. Navarro, *What Every Body Is Saying,* 88.

4. In addition to macro- and micro-expressions, human beings also mobilize so-called conversational signals, facial expressions and other bodily movements that don't express emotions per se but rather ideas. If you tell me about the mating rituals of your pet African ringneck parakeet, I might signal the idea "I am interested in this" by raising my eyebrows and nodding my head.

5. For studies documenting the mirroring effect, please see Costanza Navarretta, "Mirroring Facial Expressions and Emotions in Dyadic Conversations," conference paper, Language Resources and Evaluation Conference (LREC 2016), Portoroz, Slovenia, vol. 10, 469–74, https://www.researchgate.net/publication/311588919_Mirroring_Facial_Expressions_and_Emotions_in_Dyadic_Conversations; and Robert W. Levenson, Paul Ekman, and Wallace V. Friesen, "Voluntary Facial Action Generates Emotion-Specific Autonomic Nervous System Activity, *Psychophysiology* 27, no. 4 (1990): 363–84, https://bpl.berkeley.edu/docs/36-Voluntary%20Facial%20Action90.pdf.

6. Sourya Acharya and Samarth Shukla, "Mirror Neurons: Enigma of

the Metaphysical Modular Brain," *Journal of Natural Science, Biology, and Medicine* 3, no. 2 (July–December 2012): 118–24, https://doi .org/10.4103/0976-9668.101878.

7. Daniele Marzoli et al., "Sun-Induced Frowning Fosters Aggressive Feelings," *Cognition and Emotion* 27, no. 8 (May 2013): 1513–21, https:// doi.org/10.1080/02699931.2013.801338.

8. Jessica Bennett, "I'm Not Mad. That's Just My RBF," *New York Times*, August 1, 2015, https://www.nytimes.com/2015/08/02/fashion/im -not-mad-thats-just-my-resting-b-face.html?_r=0&module=Arrows Nav&contentCollection=Fashion%20%26%20Style&action=key press&region=FixedLeft&pgtype=article.

9. *Merriam-Webster*, s.v. "contempt."

10. "Throwing Shade: The Science of Resting Bitch Face," Test Your RBF, accessed April 4, 2020, https://www.testrbf.com/content/throwing -shade-science-resting-bitch-face.

11. Tomas Chamorro-Premuzic, "The Upside to Being Angry at Work," *Fast Company*, February 25, 2020, https://www.fastcompany.com /90467448/the-upside-to-being-angry-at-work.

12. Preston Ni, "4 Types of Anger and Their Destructive Impact," *Psychology Today*, May 19, 2019, https://www.psychologytoday.com/us /blog/communication-success/201905/4-types-anger-and-their -destructive-impact.

13. L. R. Mujica-Parodi, H. H. Strey, B. Frederick, R. Savoy, D. Cox, et al., "Chemosensory Cues to Conspecific Emotional Stress Activate Amygdala in Humans," PLoS ONE 4, no. 7 (2009): e6415. doi:10.1371 /journal.pone.0006415.

14. Ellie Lisitsa, "The Four Horsemen: Contempt," Gottman Institute, May 13, 2013, https://www.gottman.com/blog/the-four-horsemen -contempt/?rq=contempt.

CHAPTER 8: POLISH YOUR PRESENTATION

1. George Lakoff, *The All New Don't Think of an Elephant! Know Your Values and Frame the Debate* (White River Junction, VT: Chelsea Green, 2014), xi–xii.

2. Ibid., 1.

3. Quoted in Oliver Burkeman, "This Column Will Change Your Life:

The Beauty in Imperfection," *Guardian*, April 23, 2010, https://www
.theguardian.com/lifeandstyle/2010/apr/24/change-your-life-beauty
-imperfection.

4. Sarah Todd, Hanna Kozlowska, and Marc Bain, "'Aspirational Realness,'
the Instagram Cool-Girl Look, Disguises Advertising as Authenticity,"
Quartz, October 12, 2019, https://qz.com/quartzy/1722511/how
-brands-like-glossier-sell-aspirational-realness-on-instagram/.

SUGGESTED READING

Robert B. Cialdini, *Influence: The Psychology of Persuasion* (Harper Business, 2006).

The first book to define and scientifically analyze influence.

Amy Cuddy, *Presence: Bringing Your Boldest Self to Your Biggest Challenges* (Little, Brown Spark, 2015).

Helps hackers understand how body language eases our nerves before an engagement, and how we can utilize posture to enhance our communications.

Robin Dreeke, *It's Not All about Me: The Top Ten Techniques for Building Quick Rapport with Anyone* (Robin K. Dreeke, 2011).

Dreeke served as a human hacker in the FBI for years. His is one of the best books about quickly building rapport with others.

Paul Ekman, *Emotions Revealed, Second Edition: Recognizing Faces and Feelings to Improve Communication and Emotional Life*, paperback (Holt, 2007).

No scientist is more renowned than Ekman on the topic of nonverbal communications. This book describes human emotions and how they appear on the face.

Daniel Goleman, *Emotional Intelligence: 10th Anniversary Edition; Why It Can Matter More Than IQ* (Bantam, 2006).

Presents influential research on the amygdala and how it affects our psychology and behavior.

Chris Hadnagy, Paul F. Kelly, and Dr. Paul Ekman, *Unmasking the Social Engineer: The Human Element of Security* (Wiley, 2014).

An in-depth treatment of how to use nonverbals in everyday life.

Ellen J. Langer, *On Becoming an Artist: Reinventing Yourself through Mindful Creativity* (Ballantine, 2006).

This book focuses on the role of mindfulness, a skill that will benefit any human hacker.

Joe Navarro, *What Every Body Is Saying: An Ex-FBI Agent's Guide to Speed-Reading People* (William Morrow Paperbacks, 2008).

One of the best books on body language, from head to toe. Essential reading for any human hacker.

Paul J. Zak, *The Moral Molecule: The New Science of What Makes Us Good or Evil* (Bantam, 2012).

Zak's study of oxytocin has changed our understanding of trust and rapport building.

ABOUT THE AUTHOR

CHRISTOPHER HADNAGY is the founder and CEO of Social-Engineer, LLC. In his sixteen years in the industry, he has written the world's first social engineering framework, created the first social engineering–based podcast and newsletter, and written four books on the topic. Chris has spoken and taught around the globe, including at the Pentagon and other highly secure facilities on the topic of social engineering. As the creator of the world's first SECTF (Social Engineering Capture the Flag), he has led the way in educating people on this serious threat. Chris works with some of the world's leaders in scientific research to understand social engineering and even authored a book with Dr. Paul Ekman about how nonverbal communication is used by social engineers. He holds his OSCP and OSWP and is the creator of the SEPP and MLSE certifications. He is also the founder, executive director, and a board member of the Innocent Lives Foundation, a nonprofit that fights the sexual abuse of children.

Seth Schulman wields the power of the written word to start conversations, change minds, and transform lives. A master storyteller and intellectual collaborator, he has contributed to dozens of books over the past two decades in the genres of business, personal growth, memoir, health, and public affairs, including multiple bestsellers. Schulman holds a PhD in intellectual and cultural history from Brown University. For more information, please visit his website, www.providenceword.com.